# CONQUERING
# THE
# IMPOSSIBLE

*My 12,000-Mile Journey Around
the Arctic Circle*

## Mike Horn

WITH *Jean-Philippe Chatrier*

D0951072

 *St. Martin's Griffin*  *New York*

www.stmartins.com

Maps by Noël Meunier

Library of Congress Cataloging-in-Publication Data

Horn, Mike, 1966–
    [Conquérant de l'impossible. English]
    Conquering the impossible : my 12,000-mile journey around the Arctic Circle / Mike
    Horn, with Jean-Philippe Chatrier ; translated by Antony Shugaar.
        p. cm.
    ISBN-13: 978-0-312-38204-9
    ISBN-10: 0-312-38204-9
    1. Horn, Mike, 1966—Travel—Arctic regions. 2. Arctic regions—Description and
travel. I. Chatrier, Jean-Philippe. II. Title.

G850 2002.H67 H6713 2007
910.911'3—dc22

                                                                    2007009829

First published in France under the title *Conquérant de l'impossible* by XO Editions

First St. Martin's Griffin Edition: June 2008

10 9 8 7 6 5 4 3 2 1

# CONQUERING THE IMPOSSIBLE

*Dedicated to my wife, Cathy,*
*and to Annika and Jessica, my daughters,*
*who give me the freedom to do what I do*

We say something is impossible if no one has ever tried it.
—ALEXIS DE TOCQUEVILLE

The impossible is the only adversary worthy of man.
—ANDRÉE CHÉDID

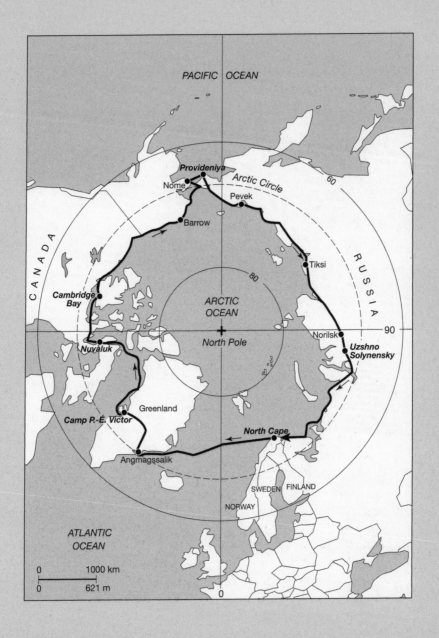

PACIFIC OCEAN

*Provideniya*

Nome

Arctic Circle

60

Pevek

Barrow

RUSSIA

Tiksi

*Cambridge
Bay*

ARCTIC
OCEAN

80

Norilsk

90

North Pole

*Uzshno
Solynensky*

CANADA

*Nuvaluk*

*Camp P.-É. Victor*

Greenland

*North Cape*

Angmagssalik

SWEDEN   FINLAND

NORWAY

ATLANTIC
OCEAN

0        1000 km

0        621 m

0

# Prologue

## Nome, Alaska, October 2003

Everything is gray—frozen solid. On the main street of town, as broad as the Champs-Élysées and lined with boxy, prefab buildings, a snow-laden wind batters the few lonely pickup trucks and makes the drunken Inuit pitch and roll. Just a stone's throw away, the Bering Strait stretches into the distance, choppy and gunmetal-gray, an unfriendly expanse of ocean. This is not a sea that welcomes sailors, and it takes cruel revenge on members of the Polar Bear Club when they practice the local tradition of going for a swim in early spring. This is the end of the earth, in a sense. You can't go any farther and still be on the continent of North America.

A hundred years ago, this godforsaken city of saloons, cancan dancers, and shoot-outs with Colt Frontier six-shooters swelled to a population of forty thousand; it was the time of gold fever. Some made their fortunes. Others were swept back south, tossed by the Arctic wind like the gold dust of their dreams. And others are still here, high atop a barren hill, with white crosses planted square in their bellies.

Just over three thousand people still live in Nome, a town whose existence seems forgotten by the rest of the world. There are construction workers, men who work on the oil rigs, and a handful of gold prospectors.

The prospectors pitch their tents on rocky beaches and obstinately dig up the sand of the seabed to pick out the last few grains of "beach gold."

During the late afternoon, this almost exclusively male tribe gathers at one of the town bars: the Breakers Bar, the Polaris, or the Trading Post. With an eye on the television set that features endless games of baseball, these living phantoms tip back their first round of Rolling Rock, the local favorite. It's the first of a long series of rounds.

Every so often I join them because in Jeff, Jerry, and a handful of others, I have found a group of warm and trustworthy friends. And because, let's admit it, I have nothing to do here but kill time.

Unless you've dealt with Russian bureaucracy, you have no idea what it really means to wait. Somewhere, in a ministry building in Moscow, my official authorization papers to traverse Chukotka (the Siberian peninsula just across the water from Alaska) sit on a desk, waiting to be approved and sent out. My permit to import a GPS device, my authorization to carry a satellite phone, and my permit to carry a gun are probably with them. Once I have these documents in my possession, I will gladly sail across the stretch of stormy ocean that is now symbolically blocking my way. Then I can begin the last stage of my round-the-world journey, the stage that will end at North Cape, Norway, Europe's northernmost point. The same place I left on August 4, 2002, when I set out to make a complete circuit of the Arctic Circle, traveling against the prevailing winds and currents. That was fourteen months ago.

Most of the time, I don't even stay in Nome; I live in a modest hut about twenty-five miles away, amid a vast expanse of tundra. Jeff, who runs an auto supplies and parts store, is letting me squat in this old cabin, which he uses as a base camp to go out hunting wolves or moose and where he sometimes barbecues on the weekend. I have fuel to stay warm, plenty to eat, and my satellite phone, which I use to call my wife, Cathy, frequently. With help from my crew, and relying upon a few well-placed connections, she is hounding the representatives of the former Soviet Empire of Red Tape with courage and persistence.

I can't say whether she will manage to wrestle those permits and authorizations out of them. But what I do know is this—if she can't do it, I'll have to go without them.

If this were to mark the end of my adventure, one year after setting out, it would mean giving up before reaching my goal. Everything I have done and endured till now would be in vain.

I've narrowly escaped dying in icy water. I've felt the fangs of polar bears brushing against my face. I've survived temperatures of seventy-five degrees below zero Fahrenheit. I've made 750-mile detours in the blackest night of the Arctic winter. I've had my fingers, my face, and even my lungs frozen. I've battled for five days and five nights running, with my boat's hull, shattered by a floating log, to reach the coast of Greenland, and then gone on to record the fastest time ever in trekking across that country. I've lost all of my gear, almost been burned alive, and all this before reaching the midpoint of my journey! This expedition is proving to be one of the toughest challenges of my career, both mentally and physically—the Arctic is a master that doesn't tolerate mistakes. However, this has also been one of the most enthralling expeditions in my career because each challenge I've faced is new to me.

I freely admit that over the past fourteen months, I mustered the courage to overcome many of the ordeals I faced only because I had no idea how much suffering remained ahead of me. Knowing what I know now, there is no way I would be able to start over.

I am totally determined not to let anything stop me now. To stay in shape during my hiatus, I cut paths through the head-high underbrush with pruning shears; I run across the tundra dragging a pair of 4×4 tires behind me; I climb the mountains all around me, driven by the question that has pushed men forward since the dawn of time: what's over the next ridge? In this case, I find that over these ridges there is nothing—absolutely nothing—for millions of square miles. Just more tundra, barren or snow-covered hills, steel-blue lakes, and not a road in sight in this land where bush planes carry travelers and goods where they need to go. I cross paths with the occasional caribou, that giant member of the deer family that can be found only in the Far North; a grizzly bear comes around my cabin from time to time; the silence is so profound that I can hear my own heart beat.

Not far from here, on a mountaintop, four rough-hewn monoliths extend their claws skyward. They are all that remains of an abandoned citadel, once part of the Distant Early Warning (DEW) Line, whose radar stations and vigilant garrison monitored the slightest troop movements, the faintest sounds of marching boots on the other side of the Bering Strait for forty years. And they, of course, were doing the same thing on the other side. And so the Russians and Americans warily kept an eye on each other, like a pair of fierce warriors, for almost half a century. And then it was over in a flash, as if those decades of madness had been nothing but a bad dream. These vestigial traces of the Cold War remain as meaningless monuments, an American-style Great Wall without the tourists.

It's enough to make you ponder the vanity of all human endeavors. Not that my own endeavors would pass the simplest test of good sense. For more than ten years now, I have been carrying out, in a thoroughly professional, highly organized, and well thought-out manner, projects that most ordinary people would consider symptoms of a psychotic death wish: swimming and paddling down the Amazon from source to mouth and traveling around the world along the equator. But this is what I do; I am an extreme adventurer the way that other people are booksellers, teachers, or butchers. I reject the "superhuman" label that some people try to pin on me. I don't want to be—and I am not—anything more than an ordinary guy who does things that are out of the ordinary. If there is anything that sets me apart from mainstream modern society, perhaps it is my intense determination, my refusal to be hindered by any obstacle. I won't be slowed down by temperatures of seventy-five degrees below zero, the murderous onslaughts of the wild beasts of the ice, or the raging waves of the Arctic seas, much less by the quibbles of some bureaucrat behind a desk.

# 1

# Three Frozen Fingers

IN 2000 AFTER MY TRIP AROUND THE WORLD following the equator, I began to look around for my next challenge with three conditions in mind: it had to be something new for me; it had to be at least as difficult as the last challenge; and, most important, it had to be something that no one had ever done before. A physical or athletic exploit is just not enough to motivate me. I need to blaze a new trail, to find my way into new territory. Otherwise, for me, the word *adventure* loses its meaning.

I quickly settled on the idea of traveling around the earth at the Arctic Circle. In terms of sheer number of miles, the distance is certainly much shorter than along the equator, but the level of difficulty more than outweighed this "handicap." The extreme cold, the icy waters, the vast ice fields, the crevasses, and the mountains that lay before me, and the ferocious polar bears all create an environment where the techniques of survival differ sharply from those necessary in the tropical jungle. All of it was totally different from anything I had experienced thus far—and that was a fundamental advantage in my eyes. What's more, many people may have attempted this same feat, but no one had succeeded. Of all the factors that would encourage me to undertake this expedition, that was surely the most important.

The Far North was a foreign landscape to me. But I did have enough experience to know one thing: I didn't have a prayer of succeeding without the kind of rigorous preparation and training that would make me capable of surviving in that environment.

My friend, the Swiss explorer Jean Troillet, had been dreaming for years of beating the world record for trekking across Greenland. He invited me to come along with him on the adventure along with another Swiss friend of mine, Erhard Loretan, who was the third man ever to have climbed, in succession and without oxygen, every mountain higher than 8,000 meters. I accepted the invitation with special enthusiasm because I had been planning to travel to Greenland to familiarize myself with the equipment, techniques, and every other aspect of Arctic travel. This expedition would serve as an initial preparatory stage for my trip around the Arctic Circle. Moreover, to have as mentors two of the world's greatest Himalayan specialists was a privilege that I hoped to make the most of.

On this expedition I basically served as a packhorse. I worked and learned. I watched, I listened, and I tried to soak up everything like a sponge. Of the many things that Erhard and Jean taught me, the most important lesson was, unquestionably, patience. In conditions of extreme cold, knowing when to stay in your tent—instead of trying to go on at any cost—can easily spell the difference between life and death. I am by nature impatient and impulsive and have a hard time staying in one place, but I learned the importance of a Zen-like self-control.

That sort of self-mastery is indispensable when, for instance, a blizzard has been blowing for two days, blowing so fiercely and intensely that you could become totally lost just two yards from your tent, the distance at which the tent would become completely invisible. In such conditions everything is a wall of white, there is no earth or sky, no features, no landmarks. Lots of people have died that way in the Arctic: just two yards away from their tent.

That's what would have happened to us if we had ventured out during the two weeks of terrible blizzard that poured its full force down on us. I couldn't stay calm. I kept showing my uncontrollable impatience, but Erhard and Jean calmed me down and kept my nerves in check; in so doing, they offered me an example of wisdom and knowledge that would be an important inspiration later on.

Shortly before leaving for Greenland, I learned that I had been named a winner of a Laureus World Sports Award, the prestigious prize given by Daimler Chrysler and Cartier. I was chosen in recognition of my 1999–2000 journey around the world at the equator.

I was invited to spend three days on Le Rocher, the famous rock of Monaco, all expenses paid, of course. Since I am not really comfortable with social occasions or awards ceremonies, I very politely declined the invitation. Erhard and Jean were waiting for me. Given the choice between the luxury of Monte Carlo and a fair likelihood of freezing to death, I didn't hesitate even for a second.

Back in Greenland, though, I told Cathy over the satellite phone that our food supplies were dwindling. Since the incredibly bad weather was showing no sign of letting up, we were considering turning back. On her end, she told me that the Laureus World Sports Awards representatives were still insisting that I show up for the ceremony; they were saying that I was required to be there. None of which appealed to me in the least. I was happy as a king where I was. If we did decide to turn back, it would be an opportunity for me to trek solo on the ice, giving me a chance to become familiar with that activity. As a joke, I told Cathy that if the people from Monte Carlo were so eager to have me attend their ceremony, all they had to do was come get me on the ice field.

My wife passed the message along, as positive as I had been that no more would be said about it. But the organizers of the Laureus World Sports Awards were not easily discouraged. They sent up a helicopter to get us: it picked up Erhard, Jean, and me at Angmagssalik, on the east coast of Greenland, and ferried us to the military base of Kulusuk. From there, a private jet that had come all the way from Europe just for us flew us back exactly as we were, fairly gamey, with all of our equipment, but without "civilian" clothes. Our civvies were still on the west coast of Greenland, where we were planning to pick them up after our trek, and, of course, we never did reach the other side of the country.

During the last stage of my trip, flying business class, I smelled so bad that the woman sitting next to me asked to be moved to another seat. I was embarrassed and could only mumble my apologies. Sweating like a pig in my polar gear and my thermal underwear, totally unsuitable for the May climate of the Riviera, I landed in Monaco, where I was informed that "my" car and "my" driver were waiting to take me to "my" hotel. I found myself in a palace where, since I had no money with me at all, I was forced to gobble down the energy rations that I was still carrying in my pockets. And since I had no clothes except what I was wearing, my hosts took me shopping, and I bought some casual clothes to wear around during the day. The following day, Cathy brought me my formal clothes, a dark suit that I refer to as my "papal costume." It was actually a suit that the Vatican had bought me, so that I would be decently attired for my audience with His Holiness.

Despite all the attention and care that was being lavished on me, I still felt ill at ease. Twenty-four hours earlier I had been on the ice field, and there was a part of me that kept wondering what exactly I was doing here. But all that changed pretty quickly when the big night arrived. A crowd of living legends showed up to pay me their respects, including Michael Jordan, Alberto Tomba, Ernie Els, Edwin Moses, Juan-Pablo Montoya, John McEnroe, Boris Becker, and Jennifer Capriati. My head was spinning! They knew who I was because, as members of the jury, they all had read my file.

I received my "Oscar" in the category of Alternative Sports, but that was not the only good thing that happened to me that night. Of the major sponsors of that event, a considerable number would become sponsors of my future expeditions, as well. For instance, my fellow South African Johann Rupert, president of the Richemont watchmaking group, which owns Cartier, offered me a sponsorship. He would also become my good friend.

+ + +

Despite the terrible weather and the relative failure of our undertaking, the Greenland expedition was a special and wonderful time for me, and I learned a great deal from it. That experience would prove invaluable to me on my second preparatory expedition for the journey around the Arctic Circle: a solo trip to the North Pole.

Objectively, I can say that I possess two main assets as an explorer: a rock-solid temperament and a solid capacity for physical endurance. But I wondered if those qualities would be enough to ensure my success without the support of Erhard and Jean, alone for the first time in the Arctic environment.

I was pretty sure that I could find the answer by going to see the Norwegian explorer Børge Ousland. He was the first man ever to reach the North Pole solo, as well as the first to cross Antarctica alone. I saw Børge as the world's foremost specialist in solo polar expeditions. Since I considered him to be an absolute master, I decided to visit Norway so that I could apprentice with him. I wanted to learn everything I could about his way of life, his personality, the way he works, his attitudes and his reactions to events—and to life in general. I even wanted to know about his everyday routines. Then I would have a better idea of whether I could match his accomplishments.

I moved in with him in his house overlooking a fjord on the coast of Norway. Børge is very, very Zen. He operates like a cold-blooded animal and conserves every last bit of energy. There are times when I think his heartbeat must slow down to about one pulse per minute, like the heartbeat of the great masters of breath-hold diving. Two solid hours could go by between the time he offers you a cup of coffee and the time you finally receive the hot beverage.

I watched and learned.

Because he had decided that my motivations were honorable—perhaps because we have a sponsor in common—Børge offered an unlimited fund of generosity to me, a South African who had never set foot on the polar ice fields.

"I want to help you become the second man ever to reach the North Pole solo," he told me. In the course of just a few days, he imparted to me the entire body of knowledge he had accumulated in all his years of experience in the Far North, and he made it clear to me that the physical condition I had needed to make it across the Amazonian jungle was nothing compared to what would be required for a polar expedition.

I returned home with the invaluable wealth of knowledge and a very busy calendar ahead of me. I needed to have shoes, a sled, and a tent custom built for me according to his specifications. Such cutting-edge equipment is expensive, and you can't buy it at the local sporting goods store. But I was lucky enough to have the financial and technical support of generous sponsors. I was all the more grateful to them because, unlike a soccer or tennis star, I could offer them only the most meager returns in terms of media attention.

As soon as my first polar tent was ready, I contacted Mercedes–AMG and asked for permission to test the tent in their wind tunnels in Munich. I needed to feel confident that it could withstand the nearly hundred-mile-per-hour winds that are commonplace on the ice field.

My Italian tentmakers brought me two or three sample tents. The shelters, made of synthetic materials, all collapsed under the powerful gusts. The test was spectacular and conclusive, and so it was back to the drawing board!

I ordered all of my clothing from the designers at Eider, the French specialist in outdoor apparel. To start with I ordered a thigh-length anorak, with huge pockets that would hold both medicine and food, and a zipper that would neither freeze nor break.

Last of all, Salomon produced skis and boots that met my specifications.

I was especially demanding because, during this expedition, my survival would depend even more than usual on my equipment. I would have to rely upon it completely because I wouldn't be able to carry a backup version of anything.

Some of the equipment I ordered was encountering delays. Organi-

zational problems began to emerge and, three weeks before my scheduled date of departure for the pole, I was still a long way from being
ready. I admitted this to Børge Ousland when he called to ask how
things were going.

"If you'll pay for a plane ticket," he said, "I'll come down to your
house this weekend." I accepted, and two days later Børge was walking
into our little family chalet in Les Moulins, near Château d'Oex. It was
hard to miss the gigantic duffel bag that he dropped casually in a corner
of the kitchen. He asked to review all my equipment, and he issued a
rapid series of judgments, "That's okay; that's no good. That might
work, but that definitely won't." He asked me what I still needed, and I
told him that I was waiting for my boots. Without a moment's hesitation, he opened the huge duffel bag and exclaimed, "Here are your
shoes!" They were his boots, the ones he wore all the way to the North
Pole. The same model that the Norwegian explorer Fridtjof Nansen,
the first man to explore the polar ice caps, wore on his early polar expeditions! Deeply moved but uncomfortable with Børge's generosity, I
said I couldn't take them. "I want to see you back here with all your
toes!" he insisted, handing me the thermal linings that went with the
boots.

The question of whether Børge's feet and mine were the same size
never came up: the boots in question were a few sizes bigger than the
running shoes or loafers that I usually wear around town. They were
built to accommodate the many overlapping layers of insulation in
which I would wrap my feet before slipping them into the boots.

The first rule of fighting extreme cold is this: it's not the clothing
that keeps you warm; it's the warm air that circulates between the layers. In other words, it's not the clothing that warms the body but the
body that warms the clothing. That was why tight clothing was to be
avoided at all costs, and why roomy, flowing clothes were ideal.

When I showed him my mittens, Børge pulled out his knife and cut
the elastic fastenings at the wrists.

"Nothing, absolutely nothing, should cut or restrict your circulation,
however slightly," he said, "or your fingers could freeze. You should fit
into your mittens the way that a car fits into a garage."

He fastened strips of synthetic cloth to the tabs of my zippers, so that I could grip them easily in all circumstances.

He took a look at my tent and asked me how long it took me to pitch it. I replied innocently that it depended on the day, the weather, the wind, and how tired I was.

"Twenty seconds!" he broke in. "At forty degrees below zero, you have exactly twenty seconds to set up your tent. Any longer than that and you're dead. Start training now, and do not stop until you can set up that tent in no more than twenty seconds, however bad the weather is or however tired you may be."

"Inside your sleeping bag," he went on, "you need to be wrapped in an insulating sheath that will keep the quart of water that you will lose through exhalation and perspiration each night from freezing inside your sleeping bag. Otherwise, the bag will be two pounds heavier every successive day, and you will go to sleep at night and wake up in the morning inside an icebox."

On top of the insulating sheath for my sleeping bag, Børge gave me a pair of ski poles that he guaranteed were unbreakable. The man who once told me that he had spent his whole life perfecting his equipment had suddenly turned into Santa Claus, and he had flown down from the Far North with a bag full of gifts, all for me!

And there were still gifts to come. The great multistar chef Philippe Rochat, who presides over the kitchen at Crissier, near Lausanne, Switzerland, is one of my warmest supporters. In his words, I am a "latter-day Christopher Columbus." He had already placed on his menu a delicious—and filling—Gâteau Mike Horn (a cake with fruit, Armagnac, sugar, and syrup), and he had handed out copies of my first book to all twenty-five of his employees, as well as to two hundred other friends and acquaintances. Now he insisted on personally preparing—for free—the entire array of foodstuffs for the expedition. It's not the kind of offer you can easily turn down. So Philippe immediately busied himself preparing and individually vacuum-packing my next one hundred "specials of the day."

Three months later, in February 2002, among the equipment and provisions I brought with me were rations that would have rated a few stars from Michelin, as I set out to try to reach the North Pole alone and on foot.

A crowd of friends from Château d'Oex—"Pipo," the farmer; "P. A.," the restaurateur; Corinne, and others—a throng of journalists, a cameraman, a photographer, a representative from my sponsor Gore-Tex, and Daniel de Bonneville from the Geneva bank of Mirabaud, along with Antoine Boissier, one of the bank's owners, all boarded a chartered jet along with me, my wife, and my two daughters, Annika and Jessica, to accompany me to the village of Khatanga in northern Russia. This would be my communications base camp, and from there we would travel as far as Cheredeny, a tiny weather station on an island in the middle of the Arctic Ocean.

The only residents of the island were a Russian who had lived there in isolation for the past ten years with his wife and son. For the past decade he had been transmitting weather reports in Morse code—he didn't even have a fax machine, let alone e-mail—to people who had never met him. Imagine ten years of living there like a lighthouse keeper, forgotten, in the middle of the sea. He told us that a colleague of his was eaten by a polar bear, right between the compound's two buildings that stand only about fifty yards apart. He showed us a home movie—not of the colleague, of the bear—and generously provided me with all the space I needed to test my tent and the rest of my equipment under the island's harsh conditions.

When the weather finally allowed, Cathy, Annika and Jessica, my brother Martin, Jean-Philippe Patthey, Sebastian Devenish, my cameraman, two of my sponsors, and a journalist all piled into the helicopter with me, and we set out on the one-hour flight to Cape Arktichesky on the edge of the Arctic ice cap. This was the closest point on the European continent from which it was possible to hike "overland" to the North Pole.

We flew over hundreds of miles of an unbroken icy white surface. When the chopper set down, I was the first one to jump down. The cold gripped me like a vise. It was forty degrees below zero and, standing there on the ice field for the first time, I wondered anxiously whether I really was capable of accomplishing what I came here to do.

Jessica, my younger daughter, hopped out of the helicopter right after me. She walked a short distance, stopped, and stared out into the immense whiteness as if she were trying to understand. Then she turned and walked back toward me with a question in her eyes: "Daddy, what are you doing here?" That pretty much summed up the general feeling in that moment.

I was now fully aware that from here on, I would be totally alone in the face of my challenge. Until now, I had been helped, surrounded, financed, supported, and conveyed by people who believed in me. But once that helicopter lifted off and carried away the last of those people, it would be up to me to play this game—me and me alone. I remembered feeling something comparable, four or five years ago, when the time came to bid farewell to my team and to set out, all alone, to cross the Amazon jungle on foot. That time, I had won the bet.

The helicopter couldn't stay on the ice field for long because there was a danger it might freeze and be unable to take off. We hurried to unload my equipment and to carry out the brief, traditional ceremony: we drank a glass of vodka and shot a flare into the sky.

Cathy, my brother Martin, and I all clustered together, embracing in a short prayer. The Lord's help would never be unwelcome.

Nobody said another word. The emotions were beyond words. Everyone knew that what I was about to try to do would define the next stage of my life. The terrible cold, which made it difficult even to breathe, and the maddening drab gray only heightened the sensation of anguish. And now the time had come to say good-bye. My daughters were crying, and so was my wife. Their tears froze on their faces. Everyone climbed back into the helicopter, which quickly took off. I turned my back on the aircraft as it labored into the air, to face what awaited me. For the moment, what I most needed to do was to forget what I was leaving behind and focus all my attention on the task at hand.

I attached the sled to my harness. The load I would be pulling was exactly eight feet behind me. That distance was carefully calculated. If it were any closer, I might find that by pulling I would also be trying to lift the sled, but on the other hand, if it were any farther away, I would be expending needless effort trying to drag it over bumps and rises in the ice because the front of the sled would remain flat, glued to the surface. The harness rope was made of a special nylon that would not absorb water, slip, or break from freezing. Last of all, the ski poles had wrist straps that were loose enough that they would not cut off the circulation at my wrists.

I tightened my hood snug around my face. The fur narrowed my field of vision to a very small circle, and I took my first step on the ice field, harnessed like a beast of burden. I realized that the 465 pounds of the sled weighed a ton. The slightest irregularity in the ice would snag my sled and stop me short. And I would have to travel five hundred miles like this! Braced against the load, I pulled with all my strength and finally developed a rhythm of sorts.

Ahead of me, a full day's march away, there was an opening in the ice field, blown apart by frequent Arctic storms. We had noticed it during the flight in, and now, to help me avoid it, the helicopter flew straight over my head, marking the line of the exact course that I would need to follow. This was a welcome pointer, as my navigational tools were limited. At this time of year, in these latitudes, the sun only jumps over the horizon for a short moment like a small, yellow flea. The intense cold freezes the liquid crystals in GPS devices, rendering them useless, and conventional magnetic compasses spin around wildly and are ineffective this close to the North Pole. In short, there was nothing to orient myself except for a little bit of sunlight and plenty of wind.

The helicopter made a 180-degree turn and passed overhead one last time, zigzagging a final good-bye. I followed it with my eyes until it was nothing but a dot in the distance, and then it vanished entirely. Nothing remained except the terrible cold, the immense emptiness, and me.

The harsh hostility of the weather I had faced since arriving at these latitudes was nothing compared to the loneliness that I was discovering now. It was a solitude rendered all the more oppressive by the certainty that, in this setting, even the smallest mistake could be fatal.

But my spirits rose again. I had plenty of excellent supplies and equipment, and I had what seemed to be a considerable store of knowl-

edge and skills. I could draw on my endless reserves of energy and determination. The only thing I lacked was experience in this kind of environment; here, everything was new to me. On the ice field it is
experience that allows you to judge the direction in which this or that
portion of the ice cap is shifting. It is experience that warns you to stay
in your tent when conditions become too dangerous to go on, and experience helps you plot the best route possible, despite the shifting
landscape and the movements of the pack ice itself, which regularly
breaks off of the main ice field and drifts away.

I picked out an ice floe on the horizon that was taller than the others
and selected it as my landmark. I headed for it. For three or four hours
I made steady progress. Then the wind started to blow harder and
harder, becoming increasingly violent. Already my lack of experience
posed a first—and serious—problem: I did not yet know at what wind
force it would become impossible for me to pitch my tent.

I decided to set up my first camp too early, rather than too late.
Then, a second problem: out of the immense variety of equipment carefully stowed under the tarp that covered my sled, I did not know with
any confidence exactly what items would be indispensable to me inside
the tent.

I set up my shelter half a mile away from the open gap between the
ice field and the piece of pack ice I was now on. I did my best to make
camp as far as possible from any fissures in the ice, which might very
well widen into yawning stretches of open water during the night. On
that issue, I had been very clearly and thoroughly briefed; on a recent
expedition similar to mine, a Japanese explorer made this very mistake,
and he and his tent were swallowed up whole.

During the night, I could hear the ice cracking over toward the open
water; it was the sound of blocks of ice breaking off and crashing together. My little "island" was breaking up; it was crumbling like a giant
cookie. Without moving at all, I could tell that I was getting dangerously close to the edge. And it was impossible to get out of the tent,
repack my sled, and move away. The wind had picked up and was blowing so ferociously that I couldn't even poke my nose outside the tent.

As long as I was stuck in the tent, I decided to take the opportunity to become familiar with my portable stove, which is not so much a heating device as it is a way of making my food edible. The food packs were frozen to start with, but now they were doubly frozen. At these very low temperatures—once my body heat "warmed up" the interior of the tent, it was still twenty-two degrees below zero—the fuel was much harder to light than under normal conditions. The flame of the lighter had to be held against the fuel for quite some time as it slowly thawed and finally caught fire. Because I did not yet have a practiced hand, I scattered fuel all over the place. I had to be especially careful not to catch my tent on fire! If I lost the tent, I was a dead man.

Finally, once I had a working camp stove, I enjoyed the first of the dishes that were so lovingly prepared for me by Philippe Rochat, a stuffed chicken that was a true culinary delight. And there was an added treat: a note, signed by Philippe's wife, Franziska, an athlete in her own right who had won the New York Marathon. "Have courage, Mike," she wrote, "we're with you!" There were tears in my eyes. With Philippe manning the stove and Franziska keeping up my morale, I suddenly felt much less lonely.

Rolled in my sleeping bag like a mummy wrapped in its bandages, I spent the next forty-eight hours a prisoner in my fabric bubble, listening to the howling winds and the ice cracking louder and louder, warning of the rapidly encroaching seas.

When the storm finally subsided just enough for me to step out of the tent, I discovered that I was a mere ten yards away from the coldest bath of my life. This discovery, along with the fact that the blizzard was continuing to gust ferociously, sort of gave me the blues. I was starting to feel that nothing was going my way. Using the satellite phone, I called my comrade in Cheredeny to ask about the weather. He told me that where he was, the terrible weather conditions had made it impossible for a helicopter to take off for the last four days. All the other polar expeditions were grounded; they were being forced to delay their departures. I was the only one on the ice.

So, in short, no one could do a thing to help me. I had jumped into the water all by myself, and now I was going to have to learn to swim. I comforted myself with the thought that at least the weather couldn't get any worse. When I used my satellite phone to call Nicolas Mingassan, who knows what he is talking about, having organized a great many polar expeditions, he supported my strategy. "Stay put," he advised.

My confidence gradually returned. I had plenty to eat and a sleeping bag to keep me warm, so I was well equipped to withstand the siege of the elements.

When the weather finally let up, it only revealed a new and truly insurmountable obstacle. The gap in the ice that lay between me and the North Pole had become a veritable ocean inlet, nearly twenty miles across!

I spent four days in the same spot, hoping that the same ocean currents that separated my piece of the ice cap from the main ice field would decide to rejoin them before much longer. There were no signs of that, however, and I couldn't stay here forever. Such big gaps in the ice field inevitably attract seals, which surface to breathe. The seals in turn attract polar bears, their chief predator. From on board the helicopter that set me down at Cape Arktichesky, I had noticed a large number of polar bears heading this way. They would certainly pounce on a tasty piece of prey like me unless I could get moving.

The helicopters were able to take off again, and now the Australian and Japanese expeditions left Cheredeny to be set down in about the same place as me, near Cape Arktichesky. Once they realized that the ocean gap that had developed was insurmountable, the pilots refilled their fuel tanks and ferried their passengers across the inlet. As they did so, they flew overhead and got a fix on me; they contacted me once they were across, asking me if I would like to be shuttled across as well. Since it looked unlikely that the ocean currents would reunite my ice floe with the main ice field, I decided to accept their offer.

Having taken advantage of this airlift, I could now make a new departure, a real one this time. The others were well ahead of me, but we weren't all boxing in the same weight class—the other expeditions were nearly all multiperson ventures. If there was anyone that I was "competing" with, it was the one Japanese trekker who, like me, was trying to solo to the North Pole.

♦ ♦ ♦

A heavy snowfall was sweeping horizontally across the unbroken surface of the ice field. I moved forward, angling slightly eastward to offset
the westward drift of the ice cap. Little by little, I tried to chip away
each day at the lead that the Japanese explorer had on me.

On the third day, I called my ice wizard, Børge Ousland, on my
satellite phone. He asked me how much progress I was making.

"Between seven and nine miles a day," I replied.

"Fantastic!" Børge cried. "I've never averaged that much distance at
the beginning of an expedition." Then he added, "If you make it through
the first fifteen days, then you've done it—you'll make it to the Pole.
Hang on, Mike!"

Day after day, I struggled to haul my sled over the crevasses in the
pack ice. One day when I was trying to cross a yawning gap that was becoming visibly wider by the moment, I took off my skis, gathered my
strength and my nerve, and I jumped, still tied to the sled. But I fell
short, slipped, and half knocked myself out, cutting my face on the
sharp ice along the edge. There I was, up to my waist in icy water, while
my sled, back on the wrong side of the crevasse, inched farther away as
the ice continued to drift.

I managed to get out of this predicament, by paddling over to the
opposite side, using jagged handholds on the wall of ice in front of me
to haul myself—dripping—up onto the steep bank of pack ice. I then
expended every ounce of strength and adrenaline I had to float my sled
across the open water and pull it up and onto the ice bank now behind
me. Somehow I made it, but I was clearly taking too many risks. If I
kept this up, I would be dead before I got to the Pole.

On the fifth day I called Cathy, who was still in Cheredeny, to give her
a progress report.

"I knocked myself out, slashed my face, and froze my ears. Other
than that, I'm learning a little more every day, and my morale is rock

solid." From her end, my wife told me that all the other teams had given up and turned back. I had the racetrack all to myself!

Stunned by the news, I hardly knew what to think. How could it be that I alone, inexperienced as I was, could keep on going when everyone else had given up? Maybe I was just too dumb to listen to the simple common sense that was telling me to turn back?

My perseverance was indeed a product of my ignorance. Apparently the others had said that they had never seen so many gaps in the ice, that they had never seen such a fragmented ice pack. For my part, I had no previous expeditions to compare this with, and so these trying conditions seemed normal to me. And I labored on.

In order to move forward while hauling a 450-pound load, it was important that my skis only slide forward, which is why the points where they made contact with the ice were covered with artificial sealskins. And since the sealskins have an annoying tendency to shrink and come unglued in conditions of extreme cold, my sealskins were screwed to the bottoms of my skis.

But in the middle of one day's slog, suddenly I felt as if I were moonwalking like Michael Jackson. I realized that I had just lost one of my sealskins. It was still attached to one end of my left ski and was dragging pathetically behind me. I swore loudly and obscenely (I doubted that anyone was going to hear me). In order to reattach the sealskin, I would have to stop, take off my boots, pitch my tent, heat up the camp stove (a waste of cooking fuel), heat the bottom of the ski, preheat the sealskin, and reaffix it to the bottom of the ski. Then, of course, I would have to break camp before I could start off again.

As it turned out, the whole thing took three solid hours, and I was livid with frustration. Then, after another hour of progress, the sealskin came loose again, and I had to start all over!


It had been twenty-one days since I left Cape Arktichesky, and—despite many further problems with sealskins—my morale was high. The days were growing longer; I could get my bearings more easily; the temperatures were becoming comparatively mild (around twenty-two degrees below zero), and the sled was becoming progressively lighter as I consumed its contents. With my goal in sight, I felt like I was on top of the world.

The icy surface that suddenly appeared before me was clamped between two giant ice mounds, thrust upward by the opposing pressure of two masses of ice. This pressure, which can snap layers of ice five yards thick like kindling, launched shards of ice into the air that, falling to the ground like pick-up sticks, created these frozen hillocks. When the masses of ice pulled apart again, they left open water between them, which the cold quickly covered over again with a thin sheet of ice. The prudent thing to do would be to go around it. But in my current state of mind, I felt as if I were capable of walking on water.

I was carrying with me a sort of waterproof outfit, which I had brought for situations just like this—in which I had to venture onto what might prove to be thin ice. This "envelope," which looked like a cross between a diver's suit and a fly fisherman's hip-waders, was loose enough that I could put it on over my regular outfit, including my shoes. It included sleeves that were closed at the ends, and it left no part of me uncovered except my head. If I were to fall into the water, it would save my life by preventing my clothes from getting drenched and by keeping me afloat with the air trapped inside. I could even use it to swim to the other side of a gap, if necessary. And once I was back on firm ice, I needed only to take it off, and I would avoid freezing instantly.

The only problem with this survival gear was that it took valuable time to put it on and take it off. At that moment I was in a hurry, and I didn't feel like taking an extra minute for anything. This valley didn't look too wide ... I decided to go ahead and run the risk of crossing without my survival suit.

As I ventured out onto this fragile surface, I checked to see how strong it was at regular intervals using a method that Børge Ousland taught me. You bring your ski pole down hard on the ice, three times in a row. If the ski pole only breaks through on the third blow, then you have a 70 percent chance of making it over. But since the ice gets thinner and thinner as you approach the middle of the new ice, the 70 percent chance dwindles to 50 percent, and then 40 percent. The ideal margin of safety is indicated when the ski pole fails to break through until the fourth impact. In this case, my ski pole broke through on the second blow. I figured that I had a 50 percent chance of making it to the other side without incident.

Two yards. Three yards. Four yards. I moved forward gingerly, doing my best to avoid sudden movements or jolts, placing my skis on the ice as if I were walking on eggshells, and distributing my 185 pounds of weight as well as I could over the surface of the two skis. Polar bears are capable of moving across very thin ice because they are masters of the art of distributing their weight. At that moment, I wished I were a bear.

I had almost reached the other side when an ominous cracking sound filled the air. As I heard the sound, I could feel the ice giving way beneath my feet. It had collapsed beneath the 400 pounds of weight that my sled still carried. A second later, I was up to my neck in ice-cold water. My skis, still attached to my feet, weighed me down and threatened to drag me under. I struggled to find a grip and clamber up the blocks of ice on the near wall, since my sled prevented me from swimming to the far side. Luckily, the sled was still floating and remained upright! If it capsized, it would sink under its weight and drag me straight to the bottom with it.

In order to free up my hands, I let go of my ski poles, and they dangled, still strapped to my wrists. Inside my head, my survival instincts rushed through my possible courses of action: "Unhook the sled! No, use it as a raft! No, it might overturn. All your equipment would be soaked and ruined, and it would take you down with it anyway."

Little by little, I regained confidence and a modicum of self-control. I gradually realized that my immediate situation was serious but not as catastrophic as it seemed at first. I was immersed in water that had a temperature of about thirty-seven or thirty-nine degrees, which was actually quite warm compared with the air temperature, which must have been close to forty degrees below zero. It wasn't in the water that I ran the real risk of dying of hypothermia; it would be when I emerged from the water. And that meant that I still had a few extra seconds to think about what to do next. I absolutely had to (1) find a way of getting back onto the ice, (2) remove my skis, (3) get undressed, and (4) get into some dry clothes.

I had kept my ice axes with me. They were within reach, in pockets that were specially added to my parka. And yet I didn't even have the reflexes to use them. It was with the sheer strength of my arms—and, above all, a miracle that I cannot understand to this day—that I managed to climb up the six-foot-high ice wall that separated me from the surface of the ice field. I was weighed down by my drenched clothing, I had my skis on my feet, and my sled was still attached to the other end of my harness, but I made it. Once I was up on the ice, I sat down and used all my weight to pull the sled up and over the wall. And yet there was no time to stop and take a deep breath—even for a second. The water that had drenched my clothing was already beginning to freeze. My first reflex was to grab fistfuls of fresh snow and cover myself with it. Because of its absorbent properties, the powdery snow "dried" me off quickly and kept me from freezing completely. Now, what I needed was to pitch my tent, so that I could preserve at least some warmth and change my clothes inside the cloth bubble. But with all the clumps of ice that were covering the landscape, there wasn't even the smallest flat surface on which to set up my tent. While I ran in place furiously to try to warm up, the ice was solidifying on my clothes and cracking with every move I made. I could feel the ice beginning to form on my flesh.

Finally, I found a clear space, just big enough for my tent. I pitched the tent—in twelve seconds by my watch—and rushed inside, ripping off my clothes and hopping into my sleeping bag.

But now I was not much warmer than I would have been standing naked on the ice. I absolutely had to light my camp stove. My daily ration for fuel was two "units," (a full bottle held six of my self-defined "units," or one liter), enough to heat up my food and melt ice for drinking water. If I used more fuel today, I'd have no water to drink tomorrow. A shame, certainly, but tomorrow would be another day, and right now I needed to worry about surviving today.

A few seconds later, I was out of my sleeping bag, huddled next to the flame of the camp stove, completely naked so that the heat did not need to pass through my clothing in order to reach me.

Because it is my body that heats my clothing and sleeping bag, not the other way around (the clothing and the sleeping bag do nothing more than hold in my body heat), the first thing that needed to be heated up was me.

As my body gradually returned to a normal temperature, I did my best to dry out my clothes but soon realized that a complete drying operation was going to use up all my remaining fuel. So I limited myself to drying off my boxer shorts and my thermals. For the rest of my clothing, I had a different idea: I threw the clothing outdoors and waited five minutes. Then I dragged my clothing, completely frozen, back into the tent and got all the ice off it by brushing the clothing vigorously. I had just invented freeze-drying: in order to extract all the moisture from a garment, first turn it into ice.

The next morning, in completely dry clothing—I changed only my wool socks and the linings of my boots, because I couldn't get the ice out of them—I started off again toward the Pole. As I went, I swore solemnly to myself that I would never fail to put on my insulating survival gear, and that I would never venture out onto thin ice. Even if I had to take a six-mile detour.

This close call made me think back to an experience I had in the virgin jungle of the Amazon. My original goal had been to make it through the jungle. Then, after being bitten by a poisonous snake and struggling for five days, balanced on the brink of death, my goal changed. It became to stay alive . . . then make it through the jungle.

In this case, survive . . . then make it to the North Pole.

The days were growing longer; the temperatures were becoming milder; my average continued to improve as my sled grew lighter; I was losing weight, but I was in great shape. Life was good.

"Look out for bears!" Franziska Rochat warned me in my fortune for the day, which came with the meal cooked by her husband. Philippe had developed seven different meals, one for each day of the week.

Thanks to him, I was dining as I never had before on an expedition. And thanks to his wife, I got "mail" twice a week.

Everything was going nicely. I had been out on the ice field for more than twenty-five days, and Børge Ousland predicted that I would be successful if I could only make it past the first two weeks. Another reason to stick to my resolution to avoid any more needless risks.

I gave Børge a call, as I had developed the habit of doing every ten days or so, to update him on my morale and my progress—my location, how much food I had left, how my sled was working, and so on. He was enthusiastic. According to him, I couldn't fail now.

And I was increasingly tempted to agree with him as I got closer to eighty-five degrees north latitude (ninety degrees, of course, is the North Pole). This far north, the ice became more uniform, smoother, and therefore easier and safer to cross. The only drawback: lost polar bears that rove the ice field may well be aggressive because of a lack of food.

I was willing to deal with the bears. The only thing I wanted was to finally experience what I had prepared for for so long, and what I believed at this point I amply deserved. I had earned this victory, and they couldn't take it away from me.

That night, I heard the usual sounds of ice cracking all around me. It sounded like a crackling wood fire or a giant hand striking thousands and thousands of matches. During the night, gaps opened all over the ice field. All it would take was for one of those gaps to yawn open directly beneath my tent, and I would wind up like that Japanese explorer.

All of a sudden, that worry disappeared, only to be replaced by another. Amid the popping firecracker sounds of the ice, I could just discern the muffled shuffling of footsteps in the snow. I could hear the faint crunching of powdery snow being pressed down by the weight of a . . .

A bear!

It made perfect sense. They are capable of smelling a fissure in the ice field from thirty miles away, along with the conditions that fissure creates—a little space of open salt water, perfect for hunting seal.

And, in fact, I felt about as vulnerable as a seal, a prisoner in my sleeping bag, with only my head sticking out. I couldn't see a thing, but I could hear the footsteps of the wild beast as he approached. Now I could hear his rough breathing . . . very close to me. And suddenly, here he was! His curiosity had been aroused by my tent, an object as big as he was, dropped here as if from another planet. He stuck his snout into the tent, in an attempt to sound out the intentions of the alien creature. The muzzle of the huge bear, its shape clearly impressed in the stretched nylon, was just a few inches from my own face. I felt as if I could count his fangs, behind which loomed half a ton of muscle, flesh, and claws. My heart must have been racing at about three hundred beats per minute. Instinctively, I got one arm free and wrapped my fingers around the barrel of the sawed-off shotgun I carried with me at all times.

The bear began to sniff around my tent, curiously trying to determine whether this unidentified object contained something good to eat. Like, say . . . me. I experienced some difficulty getting out of my sleeping bag. My breath had frozen the zipper.

I finally made it out of my sleeping bag, after warming the zipper between my hands, and I crouched, ready, finger on the trigger.

If I shot through the cloth, I would lose my tent. Better to wait and see what happened next. Of course, if the bear's next move was to attack the tent with a swipe of his claws, I might not be quick enough on the trigger.

Luckily, the bear lost interest in my synthetic shell. With the delicacy of a tightrope walker, he picked his way over the guy wires of my rigged-up alarm system without touching even one of them, and focused his attention on my sled. He shoved the sled with the tip of his snout (I could hear the runners scraping across the ice) as he tried to lift the tarp to see what was concealed underneath. All of my food was vacuum packed, and so there was nothing to smell. Despite the tense situation, all I could think about at this moment was a cartoon that appeared in a Swiss newspaper before I left: it showed me walking across an ice field, while a crowd of bears, attracted by the smell of Philippe Rochat's fine cuisine, followed me, licking their chops.

Finally, my visitor wandered away, and my pulse returned to a normal rate. The next morning, the paw prints and other tracks in the snow provided an eloquent account of the scene that I had experienced the night before through my ears and in my imagination.

On day thirty-five, a powerful blizzard whipped up, and I was forced to hunker down in my tent. That same night, the ice floe I was camping on began to drift. The next morning, I discovered that in the time it had taken to get a little sleep, I had lost twelve and a half miles without taking a single step. And I was still pinned down by the blizzard. Another twenty-four hours went by, and the ice cap began to crack loudly all around me, shattering into a jigsaw of unstable sheets of ice. This was beginning to look dangerous. I was unsure whether I should wait for the weather to clear up or push on in spite of it. The latter option would be riskier and inefficient, but at least I would stop losing ground.

I did a quick reckoning. I had spent two days in the tent and had lost twelve and a half miles—distance that I would still have to cover again—and five days worth of food subtracted from my supplies. But I still had enough food to trek all the way from Russia to Canada via the North Pole.

I decided to wait.

Forty-eight hours later, there was no break in the weather, and the cracks in the ice were getting dangerously close. Suddenly, a crack yawned open almost directly under my tent, and my sled was hanging precariously over the edge of the ice.

That mishap rang an alarm bell. I called Børge and explained how things stood. I wanted to ask him if he had ever found himself drifting south at this stage of an expedition to the North Pole.

"Never!" he replied. Still, even after I told him that I was still drifting south, he recommended that I wait out the blizzard.

"But the ice is breaking up! I can't stay here."

"Well, it's your call," Børge replied. "You're the only one who can make that decision. You've made it this far; trust your own judgment."

The blizzard was showing no signs of letting up. The ice was cracking all around me. Since I had to make a quick choice, I decided to move out. And fast. I folded up my tent, hooked up the sled to my harness, and set out. I marched north, heading into the wind, but I was drifting south the whole time. The storm was howling into my face, burning my skin, freezing my lips and the tip of my nose . . . I wasn't doing that badly, considering everything that I had going against me. And then I noticed the loose bootlace.

Under normal conditions, an untied bootlace is a tiny problem; retying it takes a few seconds. But for me, in these conditions, it was a full-fledged disaster. Every morning I would spend twenty minutes getting my boots on. I could only do it inside the tent, because I had to take my gloves off to tie the laces. It was an iron-clad rule that I could never remove my gloves outdoors. Especially when it was more than twenty degrees below zero. Well, that day the ice storm had caused the mercury to drop to seventy-six degrees below zero!

It is impossible to keep trekking with a lace untied. Just as with a pair of cross-country skis, my boots were fastened to the snowshoes only at the toe, and the heel would lift with each step. My foot would pull out of the shoe with the first step I took. That would slow me down and bring on a fatal case of hypothermia.

My only option was to attempt to tie my bootlace without removing my gloves. That's just about impossible to do under normal conditions, but at seventy-six degrees below zero, with a blizzard whipping my exposed flesh and howling in my ears . . . well, you can only imagine.

While I was struggling futilely with the bootlace, I began to notice the first warning signs of hypothermia: shivering, blue nose and lips . . . I was never going to get this done. Okay, it was time for drastic measures: I pulled off my gloves and wedged them under my arms in an attempt to preserve even a little body heat. But the gloves slipped out and fell to the ground, where the wind filled them with snow.

Before I was done tying the bootlace, my fingers were half frozen. I pulled my gloves back on: they were frozen, too. And my hands were unlikely to warm them up. I jammed my gloved hands under my arms, but it was doing no good. Now I could feel my entire body beginning to freeze. There was only one thing to do—get moving—since my frozen hands would keep me from setting up my tent. For six hours straight, I plunged forward into the blizzard like a madman. It warmed me up a bit, but my hands remained lifeless. I tapped the tips of my fingers on my ski poles. Nothing, no sensation. Now I was screwed. I took off one glove to assess the damage. The razor-sharp shards of ice had cut through veins and nerves while slowly freezing my hands; my thumb had split wide open like meat in a freezer set too low. The cold flesh was translucent all the way to the bone.

I stopped to set up my tent, using my teeth to help, as I had lost virtually all control of my fingers and was working with a pair of useless stumps. It took me two hours to set up camp, instead of the usual ten to twenty minutes. The simplest tasks had become impossible: undoing the Velcro on the tarp that covered the sled, lifting the tarp to pull out the camp stove, turning the fuel valve to light the stove so that I could melt a little snow in a cook pot. It was impossible to turn the flame-adjuster wheel with my frozen thumbs. I tried to work it with my teeth, but my tongue froze to the metal, and I ripped it half off to pull it free. My breath had coated the wheel with a film of ice, which made it even harder to turn. I finally managed to turn it with my teeth, but now I needed to pump up the fuel pressure. Despite my best efforts, I couldn't manage to work the little pump handle with my teeth, so I finally gave up and opened the fuel tank. Flammable liquid spread all over the place.

At these temperatures, a lighter is useless. The liquid gas inside is frozen solid. Only matches work in this cold. But try extracting a match from the box and striking it without using your fingers—it's virtually impossible! I tried to strike a match with my mouth, but the matches broke one after the other, without lighting.

For half an hour, I made futile attempts to catch the fuel on fire. I wasted a vast number of matches. This was serious. In order to lighten my load as much as possible, to shave ounces off the total weight, I made all sorts of sacrifices. Among other things, I cut off half the handle of my toothbrush, snipped the labels off all my clothing, and rationed myself to two matches daily.

I had an idea: I put my lighter in my mouth to thaw out the liquid fuel inside. After fifteen minutes, I figured the fuel had thawed. The problem was that, since I couldn't grip it with my fingers, I couldn't use the lighter at all. I finally wound up wedging it between both hands, and running the wheel against the floor of the tent, where it was soaked with fuel. Finally, I managed to produce a spark and the fuel burst into flame. But I had slopped so much fuel out of the camp stove that I set off a genuine conflagration in my tent! Now it looked like I might go from being frozen solid to charbroiled in a few seconds. I hastily put out the flames with my sleeping bag, at the same time trying to avoid putting out the camp stove, which had finally lit, thanks to the flames that had leaped up its side.

At first, the heat of the camp stove allowed me to regain some use of my hands. I could now bend my fingers. At first, I thrust my fingers directly into the flame, in order to try to thaw them out as fast as possible—if it wasn't too late already. Bad idea—the nerves were numb from the cold, and I felt no pain at all, but a stench of burning flesh soon filled the tent. I would need to take this gradually. The partial mobility that I had regained in my extremities made it possible for me to heat a little water. I soaked my hands in the water, but I couldn't tell if the liquid was getting hotter. And so I tested it regularly, just as if it were a baby's formula, until the water reached a temperature of ninety-seven or ninety-eight degrees to judge from the tip of my tongue. I sat there for two or three hours soaking my hands before feeling the first tinglings in my fingertips. Or seven fingertips, anyway. My right thumb, index, and ring fingers were no longer responding.

My first reaction was one of despair at the idea that I might lose my fingers when I had done everything I could to keep that from happening. Then, determination took over, and I told myself that with luck, I shouldn't have to lose more than three partial finger joints, maybe even just the pads of the fingertips. It could have been much worse: all ten fingers, or the toes ... Let's admit it, I knew from the beginning that something like this was going to happen to me. Just like I had known perfectly well that sooner or later I would wind up in the water. The only thing I didn't know was when. I had no suicidal tendencies. I just had a well-controlled sense of fatalism, a full awareness that without testing me to my limits, the Arctic wouldn't really be the Arctic.

The next morning, I didn't even poke my head out of the tent. I spent the whole day soaking my fingers in lukewarm water. I smeared my fingers with Betadine and I swallowed large amounts of aspirin to thin my blood, so that it could flow more easily to my fingertips. The ice that had formed inside of my flesh was beginning to thaw. I drove the blade of my knife into the frostbitten portion of my three injured fingers in order to determine the exact point where I could still feel the pain. In the end, I discovered that the dead portion was very small. If that's all that they would have to cut off, well . . . I'd survive. After all, I have lived without the last joint of my right middle finger for many years now; it was crushed in the breech of a machine gun in Angola back when I was serving in the South African Army in the war against the Cubans. That finger was more or less always frozen, and I managed to survive just fine with it.

These first thirty-six days had been horribly difficult. And yet, I was getting close to eighty-five degrees north latitude, while all the other expeditions had long since given up and gone home. My fuel and food supplies were dangerously low, and I was continuing to drift on my little fragment of the larger ice field. But I was still in good shape, and I felt as if I would be able to catch up on my schedule—which would make up for my supply shortages. I'd already done the hard part. Right now, there was a broad avenue stretching out before me. I had only one handicap slowing me down: my fingers. Each evening, I stopped two hours early to disinfect them and soak them in warm water. In order to prevent them from freezing again on contact with the air when I took them out of their "bath"—since even inside the tent it was thirty or forty degrees below zero—I developed an elaborate routine. I would extinguish my camp stove, carry the water, which was already starting to get cold, over to my sleeping bag, and then I would slide into the sleeping bag, quickly pull my hands out of the water, zip up my sleeping bag, and wedge my hands between my legs to keep them warm. And that's when the real ordeal would begin: it felt as if my fingers were being clamped to an anvil and slammed repeatedly with a blacksmith's sledgehammer. And it lasted all night! Actually, I should have rejoiced because this pain meant that my fingers were thawing. But it was so painful that I would almost have preferred amputation.

In the morning, as soon as I had broken camp, stowed all my equipment, slipped on my mittens, and resumed my trek, my fingers began to freeze again, despite all my best efforts. The veins that had been cut by the ice crystals were now preventing the blood from flowing to the last joints of my fingers.

Then Cathy's voice over the satellite phone made the ice field plunge beneath my feet: "Franziska is dead."

Our friend, who was also an accomplished mountain climber, had just been killed during an ascent in the Alps. A ledge had given way and taken her with it as it fell. The shocking news made me forget my injuries, my pain, the terrible cold that was burning my flesh . . .

"Franziska is dead."


I called up Philippe Rochat on my satellite phone. I'd developed the habit of calling him every so often, as I did all the men and women who had lent me their support. This time, of course, it was different. I was speaking to a man who was shattered, destroyed, and I spoke words of comfort and reassurance to him, words whose emptiness, whose uselessness, I could sense even as I spoke them. All the same, Philippe seemed pleased to hear from me, and the irony of the situation struck me. I, whose injuries had almost rendered me helpless, I, who was surviving under hellish conditions, I, who needed all the help that I could get, found myself providing moral support to a man who, without ever having ventured away from his own home, was going through an ordeal far worse than mine.

❖ ❖ ❖

A couple of days later, a number of large, swollen blisters appeared beneath the skin of my frozen thumb, index finger, and ring finger on my right hand, as well as on the thumb of my left hand. I knew perfectly well that they were warning signs of gangrene.

This time I picked up my satellite phone to call Cathy. I hadn't told her about what had happened to my fingers. I wanted to keep her from worrying needlessly, and I figured that this was my problem, so it was up to me and no one else to solve it. In the least alarmist manner imaginable, I described my symptoms to her and asked her to talk to a specialist about it for me. She put me in touch with a doctor, a woman who specializes in hands.

"Have your fingers changed color?" the doctor asked me.

Yes, and there was even worse news: my two thumbs, my right index finger, and my right ring finger had all erupted like cauliflowers, taking on the ugly appearance of frozen tripe.

"How long ago did your fingers get frostbitten?" she asked.

"Three or four days."

In response to a question, I gave as detailed a description as I could of the blisters and the open sores. She asked me if there was any smell. It wasn't a smell, it was a stench! Every time I pulled my fingers out of the warm water, a veritable wave of rot would rush into my nostrils.

"Turn back immediately," the specialist ordered me, "if you want us to have even the slimmest chance of saving your hands."

I wasn't turning back! It was pretty obvious that she hadn't spent more than thirty-five days hiking across an ice field, this so-called specialist, hauling a four-hundred-plus-pound sled harnessed to her kidneys! What did she know about my situation? What right did she have to tell me to drop everything and abandon my goal?

I hung up abruptly after blurting out, "Thanks. I'll call you if I have any other questions."

I described this conversation to Cathy, who got in touch with one of my sponsors, Groupama Assistance. In turn, they got in touch with a man who is widely considered to be one of the leading specialists worldwide in cold-related pathologies, Dr. Emmanuel Cauchy, in his office in Chamonix. In his field this French doctor is a sort of guru, and his opinion is held in the highest regard.

Over the telephone, Dr. Cauchy began by asking me roughly the same questions as his fellow doctor, and he urged me above all else not to burst the blisters. I explained to him that I had regained a bit of feeling in the tips of my fingers. He agreed that this was encouraging, but he also argued in favor of a diagnosis that I had sustained level-four lesions. "Beyond that level," he said sharply, "there will be no alternative to amputation. And that will become inevitable if you continue to expose your hands to the cold because the condition of your fingers will continue to deteriorate."

I was furious and disappointed. I needed supporters, people who would pat me on the back and give me encouragement, not vultures who would urge me to throw in the towel.

While I obstinately refused to give in to the siren song of defeat, the news of my misadventures spread over the Internet, and then in the media. Back home in Switzerland, the television trumpeted the "Mike Horn affair," and from all sides, people were calling Cathy to go on the air, live, to defend her reckless husband, who was irresponsibly refusing to listen to the voice of reason. My wife bravely replied that I didn't need her to defend me. "He's the captain of his own ship; he makes his own decisions. I don't defend him; I help him and I support him, whatever choices he may make." She refused to give the media the names of the two doctors whom I consulted over the phone, but the journalists tracked them down on their own and invited them to appear on a talk show on the subject of frostbite and the other risks run by reckless fools like me. What is going to happen to Mike if he refuses to return? That question lay at the heart of the discussion.

In my mind, the question never even arose. These were my own fingers, my own life, my own decisions . . . and no one else's.

I continued to push on, and by this point I'd even stopped soaking my fingers in hot water. That method might be effective in a hospital setting or in a temperate climate. But here, at temperatures of thirty to forty degrees below zero, all that happened was that they were freezing a little more deeply each time I took them out of the water or whenever I used them to pitch my tent, attach a snap hook, tie my bootlaces, or get dinner ready ... and with each step that I took on the ice field. Bandages were what were needed. I even learned to function without using my hands, at least not in the usual way that hands are used. I used my teeth and the palms of my hands pressed together to seize an object if it wasn't too small.

To make up for the hours it took me to perform the simplest tasks, I hiked for shorter periods each day. The result was that I was moving forward more slowly than at the beginning of the expedition, but I was still keeping up a good average—more than nine miles per day—and I had every reason to be optimistic. One reason in particular was that despite all of my misadventures, I had reached the same point, after the same number of days, as four French legionnaires who attempted the same expedition the previous year.

But the warning from the doctor in Chamonix continued to haunt me. The days that still separated me from the North Pole were very likely going to cost me my fingers, not just the fingers that were already damaged, but perhaps the others as well. That would make me a cripple and would put an end to my career once and for all. I'd reach the North Pole ... sure, I could definitely get there. I had struggled and fought to achieve that. But once I was there, I would find myself on a little piece of drifting ice field at the top of the world. Was this one expedition really more important than being able to keep going for years to come, living this life of adventure as long as possible, this life that I had chosen for myself and which I would not give up for anything on earth?

I called my friend Johann Rupert, president of the Richemont group, to tell him what I was thinking and feeling. He did not have even a moment's hesitation. "Come back immediately!" he told me.

This was the third time that I had been given that piece of advice—or, perhaps I should say, that command. I was increasingly tempted to obey but ... I had never quit before. If I gave up now, it would be the first time in my life.

"Well," I told Johann, "I just need a little more time to make a decision."

I needed time, time to get used to the idea of giving up and failing to attain my goal, throwing in the towel when I was in better shape than ever before—despite these giant blisters on my fingertips and three frostbitten fingers, which were in no way keeping me from moving forward. I needed time to get used to the idea of failure, just when I could see the finish line ahead of me. A little more time to accept the idea that I might never have a second chance. While I continued to push on, the throes of my dilemma nearly made me forget the cold, and as I continued to mull the problem over in my mind, I finally saw this expedition for what it was, first and foremost: a priceless source of lessons about myself. Among other things, it would teach me the taste of defeat and how to deal with it, a valuable lesson for someone like me who had only ever met with success. I would be forced to return to Europe, to face the judgment of others, and to look them in the eye and answer, "Well, at least, I tried." A new experience and, perhaps, a valuable lesson in humility.

Franziska continued to speak to me as I unwrapped each packet of food that her husband had prepared for me. I would read the little message that came with it: "*Bon appétit*, and keep up your courage!" "Hang tough, it'll be over soon!" "Just one more push, and then you can go home!" "It's cold outside, but they're waiting for you by the fireplace!"

Knowing this voice that kept encouraging me belonged to a woman who was no longer alive was deeply moving and upsetting, and it gave me one more reason to outdo myself.

Suddenly, an incongruous question came to me: What should I do with all these little messages, the last messages, perhaps, that Franziska ever wrote? Would Philippe want me to bring them back home?

"No," Philippe answered without hesitating. He said to scatter them over the ice field, near the North Pole. "Bestow them upon nature, give them to the wind, like Tibetan prayer flags. That is what she would have wanted, to be part of the elements for all time."

A few days later, I complied with Philippe's wishes, and I tossed a handful of little strips of white paper into the howling Arctic storms.

The gale was so powerful that they vanished the instant they left my hand ... as if Franziska were in a hurry to rejoin that wild nature that she loved so much, even to her death at its hands.

I had passed eighty-five degrees north latitude. I was practically on a highway now—the ice field stretching out to the horizon before me was as flat as Utah's Bonneville Salt Flats. At night I slept for two or three hours, thanks to the morphine from my medical kit, which helped to calm the relentless throbbing in my fingers. The pain returned whenever I woke back up, but I forgot about it as soon as I started moving again. I was only about fifteen to twenty full days away from the northernmost point on the planet: the North Pole.

It was at this very moment that I felt a liberating shift. To reach the North Pole was an obsession that had so dominated my thinking that it blinded me to everything else. That was why I would actually be disappointed when I finally achieved my goal. I now felt certain that as soon as I reached that fateful spot, I would be emptied forever of the force that had driven me here and allowed me to rise above so many other challenges.

I imagined myself circling around the Pole, sniffing at it from a few yards away—without setting foot on it. That way I would still always have that goal to achieve, that Holy Grail to grasp, like a sweet reward that you save for last, the self-deprivation making it sweeter still. I would have succeeded in dominating the elements by deciding, myself, the outcome of the battle. And even if it might seem like I had failed, I would have won a personal victory.

It had been a week since my fingers were frostbitten. That evening it was a little less cold, and I pitched my tent by the light of a magnificent sunset. All around me there was a sort of fragile and perfect harmony. Although the natural forces of the Arctic had beaten me to within inches of my life, neither the cold, nor the pack ice, nor the crevasses had managed to kill me. Because I had merely survived, the decision was still my own.

I was ready to go home.

I called Cathy, and she alerted Gouram Assathiany, a young man of Georgian descent who spoke good Russian, and he took over. Because I was in the Russian sector of the ice field, Gouram contacted a number of different military bases in Siberia. He finally turned up a pilot and a helicopter that were willing to come to fetch me.

Before they could take me home, though, they needed first of all to find me, and that was no simple matter. The good folks at Argos had offered to "lend" me a rescue beacon for a period of two years, in exchange for fifty thousand Euros. That was a little too rich for my blood. And so my friend Vincent Borde managed to obtain a beacon for me from the people at Plastimo, who sent it to Russia, and from there to an encampment near the North Pole, and then relayed it to Cape Arktichesky by helicopter. A pilot who had been asked to bring me the beacon let me know that he was coming to drop it off. But when he got there I found out that it was going to cost me ten thousand Euros! That seemed like a lot of money for a detour of a few miles along a route he follows nearly every day!

That is why, to make a long story short, I had no beacon. And without a beacon, I would be quite a bit more difficult to find. The rescue beacon beamed out a signal that any helicopter crew could pick up and find while in the air. But in the absence of the beacon, I would have to relay my GPS position to Cathy, who would then relay it to Gouram, who would relay it to my rescuers. They would then embark on their mission as soon as the weather allowed, but all the while, I would be drifting off the mark I gave them on the constantly drifting polar ice. Because the Russian helicopter crew would have no way to receive my updated coordinates in flight, they would have to sweep 150 or 200 square miles of ice field to find me, and they claimed that they did not have enough fuel to do that kind of a search. They could only agree to come get me at some specific location and take me directly from there to their base. So I gave my coordinates to Cathy, who transmitted them to Gouram Assathiany, who then organized my rescue with the Russians. I had to keep my fingers crossed that I wouldn't drift out of their range.

Furthermore, in this country where bureaucracy was still the true reigning despot, to bring someone over the border and onto their territory who had neither passport nor entry visa, and who was armed as well—I carried a gun only so that I could defend myself against polar bears—would be a major affair of state, even if it was a question of life or death. I spent two days waiting, huddled in my tent. Two days of atrocious suffering from the pain in my fingers. Two days in which the ice began to break up all around me once again, and during which I began to drift on a piece of ice field once again. In a rage I called Gouram to tell him that, since I had been drifting away from my position for the entire forty-eight hours, I was going to have to break camp and hike back to it. He told me, above all, not to move. The rescue operation was underway. For the sake of peace and quiet, I obeyed and curled up, once again, in my tent, like a snail in its shell. I stuffed myself with morphine pills to assuage the terrible pain that continued to torment my fingers.

When Cathy called me the next morning to tell me that the helicopter would reach me in eight hours, I was too weak even to try to believe her. I took another dose of morphine and slipped back into a comatose slumber. My dreams, peopled with giant ice cubes that knocked against one another in all directions, were suddenly disturbed by the hacking sound of an electric chopper . . . unless it was the sputtering of an Arctic lawn mower. Suddenly I was jolted into wakefulness by the metallic sliding sound of the zipper of my tent. The two flaps pulled open to reveal the bearded and hooded face of a Russian soldier.

"Come on, let's go," he cried. "Get moving! We're leaving! Hurry up!"

And I, my brain still swirling and foggy, replied, "Huh? Wh-wha . . . ?"

"We're heading back to the base. Right now! The helicopter can't set down because of the condition of the ice, and there is just enough fuel to get back!"

They hustled me out of my tent and told me to climb into the helicopter—in fact, it was hovering a few feet above the ice—and to leave all my equipment behind. I refused. I would rather stay right here than abandon everything by which, for which, and thanks to which I had survived for the past forty days and forty nights. Maybe it was the effect of the morphine, but it suddenly seemed to me that all this equipment had become a part of me. I couldn't even imagine abandoning it on the ice.

Faced with my stubborn refusal, the Russians chose to accommodate my demands instead of wasting another minute arguing. In the blizzard of snow being kicked up by the chopper blades, they opened the luggage hatches and tossed all my equipment inside with the distinctive brutality of underpaid moving men. It was true that there was not a single place to land between here and Cape Arktichesky, and that if we ran out of gas, we'd drop straight down into the Arctic Ocean, and that would be the end of the trip for everyone.

I jumped aboard, and the helicopter lifted off immediately. A Russian doctor who had been sent to administer emergency first aid examined my fingers with a grim expression and a series of eloquent shakes of the head. He replaced my amateurish dressings with clean bandages, treated my frostbite with an antiseptic spray, and gave me another dose of morphine, an injection this time. Apathetically, I watched him at work and a young Russian woman from a local television station who was filming everything with a TV camera on her shoulder. I could feel nothing but a profound sense of disappointment, an overwhelming sadness that brought tears to my eyes, as the miles of ice slipped away under my feet, all that ground that I had struggled to cover in the opposite direction. I was unhappy, frustrated, angry. None of it made sense. This wasn't how the journey was supposed to end!

I was suffering from emotional whiplash caused by that brutal withdrawal from a wild place that had grown to be part of me. I had been there for so long, with no one to talk to except for the ice and the snow.

They gave me vodka and steaming hot tea to drink; they gave me reindeer meat to eat. I swallowed mechanically. I was barely listening to the pilot when he came back to tell us that the fuel gauge was on empty and that we might not make it back. I listened to the signals that the navigator was sending in Morse code. Didn't he have any other way of communicating? I noticed that we were flying so low that we were practically skimming the ice; perhaps that was to shorten the fall. When a helicopter runs out of gas, it must drop like a brick....

Suddenly the rotor came to a halt with a terrible clatter at the very instant that we touched down on the landing strip of Cape Arktichesky. The entire crew heaved a deep sigh of relief. Mission accomplished.

We quickly refueled and then we took off for Dickson, a port on the Russian Arctic Ocean that was also the helicopter's base. There they loaded me into an ambulance, which raced through the snow to the hospital, an immense and sinister building made of cracked concrete that seemed on the verge of collapse. It was practically empty, lined with metal beds without mattresses. I found myself in a shower room whose tiles were half gone and where the plumbing was mostly just a distant memory. They filled the sole bathtub with buckets of water, which had probably been heated over a coal-burning stove. It occurred to me that I might be in an abandoned gulag.

But after what I'd been through, it looked like a three-star health spa, and I was going to enjoy a fairly basic cleaning. I hadn't washed in fifty days, and I was emitting a distinct whiff of polecat.

There was just one problem: I was going to have a difficult time undressing without full use of my hands. That was when a Russian nurse showed up to help me with my washing. She was quite different from the old fantasy of the Russian sex bomb, braless beneath a sheer blouse; this nurse could easily have passed for an Olympic champion weightlifter from the old days of the Soviet Union. She was so massive that she had to turn sideways to get through the door, and when she finally came to a halt in front of me, I felt like I had finally met the Yeti, only hairier. With a muffled grunt, the abominable snow woman lunged at me and ripped off my clothing. When I was dressed in nothing but my dirt, she shoved me into the tub of boiling hot water, leaving me to simmer for a while so that the filth would loosen its grip on my skin. I barely had time to begin to relax in the hot water when she reappeared, brandishing a terrifying scrub brush. She grabbed me and lifted me out of the water as if I was a newborn baby, and then set about methodically scrubbing every square inch of my body, the way you might groom a horse. But she knew her job. Soon I was red as a lobster but impeccably clean.

Clothed only in a pair of slippers and a hospital gown that was loosely tied, hanging open in the back so that my ass enjoyed a cool breeze, I met a Russian surgeon. He drew circles in felt-tip marker at the bases of my thumbs, and he explained to me that he planned to cut them off whole.

I yelled, "Nyet!"

However fatalistic I might have become since being rescued from the ice field, I was not about to allow this Siberian Dr. Frankenstein to begin to butcher me! If I lost my thumbs, it would be the same as losing my hands; and if I was going to lose my hands, then I might as well go ahead and kill myself!

I was saved by Gouram, who called the mayor of Dickson just a few minutes later to warn him that a Learjet with a doctor on board had just taken off from Paris and was flying to Norilsk to take me back to Europe, where I would be given proper treatment. In the meanwhile, absolutely no surgery was to be performed on my body. When the hospital surgeon received these instructions, he was visibly disappointed— he would have been so happy to perform a few amputations. I was placed in a bed with a mattress and a set of sheets that they found who knows where. They gave me an old-fashioned IV: the bottle was made of glass, and I screamed when a weight-lifting nurse technician stabbed me in the arm with a needle so big that it looked like the exhaust pipe of an old car.

A few minutes later the mayor of Dickson made his appearance. He had come in person to pay his respects to a man he'd never heard of in his life, but whom Gouram Assathiany had described as a famous adventurer, an international celebrity. He was clearly delighted that I had come to pay a visit to his lovely town, and he seemed to have only warm feelings toward me, though I could only guess, since I didn't speak a word of Russian, and he spoke not a word of any other language. Without a word he sat down on my bed, and with a convivial smile he pulled back the flaps of his voluminous leather jacket and took out, in order, a bottle of vodka, two glasses, three oranges, a knife, a loaf of bread, and a garlic-flavored sausage. He sliced the oranges and cut both bread and sausage. He poured out two brimming glassfuls and proposed a toast before we drank together: *Na Zdrovyeh!* Cheers!

It struck me as unlikely that alcohol—especially such high-proof alcohol—was what the doctor would order right now, especially since I hadn't had a drop of alcohol for the past forty-five days, and my veins were filled to the brim with morphine, along with other medicines. But it would seem ungracious to refuse. My host explained the art of alternating mouthfuls of orange slices, bread, or sausage, and gulps of vodka, tossed down like water. My glass seemed to refill itself magically each time I set it down. I was aware that in Russia you never open a bottle of vodka without finishing it off. In these situations, you do what you have to do. The gray hospital walls began to spin. Luckily, I was already lying down, and the bottle was empty.

But the mayor's jacket contained a second bottle! I gave up on that bottle before it was empty, and left my host to polish it off by himself. I expected by this point to see him collapse on the bed next to mine, but instead he took his leave, tottering only slightly, his face glowing in a radiant smile.

During the night I spent in the hospital of Dickson, I had some time to think. The odds were good that they'd save my fingers. I had done what I had to do, and I had accomplished what I accomplished. I had no alternative at this point than to explain what had happened to the journalists, to my friends, and to all the others . . . and to make peace with myself.

Gouram had arranged for me to be transported by helicopter to Norilsk the following day. There, the Learjet that had arrived from Paris was waiting to whisk me to Geneva. From there, I'd be taken to Chamonix, to be cared for in Dr. Cauchy's clinic. But the helicopters were all grounded by bad weather, and it took another twenty-four hours before I reached Norilsk. There, envelopes filled with cash were discreetly exchanged, and I was miraculously excused from of all bureaucratic formalities.

I later learned that the envelopes were fatter and more numerous than I had imagined, and that my rescue had been quite the Herculean undertaking, as supervised from the Paris office of Groupama Assistance.

When I had given the green light for evacuation, Gouram Assathiany immediately reached out and contacted the three nearest Siberian military bases. The first base did have a helicopter, but its blades had been removed and placed in storage; the second base had an aircraft, but no one could find the engine. At the third base, the one in Dickson, a pilot replied that his helicopter was ready to fly . . . but he, quite clearly, was not. Gouram called back the next day, once the effects of the vodka had worn off. Once he was sober, the pilot demanded a small fortune to go pick me up. After tough negotiations, Gouram and the pilot came to an agreement. I was a seven-hour flight from Dickson and the pilot demanded the presence of a second crew—and they wouldn't be doing charity work, either.

"And what about the kerosene," he added. "Do you have kerosene of your own, or would you like to buy some of ours?" Because the military base was short on fuel, it had been necessary to persuade—with U.S. dollars—the captain of an oil tanker cruising in the Arctic Ocean to make port at Cape Arktichesky to resupply the helicopter. The result? The most expensive tankful of fuel in history.

Gouram had then been obliged to reach out to his contacts in Moscow in order to obtain authorization for us to enter Russian territory—me, my gun, and my lack of papers. There, too, large quantities of cash had changed hands. And it was because the mayor of Dickson had also been generously paid off that he had been so solicitous—and so generous—to me.

It's enough to make you a cynic.

Aboard the private jet, I was welcomed by Cathy, the great Dr. Cauchy from Chamonix, a stewardess, and three pilots. Fed and pampered like a first-class passenger, I enjoyed a trip back home that would have been heavenly had the specialist, probing my frostbitten fingertips with the end of his scalpel, not delivered a prognosis of the loss of most of my first finger joints. It would be necessary in any case to amputate from the point where the bone was frostbitten, he said. We only needed to determine with greater precision just where that point was, which could not be done just yet. All the same, there was one last hope: a new type of treatment that was supposed to revive dead tissue.

I rejoiced inwardly. Whatever happened, I would be able to use my hands.

In Geneva, since the damage to my toes prevented me from wearing any shoes at all, I exited the plane barefoot and with bandaged hands. The media were there, uninvited but eager to greet me nonetheless.

After being admitted to the clinic in Chamonix, where I arrived at about one in the morning, the treatment began. The treatment consisted of injecting a vasodilator into my fingers, while my hands were soaking in a solution of Betadine; the vasodilator was to force the blood toward the extremities of my fingers. Each time the tissues became accustomed to the pressure, it was increased. I was on the verge of fainting for the three hours of the first session. There were two sessions a day for many days running, alternating with baths of Betadine.

Once the treatment had been completed, Dr. Cauchy told me that we had a choice between either amputating immediately or waiting a month, perhaps six weeks, to see how things developed. The second option was a double-edged sword, so to speak. It might help to save a little more of the joint, or it might result in my losing that much more.

I decided to run the risk.

With my fingers still bandaged, I returned home. The media peppered me with questions, and not always friendly ones. I didn't bother to answer most of them. In an attempt to escape the photographers trying to get shots of my fingers, I spent hours every day running or bicycling (even though it was difficult to grip the handlebars), both to get back into shape and in order to boost my circulation. Cathy changed my bandages every day. My fingers began to turn black, withering and desiccating, and taking on the general appearance of jerky. The fingernails fell off, and pus oozed out. I couldn't tell if things were getting better or worse. But I decided not to give in to adversity, and to do every-thing I could to get the upper hand, as it were.

After a month, I went back to Chamonix, where they injected a sub-stance into me, a radioactive compound that had the property of bond-ing with all the living tissues it encountered, so that X-rays could distinguish clearly between living zones and dead zones. This examina-tion revealed—hear ye, hear ye!—that I had recovered a bit of life in certain tissues. But the rest was dead—definitively, this time.

Ten days later, the extremities of three of my fingers were amputated, and the lifeless tip of one of my thumbs was shaved off. Later, the am-putated fingers were reshaped to look more like fingers. After the oper-ation, the surgeon decided not to close the wound but to allow the skin to grow back as much as possible, which resulted in a further layer of growth.

When I went back to see him a few weeks later, my amputations were barely visible to the naked eye. The tips of my fingers were flat, with a bevel cut instead of being rounded, and the pads of the extremi-ties had been replaced with a horny layer.

Admittedly, my fingertips had lost their sensitivity, and I had diffi-culty picking up a needle or twisting a nut onto a small bolt. But I still had ten fingers, and that was what counted.

One thing is certain, my surgeon told me: if I had spent just a few more days on the ice field, I would have lost my fingers.

I asked him when I could go back to the Far North.

"You are absolutely forbidden to expose your hands to extreme cold for at least two years, Mike," the doctor answered me.

Four months later, I set out to travel around the Arctic Circle.

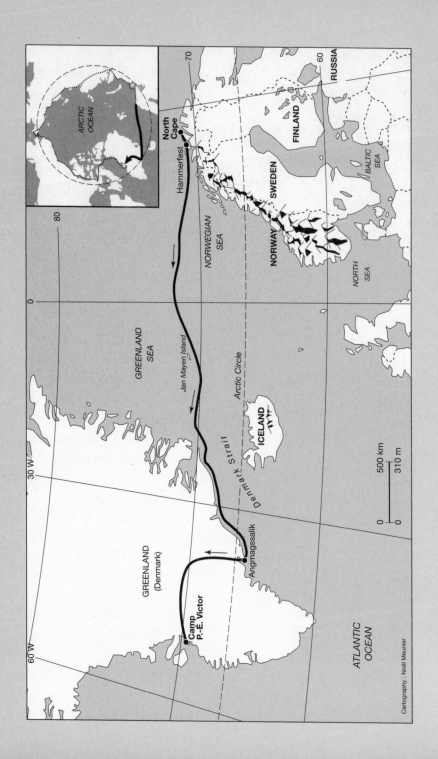

Cartography : Noël Meunier

# 2

# Terra Incognita

I WAS POSITIVE OF ONE THING. I needed to go back as soon as possible. Starting from the moment I got back home, during the treatment, during the operation, and during my convalescence, I never stopped thinking about what it was like up there. It was as if I was sitting on the bench, waiting to be put back into the game.

Regardless of what my specialist said about it, I couldn't possibly wait for two years. It would feel as if I had been buried alive. For that matter, I am a professional, and a professional could not afford to be off the circuit for such a long time. People have short memories.

I calculated that if I were to leave at the beginning of August, I would have three months of relatively mild temperatures in which to become reacclimated to the cold. Moreover, I would be done with the long maritime section of my voyage right away, and under the best conditions, since the Greenland Sea would be free of ice. Once I was on solid ground, so to speak, whatever bad weather did hit wouldn't impede my progress. And I could also expect Baffin Bay, between Greenland and Canada, to be navigable.

I had a two-month window to make it by boat across these two bodies of water before they froze and were no longer navigable. That was why I would start there, to avoid the risk that a delay in Russia or elsewhere might force me to wait for the thaw, stuck somewhere for eight months.

Now, if everything worked more or less according to plan, I would be on the shores of the Bering Strait (between Alaska and Siberia) sometime around September 2003, during the time of the year when the daunting waters of the Bering Sea observe a sort of summer truce. Two months later, the sea would be covered with ice, and I would have to wait until February of the following year for the ice to be sufficiently thick and solid to cross on foot.

In short, a relatively tight "slot." I decided to start out on my journey around the Arctic Circle on August 4, 2002.

Far from having beaten me, my relative failure in my effort to reach the North Pole had given me an invaluable body of experience and a single clear lesson. By learning to say stop, I had taken a giant step toward greater wisdom.

Everything started to move more quickly. The things that Børge had taught me were now enriched with my own hard-earned experience, which allowed me to customize my gear to better suit it to my own personal preferences. I took advantage of the four months that remained before the big departure to have new prototypes of my kites produced, both larger and smaller in size, to haul me across the ice like a sailboat in different wind conditions. When I went shopping at Salomon, I selected a pair of "improved" telemark skis, that is, skis whose width was between that of cross-country skis and downhill skis. It would take more effort to move forward, but I would also have a larger load-bearing surface, which would help me to stay on top of the snow instead of sinking into it. The company specialists worked with me to determine the ideal balance between the wood of the laths, the steel of the edges, and the Pytex of the bottom runners, so that the optimum curvature of the ski structure would be maintained, even at forty degrees below zero.

I modified certain buttons, levers, and springs so that I could work them even with frozen fingers. I selected double-sealed bottles so that I wouldn't lose the contents and the container if a stopper were to break. I carefully avoided the new high-pressure thermos bottles with springs and other gadgets that seemed certain to break in conditions of intense cold. If their contents were to leak or freeze, I would be in serious trouble.

It wasn't that I was being picky. It was that I wanted to survive. I could only recite with greater conviction what I had said before setting out for the North Pole: my life was going to depend on each piece of equipment, as it never had before.

Panerai specially manufactured for me an antimagnetic watch whose mechanism avoided all contact with the case in order to withstand the cold and was therefore suspended by means of a contrivance so secret that its inventors refused to reveal it even to me. I would wear it on my sleeve, by means of a long Velcro bracelet, and not against my skin, because the metal would stick to it in the extreme cold and—incredible but true!—it would draw the body heat out of my fingers. As for the idea of a plastic watch, it wouldn't last twenty-four hours. I would be the first person to test this Panerai watch, the Arktos model, virtually indestructible and created especially for my expedition. If it made it through this challenge, it would be marketed in a limited edition.

Yvan Ravussin specially manufactured a snow shovel for me that was a little jewel. It was made of carbon Kevlar, just like chainsaw-proof trousers and bulletproof vests; it was both unbreakable and light as a feather.

But first of all and most important, I had my tents completely redesigned by my Italian manufacturer, Ferrino, to whom I took a number of sketches and a daunting list of specifications—daunting even for them. While the company had done a lot of work with polar expeditions, it had never yet designed or produced a tent intended for long-term use in such extreme conditions.

I reexamined everything, beginning with the materials themselves. My tent would be made out of nylon composed of small squares that would prevent any tear from spreading. This nylon would theoretically remain unbreakable even when exposed to temperatures at which metal becomes fragile as glass, or elastic loses its stretchiness, or a folded tent stiffens like a sheet of steel.

At the factory, we thought a lot about the ideal shape: dome, half-tube, A-frame, or tepee? A half-tube tent—that is, tunnel-shaped—is ideal when it stands facing the wind (you get the same wing-effect as with an airplane). But in the Arctic the wind constantly shifts direction, and a side-gust will collapse the tunnel shape in the middle because there is no central arch. I decided to opt for a hybrid shape, a blend of tube and dome, with crossing struts in the middle that would provide greater strength in high winds, blowing from whatever quarter. This tent would be relatively close to the ground to minimize heat loss, but not too low, so that I would be able to sit upright in it, especially when bad weather forced me to stay inside for days at a time. In order to avoid wasting a single square inch of tent space, or carrying any unnecessary fabric (a few ounces can constitute a considerable difference), I had them narrow the tent at the base and widen it farther up, where I needed more room to move around. Suddenly, my cross between a tube and a dome was beginning to look a lot like a suppository.

Also, I didn't want a lot of guy wires or a lot of tent stakes, either. Instead of stakes I would use my ski poles and skis buried in the snow, and my sled. If there was a very strong wind, I'd drive two ice screws into the ground, and I'd moor my tent to them once it was pitched.

It needed to be perfectly ventilated in order to allow the escape of the moisture and steam I would create each time I melted snow or heated my food. Otherwise, the moisture would coat the inner walls of the tent—as well as my clothes—with ice, and I would freeze on the spot. The ventilation would work as follows: the cold air would enter the tent at ground level through a vent, and then it would be heated before escaping from a sort of chimney at the top of the tent. Moreover, the tent would be composed of two layers: the second layer, the fly, would serve as insulation. Between the two layers, the slightly warmer—or less frigid—air would help to warm the interior, and the condensation, which would form on the cover, would be easier to get rid of. Last, I asked them to create a sort of vestibule where, each evening, I could leave my ice-cold, snow-covered footwear. If that snow got inside the tent, it would eventually turn into an icy crust that would be impossible to get rid of.

I would need a window to see what was going on outside (in case of an emergency, for instance) without actually having to leave the tent. Therefore, it was necessary to perfect a transparent material that would not break when subjected to extreme cold.

The opening at the front of the tent required an oversized zipper fastening so that snow and ice would not block it, with a zipper tongue big enough that I could grab it with my mittens and injection-molded from a rigorously unbreakable plastic. To protect the zipper from the elements, it was covered with a flap. And I added a Velcro fastening as well, but at extremely low temperatures Velcro breaks. So do fiberglass tent poles when they are bent at temperatures this low. We would therefore have to use aluminum, but manufactured at a density carefully calibrated to ensure that the tent poles didn't shrink in the cold; otherwise, they would no longer fit together. There were six of them in all, about a foot and a half in length. I would also bring two spare poles.

As for the delicate matter of answering the call of nature, it was out of the question to drop my pants outdoors in the howling wind at sixty or more degrees below zero. To solve this problem I had them make a trapdoor in the tent floor with a Velcro fastening. All I would have to do was open the trapdoor, dig a little hole in the snow, and close the trapdoor when I was done.

I also had to be able to set up my tent in less than twenty seconds. With that end in mind, I needed to be able to open it as easily as an umbrella, by means of a simple, solid mechanism that I could fix myself, if necessary.

I even built in a breaking point. If the tent gave way when the winds got too strong, it would keep the whole structure from being ripped to shreds. This Achilles' heel was located at ground level near the main opening, which would make it possible for me to fix it without having to go outside.

In short, like all the rest of my gear, my tent would comply with my three basic requirements: it would be sturdy, easy to use, and easy to fix.

That, among other qualities, is what I expected from my sleeping bag as well. It would be my only source of physical comfort, the only warm place in my environment, the one thing that would absolutely need to stay dry and ice-free. To that end, the most important addition would be the insulating sheath recommended by Børge Ousland to prevent the quart of sweat that I would emit every night from freezing in the sleeping bag, making it a full two pounds heavier every day and turning me into a sleeping icicle each night. (I would have to empty the lining each morning.) Thus, it was out of the question to think of slipping my head down into the warmth of the sleeping bag where the vapor from my breath would form ice inside the bag. To hold in the warm air, the sleeping bag would have a collar that closed with a zipper, fitting snugly around my neck. There were no seams and no stitching, which would let the heat escape (and the cold in) if my knees pressed against them when I curled up asleep. At the points of support—shoulders, hips, knees—the bag was reinforced with a quilted padding that softened the thin foam mat on which the bag lay in order to allow air to circulate on all sides and to preserve the insulation. When you're sleeping on ice, it's not a luxury experience. For the same reasons the width of the base of the sleeping bag corresponded to the length of my feet plus an inch or so.

The sleeping bag's zipper opening ended midway down because I would get in from the top, and it was located on the left side to ensure that my bag stayed well clear of my stove when I unzipped it.

If everything needed to be easy to fix, I would also need materials with which to fix things. I gradually assembled a repair kit, a sort of first-aid kit for my gear, which contained swatches of wool, Polartec, and Gore-Tex; needles strong enough to pierce leather; unbreakable thread; resin epoxy cloth repair; metal wire; Kevlar thread; twine; sandpaper; glue; nails; and so on. In short, everything I would need to fix absolutely everything that could conceivably break.

Then, once all my requirements had been met, an unexpected difficulty arose. It was impossible to test this new equipment under real-world conditions. Most industrial cold chambers would not get any colder than about zero or four degrees below zero. For me on the ice field, that's so warm that I would be tempted to put on shorts and a T-shirt! (I'm only barely exaggerating.)

This situation clearly illustrated once again the need for total trust between me and Ferrino, my tentmaker. This wasn't a matter of sales or marketing. It was a life-and-death matter. This tent, this tenth-of-an-inch-thick sheet of nylon that stood between me and the elements was a barrier between life and death. If I lost the tent, it would be the end of my expedition, and possibly the end of me, too, as I couldn't afford to carry the weight of a backup tent with me.

All of this activity made me completely forget about the still raw wounds on my fingers. Mentally I was already out there, and I sensed— I knew—that this totally positive attitude could only have a beneficial effect on my body's capacity to heal.

As always, my team gave me invaluable help and support. Jean-Philippe Patthey was in charge of logistics, together with Cathy. Sebastian Devenish would be the expedition photographer, just as he had been for the trip around the equator. Raphaël Blanc was in charge of directing the video footage of my adventure. Since I would be alone most of the time, though, I would do most of the actual filming. Sebastian developed a camera especially for me, equipped with a dual battery to make up for the loss of voltage due to the extreme cold and an oversized shutter release so that I could get my finger onto it even with mittens on. Because film tends to break at twenty-two degrees below zero, the camera rolled the film into the canister as each shot was taken, rather than the other way around. With this system any photographs I took would be saved automatically.

We had to manage without digital photography because of the cold, which damages the digital medium and produces shots that look like they were taken through a kaleidoscope. That said, I planned to keep a small digital camera under my parka, where it would be warm, ready to be pulled out in case of an emergency. By the time it froze, I would have already taken a few quick snaps.

Cathy, who apparently didn't think that she had enough work to do updating my Web site and managing relations with the media and my sponsors, also made meals for me for the entire expedition and vacuum-packed them in portions that corresponded to my future daily rations. With Annika and Jessica's help, the family kitchen was turned into a small-scale factory producing enormous quantities of hyper-caloric food.

During my expedition, Cathy would be my only contact with the rest of the world. I would be calling her to give her all the latest news and report my current position. If I let three days go by without calling, she would know that I had a problem. After seventy-two hours she would call the rescue teams. To prevent that from happening, I brought two satellite telephones with me. They would work perfectly well anywhere on the face of the earth thanks to the use of three of the thirty satellites in permanent geosynchronous orbit. My satellite phones used lithium batteries, which lose less charge in extremly cold conditions in addition to being light and easy to use. If I used it sparingly, it would operate for a month and a half. I carried three with me. Like an ordinary cell phone, my satellite phone had a normal phone number so that anyone could call me when it was turned on. That was how journalists would contact me if Cathy had granted them a phone appointment.

Jean-Philippe Patthey would have to be ready to join me at any time in the most inaccessible places imaginable, to bring me supplies of food or equipment or to bring visitors for whatever reason.

Jean-Philippe, about fifty years old, was a former industrial baker from Brittany, France, who decided one day to change his life. He sold his baking business and came to offer me his services, asking nothing more than to have his expenses reimbursed. He had no experience, but his motivation—"I want to begin to live"—made me decide to make him part of the team. Enthusiastic, efficient, hard-working, and ready to plunge into things, he quickly became a member of the family.

Philippe Varrin would be in charge of translating my Web site into French. He also needed to be ready to leave on the shortest imaginable notice to go wherever he might be needed.

My brother Martin would oversee the transport of the boats.

I would need a boat to sail from the North Cape of Norway to the Greenland coast and later to go from Greenland to Canada, but it couldn't be just any boat. It would need to be a sort of miniature icebreaker with a retractable keel—a feature that's very unusual in monohull boats—so that I could "glide" over the ice. In fact, the way you break ice is by pressing down on it, not by smashing into it headlong. I wanted the hull to be made of aluminum, not steel. Steel rips on impact with an obstacle while aluminum just dents. Moreover, a boat made of steel would weigh forty tons and would slow me down considerably. The lower section of the hull needed to be at least half an inch thick; otherwise it would crack like a nutshell under the pressure of the ice. The hull would have to be sufficiently rounded that it would rise up out of the water when ice formed around it, instead of being crushed or trapped. With all these demands I might as well have been looking for a pig with wings.

To help me find such a boat I called on Steve Ravussin, my friend and mentor in the art of sailing. It was Steve who taught me on Lake Geneva how to sail the little trimaran in which I later crossed three oceans during my trip around the equator.

Together, Steve and I scoured all the marinas of the French Riviera in search of the ideal vessel. We hunted in vain. None of the fifty or sixty boats we were offered fit our needs, or else they were out of my budget. Nor did I have the money to have one custom-built. Even if I did, that would take four to six months, and I was leaving in thirty days. I was really starting to worry when somebody told us about a boat that was just what we were looking for, or so they said. It was for sale in Bénodet. I had not seen plans or photographs of this boat. I had no idea what it looked like. All the same, we hopped in the car and began driving to Brittany. When we finally got there, after an exhausting drive, we called the boat's owner to arrange to see it. Impossible, he said. He was in Paris where he practiced as a dentist. Fortunately, his wife was in town. We arranged to meet her at the marina.

While we waited for her, we looked around at the boats. One boat in particular caught our attention. It was a forty-six-foot vessel whose hull was the burnished gray typical of aluminum. "That is exactly what you need!" Steve shouted. If only that were the boat. A few moments later, the owner appeared on the deck. Then came the second miracle. According to the plans that she showed us, the boat suited my needs in every detail. Inside it was luxurious—berths, shower, hot water. It even had a ninety-horsepower engine, a crucial factor to my crew when they needed to ferry the boat around Greenland while I skied across the country. I, of course, would have no right to use the engine except for recharging my battery and for maneuvering in ports, where it is required.

I was walking on air out of happiness, until I heard the price, fifty thousand Euros above my budget.

At first the owners refused to lower their price. Perhaps the agency would agree to drop its commission, the woman said. At the broker I happened to meet a gentleman who had heard about me. He agreed to drop his commission in exchange for a little publicity. Later I became better acquainted with Jean-Yves Moysin, the dentist who owned the boat. He told me he had built it himself, and he would be proud to see his "baby" accompanying me on my journey around the Arctic Circle.

After two weeks of negotiations, we agreed on a more reasonable price. The deal was done. I had my boat!

There were a few modifications to be made to get it ready to go to sea and to face an Arctic winter. I sanded the hull, I laid down nonskid material on the deck because of the ice that would form there, and I installed a retractable propeller that would reduce drag and be less exposed to damage. The Katadyn company gave me a water purifier that would transform seawater into drinking water.

The boat was the last piece of the puzzle. Now that it was in place, there was nothing to keep me from leaving.

Another willing volunteer, Pierre-Yves Martin, stepped forward to help ferry the boat to North Cape and then around Greenland. He came on board at Bénodet in late July 2002, along with Jean-Philippe and another Swiss friend of mine, Denis, for a beautiful cruise along the coast of Norway, one of the loveliest places on earth.

I would catch up with them toward the end of their cruise. I still had to nail down my budget, obtain a few extensions, find a few extra sponsors, and do a few last lectures before leaving. These speaking engagements are my only source of revenue. I try to do as many as I can before leaving on an adventure so that Cathy will have enough money to run the house while I'm gone. (There is also a small salary for her in the expedition budget, a minor compensation for the enormous task of supporting and keeping up with me.)

I also gave interviews to journalists. Some of them criticized me for the risks I had run in the past and the risks I was about to face. It is true that if I had just stayed home, my fingers would not have been frostbitten. As I always say, "If you never use your shovel, you'll never break the handle." And my shovel could break at any time. I have had more accidents than I can count, and I expect to have plenty more of them. The next accident could even be fatal. But running risks is part of the work I do, just as risk is inherent in other professions.

In a completely demented aside, one representative of the media wondered, "How can a South African survive in the Arctic? He necessarily lacks the experience and the knowledge required." I wanted to answer him that all I need is a fire in the belly and an absolute determination to stay alive. It really all adds up to that when battling the Arctic.

Aboard our Mercedes Sprinter truck, Cathy, my daughters, and I left Switzerland on the long journey that would take us across Europe from south to north. Finally, at Tromsö, a small coastal town in northern Norway, we met up with my boat and its temporary crew. Pierre-Yves had taken care of all the equipment—halyards, generator, batteries, spare sails, tools, and so forth—and a few finishing touches. As a result, the boat was practically brand-new.

Then we traded vehicles. We gave them the truck in exchange for the sailboat. And so it was as a family that we made our three-day sail up to North Cape, spending a last brief moment together before I set off on my adventure.

Sponsors, friends from Château d'Oex, Les Moulins, and elsewhere, and a great many others had traveled to that remote spot from which I was about to set off on my new challenge. One of my cousins held the record for the longest journey; she came all the way from South Africa with her husband and her son. Everyone seemed to share the same sense of enthusiasm. As for me, I had experienced this before—the glorious part of an expedition is not so much reaching the destination but the departure, which represents the culmination of so much effort. This was the most rewarding moment because I finally had the wings with which I was going to be able to fly. I had devoted immense amounts of energy and effort for the past year and a half toward the single goal of being here, now, ready to do what I had to do. I reached this point much sooner than I ever would have believed possible. The waiting period was over. Even though they were not entirely healed, my frozen fingers—and the whole North Pole saga—belonged to the past. I was back in my element once again. For the moment, I needed only to focus all my energies on my first objective: to claw my way clear of the cliffs of the North Cape and set sail for Greenland, maintaining my course within a corridor between sixty-six degrees north—the Arctic Circle— and seventy-six degrees north.

On August 4, 2002, a number of my supporters and I set sail from Hammerfest, the little Norwegian town where their hotel was located, and headed for the tiny fishing village, Skarwag, close to where my starting line was located. Others arrived in minivans. Under a gray drizzle that was illuminated from time to time by slanting shafts of sunlight, we raised our champagne glasses in a toast to the success of my adventure, beside the wharf where my boat was moored.

The time had come to say good-bye. Cathy and my daughters were the last people I wrapped in my arms before hoisting the anchor. As the boat began to pull away from the wharf, Annika and Jessica leaned out for one last kiss, to tell me that they both loved me and to say that they were sure that I was going to make it. My heart was in my throat. Now, more than ever, I knew that I had to make it back alive. The euphoria of departure did not prevent me from seeing that this separation would be painful for my wife and my daughters.

On the stormy sea my friends accompanied me a little way aboard a trawler, taking photographs and making sweeping gestures of farewell. Standing in the bow, I answered them. With the mainsail set, but on autopilot, my boat pitched into the trough and rose again, bow pointing at the sky. I disappeared and reappeared among the tossing waves, my face lashed by the gusts of wind. The gray water burst beneath my haul, spraying geysers all around me. I was happy. Here—and now—was where I wanted to be; I had fought to be here, and this was the first victory in that battle.

I turned around for one last glimpse of the boat that was carrying my friends and my family. It vanished in the distance, and I didn't turn around again.

For me, this was the beginning of the adventure. For them, the beginning of the wait.

The giant cliffs of North Cape formed a wall of rock that rose a few hundred feet into the sky. The gray waves crashed repeatedly against it. Atop the cliffs stood a bronze globe that marks the exact location of the northernmost point in Europe.

Just at that moment, my GPS indicated that I was crossing the imaginary starting line. I gathered all my strength to fix in my memory all the details of my surroundings, every rocky crag of the cliffs, every jutting relief, every bit of greenery . . . right down to the fierce whirlwinds in the sky and the somber swells of the sea. I wanted all this to stay with me. I wanted to be able to compare this image to the one I would see when I would reappear here, moving in the same direction after having traveled the length of the Arctic Circle. Of all the seas, rivers, and lakes that I was going to cross, of all the ice fields, barren tundra, and vast icy expanses that I would have crossed by then, all the cliffs, crevasses, mountains, and so on, this view would be the only one that would not be appearing to me for the first—and the last—time.

More important, this would be my finish line, my final destination. I wanted to be able to visualize it at any moment, even from twelve thousand miles from now, and say to myself, "That's where I'm going."

I had settled on traveling around the Arctic Circle against the winds and against the ocean currents for one very simple reason: if I had succeeded in the challenge by going in the opposite direction, I would have spent the rest of my life wondering what would have happened had I gone the more difficult way.

There were no ships in sight—nothing but menacing seas and wind. It was sobering to think that the ocean stretching out in front of me was virtually unknown. So few people venture onto these waters that there is practically no information about them at all. Far from frightening me, the idea struck me as exciting. Whatever I was going to run into between here and Greenland, I looked forward to it with impatience, and I felt sure that my experience as a sailor would allow me to deal with it. I was so pumped that I was beginning to look forward to obstacles and difficulties as a bundle of tasty treats.

But the first challenge had a funny flavor. Shortly after my departure I realized that my automatic pilot seemed incapable of holding a course; it was wandering all over the compass. And yet it had a gyrocompass, indicating true north and not magnetic north, something indispensable at these northerly latitudes.

After struggling with the autopilot for ten hours, I phoned the Raytheon representative, who told me that my automatic pilot was the most sophisticated model available on the market. It simply *could not* break down. I replied that it *had* broken down, that I was being forced to adjust my course repeatedly, that I was wasting time . . . and that I was getting annoyed.

"All right, all right." The manufacturer said to me, "Head back to Hammerfest. We'll send one of our Norwegian reps to meet you."

So I turned around and I called Jean-Philippe Patthey, who was getting ready to head back to Switzerland with the truck (everybody else had already taken the plane back), and asked him to wait for me.

Back at Hammerfest, everyone took turns examining my automatic pilot; they disassembled it, reassembled it, tested it, retested it—and finally declared that it was functioning perfectly. I kept on tinkering with it and realized that the fire extinguisher was fastened to the other side of the wall from where my automatic pilot was normally hung—the automatic pilot whose compass had to be kept as far as possible from all metal objects.

I removed the fire extinguisher and went back to sea with Jean-Philippe. We recalibrated the automatic pilot and its compass by slowly sailing in a large perfect circle. Then we tested the recalibrated autopilot. Now it held a course perfectly. It had indeed been the metal fire extinguisher that was causing problems, mixing up the compass and scrambling the automatic pilot! As we were readying the boat neither I nor any one else had noticed how dangerously close the metal fire extinguisher was to the automatic pilot.

The technicians went back home, Jean-Philippe went back to Switzerland, and I departed a second time.

As soon as I left Hammerfest, a perfect wind sprang up to fill my sails and send me straight along my course. Sailing straight as an arrow, I went shooting at ten or twelve knots through the spray that sprang up all around me, a perfectly respectable speed for a single-hull vessel like mine. I was happy as a clam; I was a free man.

A steady wind, a clear horizon, conditions remained ideal day after day. I sailed straight along without varying my course an inch, heading for the Scoresby Sound on the east coast of Greenland, which I hoped to reach in just fifteen days or so.

It wasn't until three days after weighing anchor that I finally got a real night's sleep. The adrenaline was keeping me awake. Now that the tension of logistical preparations and the stress of the actual departure were beginning to wane, my body needed to make up for lost sleep. The rolling of the boat helped me relax, and I slept like a log.

Two days later I sighted the only piece of dry land between North Cape and Greenland, Jan Mayen Island. I made a radio call and a woman's voice replied. The young woman who ran the meteorological station on the island was amazed to learn of my presence in these waters, where a sailing ship had almost never been sighted. In excellent English she forecast relatively stable weather for the rest of my journey. On the other hand, along my course there was a substantial likelihood of encountering a great deal of ice drifting from the north.

I thought of the great Fridtjof Nansen, the first man to explore the polar regions, who sailed from Norway on a trip to Greenland. The accumulation of ice blocked his whaling ship, and he and his men had to launch boats and row, hauling their ships between cliffs and icebergs. That was a century ago, but I was afraid the same thing might happen to me.

In the meantime, the weather suddenly warmed up. I sunned myself like a tourist, wearing shorts and a T-shirt.

But the sun-worshiping interlude was soon over. Five days after set-ting out, the winds began to quicken angrily, the swells began to rise, and my hull thudded over the choppy surface as if on a poorly paved road. Things started to get serious. Waves crashed over the deck, and the water that soaked the upperworks began to form ice in the chill wind, but it was not yet cold enough for the ice to weigh down the masts sufficiently to capsize the boat. All sails set, I was still sailing at ten or twelve knots before the wind—like a gentleman, as the phrase goes. Or in the words of Mick Jagger, "It's only rock 'n' roll, but I like it."

I was liking it until a veritable explosion shook my boat from the hold to the topmast. I barely had time to grab a backstay to keep from being tossed overboard. As I turned to look aft, I saw floating away in the gray waters in the evening light an enormous tree trunk, which I had just slammed into at full speed. I hurried down into the cockpit and carefully examined every corner in search of a leak. Nothing. Re-lieved, I took the helm again. But two or three hours later, it became alarmingly heavy. The boat was no longer responding to the helm, and it was traveling more slowly. I went belowdecks again. Now there was four inches of water in the cockpit, which meant that the hold was full and that there was more than three feet of water in the boat!

The first thing that came into my mind was that I had waited too long before checking the water level a second time, which meant that the situation might now be irreparable. Instinctively, I turned on the bilge pump. The motor that drives the bilge pump was underwater, but it was turning all the same—for now. But that wouldn't prevent the level of water in the cockpit from rising inexorably.

And to top things off, I was just entering the danger zone—less than 185 miles from the Greenland coast—and I was beginning to see my first icebergs. Obviously, I wouldn't be stepping away from the helm again. Hitting an iceberg after hitting a tree trunk would be a little much for just one boat.

Luckily, I also had a hand pump that could be operated from the helm. I worked the pump with one hand and held the rudder with the other hand, while the main pump continued to operate as well.

After a while I could see that the level of water in the cockpit was holding steady, but it wasn't dropping, either. And one thing became horribly clear. With all the determination and energy I could muster, I could certainly continue to man the helm and pump simultaneously for a number of hours—maybe even for a whole day. But I could never hope to do it for five days in a row, which was how long I figured—at my boat's now sluggish rate of progress—it would take to reach Greenland! Sometime or other, I would certainly have to sleep.

I had activated my iceberg-detecting radar. It can warn of icebergs miles away; if we were heading right for one, it would sound an alarm. But it can't pick up growlers, the chunks of floe ice that break off and float along just beneath the surface. Even with an aluminum hull like mine, designed for polar navigation, those huge slabs of ice with sharp angles would have the same general effect that a chainsaw would have on a shoebox.

For the immediate future I could see only one solution—set my course straight for dry land and make it as far as possible. Then, when the boat sank beneath me, I would pile all my polar equipment in the inflatable life raft and do what Nansen did, paddle and hope to make it to the coast.

I made a stab at calling the former owner, but Jean-Yves was not aware of any particular weak points in his boat.

I turned on the automatic pilot, feverishly stacked all my land equipment atop the sled, and then placed the sled on the inflatable life raft. Faced with the imposing mass now piled in the raft, I said to myself that for whatever paddling might accomplish, I would paddle.

I called Cathy to warn her that I was certainly going to have to abandon my boat and reach Greenland by paddling.

Lost amid the icebergs and growlers, exhausted and disappointed, I was filled with rage at the injustice of the situation. I had plowed straight into that goddamned tree trunk, probably the only one for hundreds of miles in all directions. And now it was going to cost me my boat, less than a week after the start of the expedition!

The boat was riding so low now that the water was coming in through the through-hull fittings, a set of small openings above the flotation line through which I discarded my used water. I closed the through-hulls, returned to the helm, and started pumping again. But the hand pump was just not powerful enough; I had to go back down and start bailing with a bucket, which I would then have to empty into my shower, which drains out by means of the through-hulls, which I had to open again. On my knees on the cockpit floor, I was emptying bucket after bucket of water while the electric pump went on emptying water, doing its part.

And slowly, at long last, the water level began to drop . . . Once it was below the floor boards I climbed down into the hold and kept on bailing. When finally there was no more than ten inches or so of water at the bottom of the hull, I made a careful examination of the whole interior, inch by inch, in search of the leak.

There was no leak that I could see, but I did notice one important thing. The tree trunk had somehow smashed into the stern and hit the propeller. The propeller shaft is enclosed in an aluminum casing that is equipped with a "stuffing box," a carbon disk that, through a valve mechanism, prevents water from leaking into the hull around the propeller shaft. It turned out that the motor that was driving the pump was actually spilling water into the boat after the tree trunk split the casing of the propeller shaft.

There was no way that I could repair it, but I did see a way to reduce the flooding considerably. I sliced the inner tube that I always carry with me aboard a boat into strips and stretched these strips of rubber to create a sort of supertight bandage around the aluminum casing. At the same time, I kept on bailing to bring down the water level a little farther, in an attempt to make the work a bit easier. I was crouching in the dark, bent over double, working with my hands plunged into the icy water that kept flooding into the boat. My fingers, barely recovered from the frostbite, partially amputated and practically numb, were making the job especially challenging.

The whole time I was working like this, the icebergs—more and more of them as I neared the coast—were sliding past me in an endless procession. If I hit one of them, the boat would sink for sure. On the other hand, if I did nothing to stop the water from pouring into my boat, the end result would be no different. I knew that if I could only stop the leak before I hit something, there was at least a fifty-fifty chance of making it to dry land. In any case, sitting there at the helm of a sinking ship, with no idea where the water was pouring in from and without doing anything to try to stop it, was more than I could stand.

So I kept stretching my strips of inner tube, which I forced into place with pliers and wire. When I was done, the water pressure from outside was still too great for there to be a perfect seal, but it was pretty close. Now, the hand pump and electric pump combined ought to be sufficient. I went back to my place at the rudder, content and relieved. I'd made my bet and I had won. I had made it through the icebergs and the growlers; my boat was sailing serenely over the gray swells. I had saved the boat and my expedition, too.

Next, I called Jean-Philippe to alert him that I was going to need a new aluminium casing for my propeller shaft. Was there, by any chance, anywhere around Scoresby Sound a boat repair shop or even a garage—anyplace at all where I might be able to leave my boat for repairs while I trekked across the country?

"Absolutely nothing," came the answer, two hours later. "Moreover, there isn't even an airport, however small. There is no way to meet up with you there. You are going to have to sail directly to Angmagssalik."

This tiny port village, with a population of three hundred, was located just below the Arctic Circle. It was no better equipped, but at least it had an airfield so that my team could meet up with me, bringing the necessary spare parts.

I set my course southward, sailing along the coast.

Not everybody has friends in Angmagssalik, but I do. My friend Robert Peroni lives there. I had asked him to procure the permits necessary for crossing Greenland. Unfortunately, Robert had informed me by radio a few days ago that things were becoming more complicated than he expected and that I was going to have to wait there for a month before I could hope to have the necessary permit. I was furious, but I wasn't about to turn back a second time. I decided to go on.

With the background noise of the constant chugging of the engine running constantly to operate the electric pump, I discovered the savage beauty of the immense cliffs of Greenland, those gloomy walls of rock topped with snow. My readings of Nansen's memoirs resurfaced in my mind, stimulating my imagination, and I felt as if I could see the great explorer paddling across these same roaring waters, he and his men dreaming that they would be the first to cross this wild land.

The wind shifted suddenly, and enormous sheets of pack ice began to drift southward, following the same course I was. Pushed by winds out of the west, these huge sheets of ice are driven out into the open ocean where they ultimately melt. But now they were pushing back in the opposite direction, and I found myself caught between the coastal cliffs and blocks of pack ice many miles in length. I could sail out of this situation, but I didn't want to run the risk of heading back out into open sea. I preferred to stay close to dry land. Here at least, should the worst case arise—that is, if I was forced to abandon ship—I could still reach the mainland with my equipment and continue on my way. And from my point of view, that was the only thing that mattered.

The battle lasted five days and five nights. All sails set, I slipped among the icebergs, ramming slabs of ice that lifted the boat up and then let it drop again with a thump. Wedged between the granite cliffs and the giant blocks of pack ice, I tacked and veered to avoid being crushed or colliding with the icebergs which, just to make things harder, did not always seem to move with the wind or the current. In fact, the immense segment of the iceberg that jutted out of the water acted like a sail, with the same angles of thrust. It was impossible to think of abandoning the helm, and so I struggled to fight off sleep. But fear, and the need to bail constantly to reduce the level of the water that was once again filling my cockpit, were enough for the most part to keep me wide awake.

When I could no longer stay awake, I would drive the boat onto one of the little flat ice floes and leave it grounded there, bow in the air. I would let the boat drift with the floe, confident that it wouldn't collide with anything for the time being. That would let me close my eyes for minutes, even hours, until the hull of my boat would finally slip off the floe by itself. The smack of the hull hitting water would wake me up, and I would set off again, taking care not to run into any of the many icebergs lurking in the fog.

When I finally sighted the fishermen's houses of Angmagssalik, little multicolored wooden boxes scattered on the ice high atop the cliff, I felt as if I had been saved by a miracle. I had sailed along the Greenland coast for hundreds of miles; I was completely exhausted, half-asleep at the helm; my hull was full of water and badly dented from all the collisions; but I had arrived.

My crew landed at Angmagssalik the same day, after a journey that had certainly been less trying than mine.

Before leaving Switzerland, Jean-Philippe had placed a small classified ad in the newspapers: "Wanted: volunteers to take Mike Horn's boat around Greenland." He had received twenty-four responses and had chosen two prospective pilots. Angelo and Pierre-Yves arrived with him. Dominique, another companion, was waiting in Switzerland so that we could send him a detailed order for other spare parts and tools to bring on a later flight.

Working with the tide, we got the boat out of the water, using its winch to haul it along a ramp, the only piece of maritime equipment in the place, which is more of a natural harbor than a real port. Once we had the boat in dry dock, the *Arktos*, the name I had given the boat and my expedition, became a dorm where all four of us crashed, crammed in together for as long as it took to repair the boat. Angelo proved to be a gifted mechanic and handyman. Soon the boat was as good as new and perfectly watertight, as proven by the test runs we took in the open waters.

On the administrative side, things seemed to go as if by magic. After a few discussions with the authorities in Angmagssalik, my permit was issued in no more than twenty-four hours. Work on the boat took ten days, and I was becoming impatient. If I got too far behind schedule, my whole calendar would be thrown out of whack.

Wasting no more time, all four of us boarded the boat and left Angmagssalik for good. A few hours later I was leaving the boat again, setting out with all my polar equipment a short distance farther south, at a landing point where the slope of the terrain ran straight up from the water's edge all the way to the ice cap.

Last farewells and a round of hugs. My teammates all urged me to keep my spirits up, and I wished them good luck. If God and the ice field were both willing, we would meet again at Ilulissat, on the west coast of Greenland, where I would be counting on them to be waiting with the boat.

I no longer had to worry about my boat; it was in very good hands. Now I could focus on my next goal: the 450 or 500 miles of ice field that I would have to traverse in my solo trek across Greenland.

First of all, I would need to climb. A long gradual climb up to the main plateau, which stretches out at an elevation of ten thousand feet above sea level. The delay that had been caused by the problems with my boat had forced me to start across Greenland at the beginning of autumn, and I was greeted by snow squalls and a head wind blowing in my face. None of this was at all encouraging, since I had allowed myself only about twenty days—with a ten-day margin—to make my crossing (and so I had allowed thirty days for Jean-Philippe and the others to reach Ilulissat).

I wanted to beat the speed record between Angmagssalik and Disko Bay, which is just south of the camp from which Paul-Émile Victor set out to discover the Greenland ice cap. The speed record was set by a four-man German team, and they had taken forty-five days to complete the same route. (There is also an "official" record of nine days, but that did not apply to me because it followed a different route, a straight line along the Arctic Circle from Angmagssalik to the west coast.) But I hadn't forgotten that on my first attempt, with Erhard Loretan and Jean Troillet, we had been forced to spend two weeks in our tent without being able to venture outside at all, and had finally been forced to give up. I thought about them and the lesson of patience that they had imparted to me when, immediately after beginning my ascent, bad weather confined me to my tent for twenty-four hours. During the night I had to get out of the tent every half-hour to shovel away the snow, otherwise its weight would have crushed the tent. My sled, on the other hand, was completely buried in snow.

This sled was originally designed by Børge Ousland for use on ice. I adapted it to work on any surface I might happen to encounter—snow, ice, rock, tundra, brambles—by making the bottom of the sled thicker and stronger. Same thing for the runners, which were the same width as my skis, so that they would naturally run in the ski tracks. If one of the runners was damaged, it would cause the sled to steer toward the damaged side and that would force me to expend a considerable amount of extra energy to pull it back straight. I needed to be able to fix any such damage quickly and easily by remolding the Teflon with the flat of my knife blade. The front of the sled was rounded and raised so that it would rise up over bumps and slide over them without snagging. The sides of the sled had a rounded bulge so that the entire sled would tend to stay upright rather than overturn in case of violent impacts. The sled was unsinkable, superdurable (it would survive falls of several feet on the ice), and very light when unloaded. I hooked myself up to it with a harness that I had dug up in the back room of Ferrino, my tentmakers. After trying on countless climbing harnesses that were fairly comfortable, I asked to see the most comfortable backpack that they made. With a few quick cuts of my knife, I had separated the backpack and its harness; I added two polyester rings to the harness, big enough to clip carabiners onto even when I was wearing my mittens and in the middle of a raging blizzard.

The 265 pounds of the sled's weight consisted almost entirely of the weight of the load. That load consisted of one month's food supplies and ten aluminum bottles, each holding a quart of the benzene fuel that my stove burned. Each bottle weighed about two pounds. I could have carried a single large jerrican but if it leaked or there was a fire, that would have been the end of my fuel. By breaking it into separate compartments, I would reduce that risk.

The bottles were packed separately and insulated from each other to limit impacts. They were sealed with a plastic stopper that accommodated the expansion and contraction of the aluminum under conditions of extreme cold, which increases the volume of the liquid. For that reason the bottles were not completely filled. The bottom of each bottle was reinforced with a layer of rubberized foam to prevent the thousands of hours of constant rubbing against the Kevlar surface of the sled from wearing a hole through it. If that were to happen, not only would I lose my fuel, but I would also lose my food, which could become contaminated with benzene and rendered inedible.

Without a teammate to take turns beating a track with me, I struggled to open a path through the snow, which varied greatly in depth. But weather conditions would eventually improve. They couldn't have gotten any worse, and the fury of the wind would actually work in my favor by compacting the snow ahead of me.

I couldn't see any farther than the tips of my skis, and I would constantly stare at these two boards that were carrying me. I needed to make sure that they were always perfectly parallel, otherwise I might begin to drift off course. Because I am right-handed, my right leg is a little stronger than my left leg, and it always tends to push me to the left. I have to compensate for this on a regular basis.

My skis were white, and they would have blended right in with the color of the snow-covered ground if Annika and Jessica hadn't been allowed to express their youthful creativity. With tender, loving dedication, they had drawn our home in Switzerland in black magic marker. Plumes of smoke curled out of the chimney, and little people at the windows were speaking in word balloons: "Daddy, we miss you.... Come home soon." A little farther along, a seal was poking its head up through a hole in the ice, and a polar bear was smiling at me and saying, "Good luck, Mike!" At the tip of one ski my daughters had drawn a cat; at the tip of the other, a mouse; and they whispered in my ear that the cat would catch the mouse when I got home, when my skis were finally standing side by side, with the tips close together.

Progress was already difficult, and it was made even harder by the countless crevasses that were opened in the slope by the contrasting movements of the glaciers and the ice fields calving icebergs into the ocean. Those crevasses were fatal traps. The unfortunate soul who falls into one is wedged helplessly in the sharp angle at the bottom of the crevasse and is gradually swallowed by the ice as his body heat melts the walls. The effect is something like being digested alive by a very large, very cold creature.

When there are two teammates traveling together, one teammate can help the other one out, especially if they are roped together. That is why it was theoretically forbidden to venture into that region alone. And that is why I obtained a permit in the names of two people from the authorities in Angmagssalik, knowing that once I was far away from civilization, no one was going to come after me to ask about it. Unfortunately, that also meant that nobody would come to my aid if I got into trouble.

During the three days of my ascent, my heart would race every time I had to thread my way, with my sled, between two of these bottomless chasms. Or whenever I would prod the ground with the tip of my ski pole to discover invisible crevasses covered with a bridge of fresh snow that would never hold my own weight, much less the weight of my sled.

Luckily, there was still daylight twenty-four hours a day. The harsh light that reflected off the ice would have burned my eyes if I hadn't been wearing sunglasses that adjusted to variations in light intensity and whose unbreakable plastic stems would not adhere to my skin under conditions of extreme cold. The positive side of all this sunlight was that it allowed me extra time to wend my way carefully through this mortal labyrinth, making detours lasting several hours around some of the crevasses.

I crossed the narrowest ones using a method borrowed from mountain climbing. I took off my skis and put on long, pointed crampons. Then I drove a titanium piton into the ice on the inside face of the crevasse through which I slid a rope that was fastened to my harness. Then I climbed down into the gap and jumped across to the opposite face, hooking on with the help of my crampons and my ice ax. I would climb back up and drive in a second piton. Now, I would have a piton on each face of the crevasse and that would allow me to install a network of pulleys and ropes between my two anchoring points. I would stretch the cords as tight as possible and shuttle my sledge across, hanging from its two portage hooks. And then all I would need to do was recover the piton screwed into the "wrong" side of the crevasse, haul myself up out of the crevasse on the "right" side with the aid of the other piton, unscrew it, and continue on my way.

Of course, all this took up a lot of time, and I wasn't making much forward progress—three, six, eight miles per day. That fell far short of the distance I was hoping to make, and my dreams of setting a record were beginning to vanish before my eyes. All the same, I held out hope that once I was on the plateau the relatively flat surface and the slight downhill slope would allow me to make better time.

When I reached the plateau, the wind suddenly shifted as if it had only been waiting for me. All the conditions had lined up perfectly. I was finally going to be able to use my kites.

I had five of them, each suitable for a different wind speed. They had been custom-made for me by Eric at Vade Retro, and they had the unusual property of working not only when the wind was blowing from behind you but also in crosswinds and even when the wind was blowing almost from straight ahead. The inventor called them the Edge, with a clear reference to the aeronautics term "leading edge." To me, though, they were sails, and I was hoping to convert them into wings.

Doubly harnessed—to my sled behind me and to my kite in front of me—I headed through the powdery snow, traveling north to skirt the major glacier formation that prevented me from following a straight line between Angmagssalik and Ilulissat. This lengthy detour was made up for by the speed that my kites gave me. The smallest of the kites was twenty-two square feet; the largest was 237 square feet. To make them more visible—but also to cheer up my days and to put a little color into this pale landscape—I ordered them in a multicolored array of blue, green, and orange. You use them just like the sails of a boat, choosing a size inversely proportional to the force of the wind. The wind force also determined how far out I would play the line. I would let the smallest kites out to about fifty feet's distance, and sometimes I would play out more line to get the kite higher to catch an elusive wind. The larger kites, in an ordinary wind, would be played out four or five yards ahead of me, like imposing spinnakers. The effectiveness of this technique immediately translated into greater distances covered—fifteen, twenty, even twenty-five miles a day! And I didn't even need to use my legs. I was just letting my skis slide over the snow!

Unfortunately, there were many disadvantages to this kind of travel that detracted from the speed I gained. First, because I was following my kite, pulling on the line as if on the reins of a horse, I might veer off course by as much as fifteen or twenty degrees without even realizing it. The kite kept my hands full, so I couldn't check my navigational instruments. I had to use the angle of the wind against my face to determine and correct my course as best I could.

Another problem was that my legs would plow down through the snow, which would pile up to my knees, and it was hard work to maintain my balance against that pressure. I would eventually fall down, get back up, and start off again. The physical effort was exhausting. Finally, I was traveling practically blind because my view of the horizon was blocked by the cloth of the kite spread out in front of me. It was difficult under such conditions to maintain the focused concentration that I needed to stay upright, as well as anticipate irregularities in the terrain and the sheets of ice jutting up under the snow. In this last respect I was happy that the crevasses were behind me for now.

Despite everything, with the help of the wind the advantages of kites clearly outweighed the disadvantages. As I became more expert in handling this new tool, my improving skills had noticeable effects on my daily performance. One day, when the wind was steady and the snow was stable, I made sixty-six miles, which consoled me the next day as I sat in my tent all day, held prisoner by the suddenly nasty weather. The following day, without the help of my kites, I did a veritable marathon distance of twenty-three miles. The day after that I racked up forty-six miles, half of that with the help of my kites and half without, since the wind had shifted direction in the middle of the day. On the tenth day I set a record with eighteen hours of kite-aided travel and eighty-nine miles covered. I was back in the race! If I kept this up, I had a good chance of beating the speed record for crossing Greenland.

I was just 137 miles from the finish line when catastrophe struck. I was hooked up to my 237-square-foot kite, and I didn't realize at first that the wind was beginning to pick up speed. When the wind sud-

denly dropped, it was the calm before the storm, too brief a calm for me
to react. A moment later, a terrifyingly powerful squall came rushing at
me and literally lifted me into the air. This was the katabatic wind that
blows off the center of the Greenland ice cap and down toward the
coast. This country is also known for the "pittarak," a type of typically
Greenlandic hurricane that blows flat along the ice and whips up such a
flurry of snow that you can no longer see your own legs. When the
weather forecasters warn that a pittarak is on the way, people batten
down their roofs and tie down their sleds, their snowmobiles, and anything else that is not solidly anchored to the ground.

In just a few seconds I had gone from a standing start to thirty miles
per hour! That's fast on the ice. Especially with a sled weighing 265
pounds harnessed to your hips and a visibility of roughly zero. At first,
all I could do was try to stay on my feet, holding on with all my strength
to the cables stretching out to my kite. I went tearing through deep piles
of powdery snow, sailing over sheets of ice, bumping over hillocks,
hurtling over mounds, and whipping across hollows. The violence of
the squall kept me from reeling in my kite, which had gone completely
mad, jolting me in all directions, slinging me right and left as if the kite
were the puppeteer and I was the puppet dangling at the end of the
strings. I could have cut loose from the kite, thanks to an emergency release device that worked with a carabiner. But I didn't even want to consider it; I couldn't stand the idea of losing my kite. The only thing I
could do for the moment was to keep up with the kite and hold on.

So I held on. But after four minutes of this bouncing and jolting, I
could tell that my legs were not going to last much longer. Completely
exhausted, I finally decided to release the kite.

It was at that exact moment that I plunged into a hollow filled with
soft snow. One of my legs sank into the snow, and the other leg kept on
traveling. I was spun around and then hurled against the ice.

I stood there, motionless, for a fraction of a second. That was
enough time for the 265 pounds of my Kevlar sled, hurtling along at
thirty miles per hour, to catch up and hit me flush in the head. Half-
conscious, covered in blood, I was dragged across the ice by my sled like
a runaway horse. Out of the thirty lines that run out to the kite, many

had parted, but the ones that were still attached were sufficient in number to drag me along, at least in this raging wind. I desperately tried to reach the emergency release carabiner, but, caught in a welter of lines where the straps to my sled and the ropes to the kite were tangled together, I couldn't move at all. I couldn't get my legs free because of the skis. Snow was packed into every tiny opening in my clothes, and my body began to freeze. I slammed against something and lost my glasses, as well as the GPS that I wore around my neck. Luckily, I had a second GPS in my sled, and I still had my compass! I was sliding at top speed along the ice, and the bumps and razor edges of the surface tore at my face like a grater. Snow filled my nose, my mouth, and my eyes. A thought began to form in my head: if my sled hits me again, it'll kill me.

I would have given anything to make the wind die down, but instead it began to blow twice as hard. The situation had become so dire that I started to wonder if I would ever live to tell the tale.

But I refused to give up. By struggling with the lines and ropes that wrapped me up like a kitten in a ball of yarn, I finally managed to get one leg loose and extend it ahead of me. Then, since I was still unable to get a hand free to reach the release carabiner, I started sawing the lines of the kite that were still intact with the metal edge of my ski. Those lines are made of Kevlar, and they were theoretically supposed to be unbreakable. But because they were stretched out by this extreme tension, they finally wound up snapping, one after the other.

There must have been fifteen of those lines. Each time that I managed to saw through one of them with my improvised rasp, the cloth of the kite collapsed a little, and my speed would drop a little. My leg got tangled up again, and I managed to free it again. Once I finally managed to recover the use of my arms, I immediately snapped the release carabiner. My kite flew away, tumbling in the furious gusts of wind and vanishing into the blizzard.

Finally, lying motionless on the ice, I slowly calmed down and did my best to evaluate the situation. With the exception of my lost glasses and the kite, I still had all my equipment. I took stock of my physical condition. Nothing seemed to be broken, but I was shaken and could barely stand up.

I hastily pitched my tent, squirmed into my sleeping bag, and was soon fast asleep.

The next day, after many hours of skiing, I finally spotted a tiny patch of color on the white horizon. As I drew nearer, I could see that it was my kite; its lines had caught in a crag, and the snow squalls had flattened it to the ground. It was unusable, but I was overjoyed at having found it. The next time I met up with my team, I would have them take it to the manufacturer to see if it could be repaired.

According to the last position recorded on my lost GPS and my current position, shown on the other GPS, I had been dragged more than two miles. On the ice, at that speed and under those conditions, that was a long way! The moral of this misadventure—which could so easily have turned to tragedy—was that once again I had been reckless. I just wanted so badly to beat that speed record for crossing Greenland.

I had narrowly avoided being killed, but my average speed was far better than I could have dared to hope. Twelve days after leaving Angmagssalik, I was no more than fifty miles from Ilulissat. If I managed to keep up the pace, I would have completed the crossing in fifteen days, not twenty!

On the thirteenth day I made thirty-seven miles. Unfortunately, I was going to have to slow down now. As I began my descent to the coast, I entered crevasse territory again.

A steady wind was pushing my kite and I kept sailing along on the smooth surface of the glacier. Everything was cloaked in an unbroken grayish-white fog all the way to the horizon. I felt as if I were a pilot, flying through the clouds.

Suddenly, a shadow flitted across my field of view, so quickly that only my subconscious must have registered it. I would never have noticed it if it weren't for the expanded field of view that you tend to acquire on the ice.

But I still couldn't process what I had seen.

I had a sudden surge of adrenaline as it dawned on me that I had just seen the steel-blue mouth of a giant crevasse. And where there was one, there were more—ready to devour me.

I had reached dangerous territory sooner than expected. I absolutely *had* to come to a halt. But at the speed I was traveling, there was a considerable stopping distance. I would have to haul down my sails and slow down gradually; otherwise my sled, moving along at nineteen miles per hour, might hit me once again. I let out the kite cables little by little to give some slack and reduce my speed. When I had finally come to a stop I strapped my kite cables to my sled, and once I'd struggled out of my harness I ventured out into the pea soup of fog in which I couldn't even see the tips of my skis. A few yards farther on, my heart skipped a beat. Half of my kite was dangling down into one of the largest crevasses I had ever seen!

The kite had twenty feet of line. Another twenty feet and that would have been the end of me.

I realized that I must have overflown a certain number of narrower crevasses, whose frozen snow bridges only supported the weight of my rig because of the speed at which I was traveling. And now, in the blinding fog surrounded by mortal traps that I could sense all around me, I no longer dared to move even an inch. I feverishly pitched my tent exactly where I had come to a halt and settled in for the night.

The next morning the weather cleared up, and my fears proved to have been justified. I was in middle of a veritable labyrinth of crevasses. That I had made it as far as I did without being killed was a minor miracle!

All this merely confirmed what I already believe. There is a God, and he even has time to look out for me. On this segment of the journey alone, that would actually be a full-time job.

It took me two whole days to get out of the crevasse-filled area and back onto the steep slope that ran down to the coast. Those were two days during which a furious gale never stopped howling in my ears. At a distance of six miles from the camp of Paul-Émile Victor, I contacted Jean-Philippe Patthey and suggested that my crew come to meet me. Jean-Philippe reported that my boat was shipshape and ready, and awaited my arrival. It didn't take me long to spot the boat, in spite of the snow blindness caused by the loss of my sunglasses. There it sat, far below me, riding on the luminous surface of a fjord like a tiny scale model on a mirror. To reach it, I would have to cross an area of streams whose beds were cut into the surface of the ice and whose raging flows could easily pick me up and toss me into the crevasses before I could resist. My feet were freezing from tramping through the water, but I made it through.

I had crossed the Greenland ice cap in fifteen days and eight hours, setting a new record.

This first land segment of my journey allowed me to get familiar with my gear, and I now knew how to coax maximum performance from it. My gear and I were ready to face the impending Arctic winter. One part of the journey had just ended, and another was about to begin.

Upon arrival, my most immediate concern was the extra food that I had on hand, having taken less time to make the crossing than expected. There was no thought of abandoning that precious cargo on the ice field, and so I stuffed my face out of gluttony and in order to increase my fat reserves to protect against the coming cold . . . and because I definitely deserved a banquet!

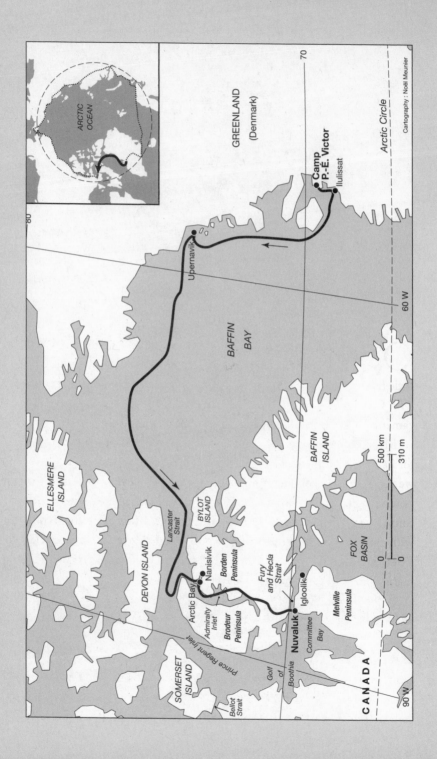

Cartography : Noël Meunier

## ( 3 )

# The Courage of a Bear

ONCE AGAIN AT THE HELM OF THE ARKTOS, I sailed out of the camp of Paul-Émile Victor heading for the village of Ilulissat, a little farther south, accompanied by my logistical team. There I met up with Cathy, three representatives from the Banque Mirabaud, and my cameraman, who wanted to get in a few photo sessions.

My five days in Ilulissat were primarily devoted to readying my boat for its next big journey, which mostly involved filling it with all the food we could fit, and completing my polar outfitting with a view to all the potential situations I might encounter on the Canadian ice field. Because I had prepared for everything imaginable, I was more concerned with what I would encounter that was unimaginable to me now. And so I brought as much gear as I could in order to handle a variety of climatic and geographic contingencies.

After leaving Ilulissat I sailed around Disko Island and then, instead of heading directly northwest toward Canada, I sailed north along the Greenland coast, toward Upernavik. That way I could take advantage of the favorable currents and microclimate that brought unusually fair weather to that region. The landscape was magnificent, but there were more icebergs than there are eighteen-wheelers on the turnpike. And they were much bigger than the eighteen-wheelers, too, these huge

masses of ice many miles long, which would sometimes take me hours
to sail around. As I admired the base of the icebergs immersed in the
crystalline water, I thought to myself that the amount of floating ice
that broke loose in that area every year held enough freshwater to supply the United States for ten years! This section of the Greenland ice
cap was the largest source of icebergs in the entire Far North. If it were
to melt completely, it would raise sea level around the world by thirty-
five feet. It was a disaster movie whose screenplay the directors of our
environmental agencies should read carefully.

Upernavik was a legend to me. It was part of my personal mythology
after reading, among the many books I devoured while preparing for
this expedition, *The Ghosts of Cape Sabine*, which tells the story of Lieutenant Adolphus Greely. The American explorer attempted in 1881 to
reach the northernmost point of the American continent. The members of his expedition, after committing a number of blunders, ran
short on food and wound up resorting to cannibalism.

Upernavik was their last known port of call.

The place was certainly charged with history—with all the histories
of polar exploration, stories that so often ended in tragedy. I wanted to
set foot there myself, if for no reason other than to catch a whiff of the
adventures and legends that still float in the air there.

After just a day and a half on the ocean, I dropped anchor off a fishing village that was even more modest than Angmagssalik. It wasn't
even a port. It was a cove where the wind that gusts constantly had
wrecked a great number of old steamships, whose carcasses blended
into the gray haze of water and sky.

Two Greenlandic helicopter pilots, surprised to see me there, asked
me all sorts of questions and told me they couldn't take off. "They are
forecasting winds at fifty to sixty knots," they told me. "It'll be impossible to take off from Upernavik for at least two days." Fifty-knot winds
with all those icebergs—I wasn't very eager to set out in those conditions, either. I decided to wait for a day and see how things would develop.

I had barely fallen asleep when I was jolted awake by ocean rollers
crashing against the hull. My anchor was dragging! *Arktos* was in dan-

ger of being hurled onto the shore and winding up like all the other
ship skeletons, which had certainly met their fates in similar conditions.
I had no choice but to weigh anchor entirely and put out to sea where
my boat would be safer than in port. Running on autopilot with only a
storm jib the size of a sheet of writing paper rigged, being tossed over
mountains of water, and then plunging between them into troughs that
looked eager to swallow me, I slalomed crazily between icebergs. It was
never completely dark, but visibility was sharply reduced by the heavy
fog that had set in.

The storm forced me to stay at the helm for forty-eight hours
straight, without a minute's sleep. Then things calmed down.


In a sense, the weather forced my hand and obliged me to forge ahead
faster than expected. Rather than return to Upernavik, I crossed Viscount Melville Sound and Baffin Bay, where icebergs were fewer.

After a few days' sailing, I arrived at the mouth of Lancaster Sound.

This was the beginning of the famous Northwest Passage, which
then follows the Bellot Strait, runs around King William Island, passes
through Cambridge Bay and Amundsen Gulf, curves over the top of
Alaska, and runs through the Bering Strait. I had planned to be able to
sail at least as far as Cambridge Bay, to the large island of Victoria, before my boat became trapped in winter ice and I would have to continue
on foot.

Six-knot currents rush into one end of Lancaster Sound and rush
out the other end with the same power. I was trying to make the best of
things, so I sailed along a heavy snow that transformed my boat into a
Popsicle. The wind shifted. If it suddenly began to blow hard, it could
freeze the halyards and make it impossible to work the sails. And so I
was obliged to change the setting of the sails constantly, in order to keep
the cables from freezing solid in the pulleys.

But actually things were looking pretty good. According to the
Coast Guard officers aboard a Canadian icebreaker named the *Terry
Fox*, Bellot Strait was open. If I hurried, even though it was late in the
season at the beginning of October, I would be able to make it through.

Incredible! I could already visualize myself, sails bellying, making good time all the way to Cambridge Bay.

Two days later, I had a cold shower in terms of morale. Just as I was rounding the Brodeur Peninsula, the *Terry Fox* warned me that five miles of ice blocked the Bellot Strait between Somerset Island and the Boothia Peninsula.

"You could have made it through just two days ago," the Coast Guard officers told me, "but not now."

A matter of two days—forty-eight hours—had just foiled my plans.

It seemed that the storm that I weathered in Viscount Melville Sound had pushed the ice into Lancaster Sound all the way up to Bellot Strait, where enormous chunks of pack ice now blocked the passage. There wasn't even the narrowest channel of navigable water. The *Terry Fox* questioned me about the specifications of my boat—size, engine power, thickness of the hull, and so forth—and confirmed the bad news. There was no way I could get through.

And to think that after Bellot Strait there was clear sailing all the way to Cambridge Bay. I was out of my mind with frustration.

And that wasn't all. My friends in the Coast Guard informed me that the temperature had just gone into free fall and that the ocean was beginning to freeze over.

"If you keep on going," they told me, "the ice will close up behind you. You will leave your boat there, and we won't even be able to come look for you. Turn back. Come back and meet us at Nanisivik!"

Nanisivik? I'd never heard of the place, but the pessimistic predictions of the Coast Guard men proved to be accurate. I decided to follow their advice and turn back. The ice did indeed solidify behind me as I entered the narrow Admiralty Inlet. This was the beginning of a mysterious journey as I plunged into the unknown expanses of this region for which I had no maps, since I had not expected to venture in this direction. Blindly following the instructions of the *Terry Fox*, in a strange half light that was neither day nor night, I sailed along in silence beneath the walls of a menacing gorge with a mixture of anguish and excitement that the first mapmakers certainly must have felt, sketching what greeted their eyes as they moved forward on a path of discovery.

When I reached what should have been Nanisivik, I couldn't see a thing. There were no lights except those of the *Terry Fox*, the Canadian Coast Guard icebreaker, toward which I was sailing at a cautious six knots.

I was absolutely exhausted. Ever since Upernavik the incessant work and the bad weather had conspired to deprive me of both sleep and food. The constant cold and clamminess—there was no heater in the cockpit—had brought my frostbite back to life, and my hands were terribly painful. After the hellish journey across Baffin Bay with sixty-knot winds and the brutal currents against me, after turning back, being gradually encircled by ice, and the battle to save my boat, I felt as if I were coming home.

The crew of the *Terry Fox*, who had noticed my arrival on their radar screen, tossed down lines and we moored the two boats together. They gave me hot soup, cold beer, and some sharp questions, which amounted to, "And just what do you think you're up to out here all alone?" As you can imagine, the answer was a long one.

The *Terry Fox* was heading back tomorrow to its home port on the Saint Lawrence Seaway. The icebreaker—even though it was a class four vessel—was in danger of being trapped by the cold and there wasn't a day to waste. I asked, just for the sake of trying, whether the captain might be kind enough before heading back to Quebec to break the ice blocking the Bellot Strait so that I could make it through the passage.

"Sorry, Mike," he answered. "That ice is too thick. Even for me."

At least I had tried everything. The ice was closing in behind me, preventing me from turning back. That decided it for me. My cruise was ending here.

Nanisivik was neither a port nor a village. It was a zinc mine, and the miners were the inhabitants. They lived in prefabricated huts around an ore crusher whose dull rumbling was a constant and unsettling presence. Men only stayed for fifteen-day shifts—any longer and they would go mad.

*Arktos* was the first sailing vessel ever to drop anchor at Nanisivik—a minor landmark event, quickly overshadowed by another, much larger development. The day I arrived was the last day of Nanisivik's existence. The mine was shutting down for good after twenty to twenty-five years of continuous operation.

By an odd and almost frightening coincidence, the minute I set foot there, the town vanished. Everywhere there was a hustle and bustle of trucks and pickup trucks being loaded. Helicopters and planes were taking off, carrying off light equipment and materials. Miners and engineers were leaving for other jobs.

I had the weird impression that I had somehow triggered this hurry-scurry exodus. I felt like yelling, "Hey, guys, hold on! It's only me!"

Canadian environmental laws require any company operating a mining concession to return the site to its original state once the deposit has been fully exploited and operations have ceased. And so crews were out bulldozing all the houses without exception, filling in the swimming pool, demolishing the gymnasium, the restaurant, the post office, and all the other facilities that had been used for the past two decades by the almost exclusively male population. In quarries and mine shafts they parked 4×4 Toyota Land Cruisers, earthmovers, steamshovels, Caterpillars, bulldozers, and other vehicles—all of which looked brand-new. And then they buried them all under thousands of tons of rock, blasted loose with dynamite! Huts filled with enough spare parts, drilling equipment, and other mechanical equipment to dig shafts and rebuild any engine imaginable ten times over—met the same fate.

I was fascinated (and horrified) by the sight of millions of dollars of equipment buried like a pile of junk. I knew perfectly well that, since planes are the only means of transportation up here, moving this material out would have cost far more than its market value. Moreover, the mining company, having established this site with the idea of operating it for ten years, had more than doubled its expected revenues and had enjoyed an excellent return on its investment. All the same, I couldn't help thinking that it was all a gigantic waste.

But at least I was able to observe this incredible, once-in-a-lifetime spectacle!

The setting was melancholy, even tragic. Nanisivik had never been a real town, but it still represented twenty years—in some cases, longer—in the lives of these men who were now beginning to worry about their futures.

As with any other dramatic conclusion, there was a farewell party, and I was invited. Alcohol, normally forbidden in order not to "contaminate" the Inuit, reappeared and flowing freely. One man named Bill, the chief engineer at the mine, told me that a cargo icebreaker, the *Arctic*, would embark with the last load of zinc from the mine in a few days. After that they would demolish the ore crusher and the mine would shut down for good.

Since Bill seemed to be fascinated by my adventures, I gave him a brief summary of my situation and explained to him that, unless I could sail all the way to Cambridge Bay, as I had planned, I was going to have to trek the whole distance on foot. To make things worse, I would have to follow a much longer route since ahead of me, between Baffin Island and the Barren Lands, extended the Gulf of Boothia, which never freezes over. If my boat was stuck here, I would have to walk all around the Gulf of Boothia until I could find a way across.

As for the idea of waiting for the thaw so that I could take my boat and continue, as planned, by water . . . that would take eight months! And without wishing to offend a resident of the place, I didn't want to spend eight months in this hole, which was going to disappear in a matter of hours anyway.

I was disappointed even though I was certain that I had made the right choice to take shelter here. I couldn't wait until springtime, and I couldn't leave right away. It was the end of October, and the snow was not thick enough or compact enough for me to set out across the vast rocky expanses of Baffin Island. The snow takes a while to accumulate in this frozen desert where precipitation is infrequent and gales are almost continuous. It's a no-man's-land less reminiscent of an ice field than the surface of the moon.

Some Inuit whom I happened to meet confirmed this. It would be at least three or four weeks before the snow would be safe to travel across. So I might as well make the best of it and settle in as comfortably as I could. Bill gave me his house, one of the last ones standing. A crane that had miraculously survived the general destruction delicately hoisted my boat, which had been anchored in the shelter of a natural deepwater cove after the *Terry Fox* left, and set it down on the ice. Considering that the ice would not fully melt before next August, I wasn't worried. There was no danger of *Arktos* drifting away or sinking while I was gone.

Since I had some time on my hands, I called Cathy and asked her to join me with Annika and Jessica. I hadn't seen my daughters since my departure from North Cape and, once I left Nanisivik to set out into the Arctic winter, it would be at least six months before I could hold them in my arms again.

A few friends traveled along with my family, and the little group arrived without encountering any problems. Though Nanisivik was nothing more than a barracks community, its airport—given the importance of the air freight generated by the mine—could accommodate passenger airliners.

On the rear section of my skis, Annika and Jessica, who had already richly decorated the front of the skis, drew a number of *inukchuks*. That is the Inuit name for the mysterious piles of huge flat rocks that you can see here and there atop hills, almost everywhere in the immense territory of Nunavut. Their origins shrouded in the mists of time, *inukchuks* are used to point the way to the next village. To a traveler seeking the right road, they call out, "I've been there. This is the way to go." The *inukchuks* on the back of my skis and the house on the front of those skis would now call out together, "I've been there. Now I'm going back home."

After camping out for a few days in the four or five remaining houses, my visitors left me to a solitude more intense than before. In all of Nanisivik, besides me, there were only five men in charge of the cleanup. They were cutting off the water supply and the electrical generators. There would be nothing but a minimal infrastructure operating at a low level throughout the winter so that people would be able to come back next summer to finish the renaturalization of the site.

The mine had finally shut down, the *Arctic* was loading the last shipment of zinc, and they shut up the last house—mine.

Now I was homeless, with no roof to protect me from an increasingly biting cold. Luckily, I knew that I could rely upon Claude, who generously offered to let me stay in the tiny cabin where he stores his sealskins and his tools at his home in Arctic Bay.

Corey, one of my new miner buddies, first introduced me to Claude Lavallée. The thirty-two-year-old native of Quebec had come to live in the Arctic when he was thirteen, accompanying his father who was installing phone lines for the mining companies of the Far North on behalf of Bell Canada. As a very young man, Claude began to work with him. But when he was fifteen he met Lily, a young Inuit woman. When Lily became pregnant Claude went to live with her in Arctic Bay, an Inuit village located twenty-two miles south of Nanisivik. They were married, and to earn a living Claude took the bus from Arctic Bay to the mine every day together with his new Inuit "brothers." It was one of the longest bus routes in the entire Arctic. Lily's father, Johannessy, taught Claude the arts of hunting, fishing, and survival in the Far North, but shortly after the birth of her baby, Lily's parents broke up. Her mother moved not far from Arctic Bay, and her father went much farther south to Igloolik. Thus Claude, at the age of sixteen, found himself the head of a large family, and he supported and raised all of Lily's brothers and sisters by himself by working at the mine.

While the last traces of life were being eradicated for all time in Nanisivik, I set out for Arctic Bay. The village is located well to the north of the Arctic circle but still within the geographical limits I had established for myself when I began the trip. Claude's toolshed had only a tiny wood stove, and it was freezing cold inside. I felt like I was sleeping in my tent out on the ice field. But accommodations were free of charge, I was still completely in contact with nature, and I didn't have to deal with anybody if I didn't want to.

Once the mine was shut down, Claude relied upon the centuries-old strategies of his adopted ancestors for the care and feeding of his little tribe. He fished, hunted on foot or with his sled dogs, and became a skilled mechanic, fixing snowmobiles and various other machinery. He was a master of jury-rigging and improvisation, a MacGyver of the ice field, capable of making anything you can name out of the materials he had on hand. Supplementing his income was the generous monthly subsidy that the Canadian government provides to every Inuit family. However, up there that stipend only went so far, considering the scarcity of supplies and the difficulty of shipping anything.

I shared their family meals, fed the dogs, helped out in the shop, and did whatever I could to make myself useful. While I was a member of the household, Lily made me a pair of sealskin gloves and boots.

At the beginning of November, when my route showed promising signs of becoming passable, Claude helped me reinforce the runners on my sled and bolster the sled's framework. If everything had gone according to plan, I would have traveled only over ice, and my sled, in its current condition, would have been perfectly adequate. But modifications were going to be necessary for travel over the soil, rocks, and mountains, which awaited me on the route from the northern tip of Baffin Island.

Claude gave me GPS positions for fishing holes and liquid obstacles located along my route. He told me everything he knew about the ways and habits of polar bears, their migratory routes, and their gathering spots, which he suggested that I avoid assiduously. He also initiated me in the mysteries of seal hunting. In short, he helped me with the unstinting generosity of a simple, honest man.

We became close friends, but I felt that in his eyes I was just another extreme hiker, like the three adventurers he had helped to prepare for a trek three years before. They set out to travel by foot from Arctic Bay to Igloolik, the last village on the Borden Peninsula, just before Fury and Hecla Strait, but they gave up along the way. Now it was up to me to show him my worth.

After three weeks in Nanisivik and nearly a month in Arctic Bay, I was growing restless, to say the least. But Claude insisted that I should wait just a little longer to be certain that all the conditions were right.

I got to know Lily's grandmother, whom Claude supported just as he did the rest of the tribe. She lived in an igloo-sized wooden cabin lit by an oil lamp, and she sewed with a seal-bone needle. With Lily as an interpreter—the old woman spoke only Inuktitut—I told her about where my expedition would take me next and my planned passage through Cambridge Bay. The old woman told me a story of her parents, who had once spent five years of their lives finding and retrieving a boat—an abandoned schooner—from Cambridge Bay. Back then, the Inuit of the region used these schooners for hunting seals and narwhals, to sell their furs and ivory to the Hudson Bay Company. Lily's great-grandparents set out with their sled, dogs, and children, and they sailed the schooner back on the tiniest patches of navigable water, hauling it over the ice the rest of the time. They all camped out together on the spot in igloos whenever conditions became too harsh.

Then when Lily's great-grandfather finally returned to Arctic Bay five years later with his ship, the result of so much hard work, the village shaman demanded that Lily's great-grandfather give him Lily's great-grandmother. When he refused, the covetous shaman cast a curse on the schooner. Lily's great-grandfather, who believed in enchantments and curses, never set foot in the schooner again.

The day before I was finally planning to set out again, some hunters contacted Claude by radio and informed him that the ice had suddenly melted in the Prince Regent Inlet, which had become a stretch of open water, impossible to cross on foot.

"We're stuck on the other side!" they told him. And I was stuck on this side.

I gnawed on my leash for another week. The temperature dropped to twenty-two degrees below zero, and the ice froze over again, in part. It was mid-November, and by now it was almost perpetual night.

I finally ran out of patience. I decided I had spent enough time waiting, and it was time to move. Forget about Prince Regent Inlet. It was either that or wait for the twelfth of Never. So I decided to abandon the route entirely and go around the Gulf of Boothia to the south—unless I could find a way to cut across it. I'd likely have to go all the way around, which meant heading as far south as Melville Peninsula and then passing through Committee Bay before heading north again to Kugaaruk. It doesn't seem like much when you look at a map, but in reality, this was a 750-mile detour to Cambridge Bay by way of a vast icy wasteland, extremely inhospitable and plunged into the relentless darkness of winter. It would lengthen my expedition by at least four months!

To add insult to injury, I would be traveling directly along the migratory route of the polar bears who pass through Committee Bay on their seasonal migration to their winter seal hunting grounds. The female bears with their newborns are especially ferocious. It all amounted to being in the wrong place at the wrong time, but I had no choice.

Dealing with this situation struck me as more than I could handle, and I didn't even really want to consider it for the time being. I would just hold out hope that I could find a shortcut.

Then on November 16, just as I was getting ready to depart again, the ice melted, but this time in Admiralty Inlet, a body of water that had never before had open water at this time of the year.

Admiralty Inlet, which runs north-south between Borden Peninsula and Brodeur Peninsula, was my route south. It was a frozen highway that ran between mountain ranges that were impossible to cross on foot, and I needed to use it to get at least as far as Nyeboe Fjord. By the time I got that far, the ice should be thick and dense enough to allow me to continue to Kugaaruk, on the far shores of the Gulf of Boothia.

But now Admiralty Inlet had become a navigable channel!

I was disappointed but not beaten. I have always believed that things always happen for a reason, even if it sometimes takes a while to figure out what that reason might be. A defeat, for me, is never anything other than one step on the road to victory. I have never thrown in the towel without a very persuasive reason.

So I bided my time until the end of November. The ice had finally frozen over again in Admiralty Inlet, and the thermometer was dropping further. I had green lights all the way.

Claude, who continued to share his invaluable knowledge with me, suggested a number of potential routes and showed me which islands to go around between Arctic Bay and Pelly Bay. No one had ever managed to travel between those two villages on foot in the heart of winter, and so no one knew exactly what I would be facing. There were only three things we knew for sure: it would be terribly difficult, I would be far from help in an area swarming with polar bears, and I could not afford to make even the slightest mistake.

After he had so generously shared with me so much of his time and experience, I was delighted to have an opportunity, in turn, to do something to help Claude. When the engine of his snowmobile locked up because of some poor-quality fuel, which had reportedly been destroying engines all over the Arctic, I helped him buy a new one. He depended on that vehicle for his survival because it was indispensable for the hunting he did to feed his family and his dogs. He would pay me back when he was able. Compared to everything he had done for me, it was a small favor.

Two days before my departure, at the invitation of the Royal Canadian Mounted Police (RCMP), I enjoyed a delicious impromptu banquet. I spent the evening in the company of some exceptionally fine people. I could truthfully say the same thing about every member of the community of Arctic Bay, which, in the course of a month, adopted me as if I were one of their own.

When the time came for me to set out once again into the unknown, they all began to worry at the idea of seeing me go, willing prey to the night and the bears. Each member of the community tried to convince me not to go, and I could see the sadness in their eyes when I courteously but firmly refused to heed their advice.

* * *

It was two in the afternoon when I departed, but it was so dark that I couldn't see a thing except for the headlights of Claude's new snowmobile. He had come to bid me farewell. Without a word he wrapped me in his arms. In the darkness his eyes were glistening with tears, and he turned his head away to conceal his emotions. Although I may have been just another professional adventurer to him at first, I was now a true friend.

But I felt certain that we would meet again before too very long. If, as I feared, I was going to have to trek all the way around the Gulf of Boothia, I would certainly be needing supplies around Christmas. I already expected to rely on him for that.

I set off, and when I turned around to take one last look, I saw Claude's silhouette, dwarfed by his surroundings, as he waved slowly in the frozen air, as if he were waving the flag of our friendship. Then he was gone, and I had nothing ahead of me but the icy night of that late November of 2002, as I set out to walk along the length of the Borden Peninsula.

It wasn't the first time I had left a place where I had made friends—probably leaving it forever. However, it was the first time that I was leaving the human warmth of an adopted tribe and striking out into the utter darkness of the Arctic night. You can't change your nature, and I am a man of the south and require sunlight. To make things worse, I knew that every step was taking me farther and farther from my intended route because I was being forced to make this huge detour.

For all these reasons, my departure from Arctic Bay remains one of the most heartbreaking that I have ever experienced.

My eyes quickly became accustomed to the half-darkness into which my forehead lamp cast a pitifully small shaft of light. There was no risk of losing my way because I was following a clear course between the two long lines of cliffs that enclose the Admiralty Inlet. I had to get used to being a beast of burden again, an exhausting experience that I had not enjoyed since crossing Greenland two months before. My cargo, which back in Greenland had included just ten bottles of pure benzene, now included thirty bottles and weighed forty-five pounds more.

In order to ease myself back into shape, I covered only a modest distance the first day before pitching my tent for the night (that is, the darkest few hours of the day).

After the first five hours of travel each day, I began to suffer from hypothermia. In that relatively fragile state, I had just seven minutes to pitch my tent. Any longer than that and I would begin to die of cold. If anything delayed me, it meant death. In those temperatures that would be the situation every time I stopped.

Four days after leaving Arctic Bay, I had a great surprise. When I emerged from my tent I found myself nose-to-nose with an Inuit family. They were on their way back from a fishing expedition for Arctic char and had stumbled upon a lunatic camping in the middle of the ice field: me. Guessing that I was on my way somewhere, the man asked me my destination. When I answered, "Alaska," his almond-shaped eyes grew round with astonishment. He shot back, with the brevity that is so typical of the Anglo-Inuit language: "And plane?" I felt like I was dreaming! He, an Eskimo muffled in his seal and caribou skins, dressed the way his ancestors have for centuries, was pointing out the advantages of flying.

The Inuit woman was looking at me with a sense of concern that I could clearly read on her tanned features, prematurely aged by a life that was as harsh as the climate. "You come back with us to Arctic Bay," she said. "Winter coming; night fall; temperatures drop real low; bears in migration. You go die."

I replied as diplomatically as I knew how that I was deeply touched by her concern, but that with all due respect for her and her family, I knew what I was doing, why I was doing it, and that I was quite determined to continue. Again, the man and the woman tried to persuade me to go back with them, to give up, to turn around, and after we said good-bye, they came after me again to beg me to reconsider one last time. Once it became clear that they could not change my mind, the Inuit man told his son to offer me his second pair of fur gloves.

By the way, the only reason I hadn't adopted the local style of dress, which would certainly have been less complicated, was that it was not well suited to long expeditions like the one I was undertaking. The natives of the Far North go out into the wild to hunt or fish, but when the distances grow longer they allow themselves to be pulled by their sled dogs or else they ride on their snowmobiles. To each his own way of life and to each his own equipment.

The friendly harassment to which I had just been subjected might seem excessive, but I didn't see it that way. It is theoretically impossible for human beings to survive at the extreme temperatures that prevail here. You cannot survive in the Arctic winter unless you stay in one place, as the Inuit do, living on their supplies of food and on their body fat. Walking requires considerable effort and uses up an enormous amount of calories—in my case, between eight and ten thousand calories a day, five times the normal rate. Chocolate, nuts, unsaturated fats, starches, butter, and vegetable oils—my entire diet was swimming in oils and fats. I was basically living on fats. All the same, I was losing weight every day, which was a bad thing for two reasons: first, because every extra pound of fat on my body would offer extra protection from the cold; and second, because if I was carrying that weight on my body then I wouldn't have to weigh down my sled with unnecessary supplies.

I drank nothing more than the strict minimum during the day in order to spare myself the ordeal of urinating outdoors in conditions of extreme cold. After my breakfast—tea or coffee with a big bowl of cereal—I filled two thermoses with a hot vanilla-flavored energy drink with a milky consistency. I took a few gulps of this drink approximately every two hours. This "liquid nutrition," as I called it, rehydrated me, warmed me up, and quenched my thirst and hunger. However, that didn't keep me from munching all day long on cashew nut bars or dried fruit, chocolate, or homemade brownies packed for me by Cathy. I also avoided wearing red-tinted sunglasses because experience taught me that the color red tended to make me hungry.

Ten days after leaving Arctic Bay, I called Børge Ousland on my satellite phone to give him a progress report. But instead of receiving congratulations, I was greeted with a brusque, "That's too cold! I have never traveled in that territory during that time of year. Head back to civilization."

In my situation I needed someone to urge me to outdo myself, to win, not to give up. The situation was eerily reminiscent of my earlier attempt to reach the North Pole. I ignored his advice, but each time I turned a deaf ear to good advice—each time I refused to heed the call to reason—I could feel a heavier burden of responsibility on my shoulders.

A few days later, I met my first polar bear.

It was one of those days when my kite, buffeted by only a slack breeze, dragged me forward with intermittent jerks like an old jalopy on its last legs. The polar bear that suddenly ventured across my path about a hundred yards away seemed less interested in me than in the large colorful rag that I appeared to have on a leash. Startled by the bear's presence, my reflex was to shake the kite with all my strength. The result was immediate. Frightened by that unidentified flying object, the bear turned and galumphed away. I could see his sizable white posterior as he took off at full speed over the ice.

I had just discovered a secondary use for my kites, unexpected but valuable.

Since I couldn't sleep with a kite fluttering overhead, I also used a nocturnal antibear alarm system that was developed by my friends Laurent and Daniel during their time in the Swiss army. This system, which we refer to as "bearwatch" required that I surround my tent with a wire hooked onto three stakes about twenty yards away from the tent and about a foot and a half above the ground. Polar bears, which drag their paws as they walk, have almost as much difficulty stepping over the wire as they would slipping beneath it. The slightest contact between the wire and a foreign body will trigger the launch of a flare. The sound of the flare blasting off would frighten the animal, and the light of the flare as it drops back to the ground suspended by a parachute would allow me to see the bear clearly.

My bearwatch alarm system allowed me to sleep soundly. It had only one small defect—its sensitivity meant that it could be set off by a moderately rough windstorm.

One day the roar of a snowmobile in the distance announced the arrival of a visitor. When the engine drew close and came to a halt, I discovered to my joy that it was Claude Lavallée. It had only taken him a single day to get here from Arctic Bay, whereas I left two full weeks ago. Before the ice got too thick, he was going fishing one last time on a lake not far away from here for fish to feed to his dogs.

"I needed to come," he said, "to give you one more chance to turn back." And, once again, I politely declined. Since accompanying him to the lake did not involve much of a detour, I agreed to go. During the forty-eight hours that we spent together, I slept under his canvas tent and I fulfilled my duties as apprentice by helping him to set his nets and haul the big fish out of the icy water.

Before long, the weather started to turn ugly and Claude was forced to hurry back to Arctic Bay. Otherwise he ran the risk of being pinned down out here. While breaking camp and packing and loading his equipment, he asked me one last time if I was absolutely dead set on going on.

"We are friends now," he said, as if to excuse his nagging. He already knew my answer, but I could sense that he wasn't so much trying to keep me from going on as he was trying to be certain that I understood what I was taking on.

For a good long while, Claude Lavallée would be the last person to have seen me alive. I was hoping that this "good long while" would not take on a sense of finality.

This time, roles reversed, it was Claude who left me. I found myself alone again in a night filled with ice and rock and hellish cold.

I was alone again and contemplated my situation. What had driven me to ignore so stubbornly the advice of everyone I knew, including people who live here and know this country much better than I do? Pride? Stupidity? As the days went on, I determined to stop questioning myself. If I let myself be consumed by doubt, I was certain to be beaten by the forces of nature, which sharply outnumbered my own.

The landscape around me slowly shifted as I marched along day after day. The Admiralty Inlet extended before my skis like a broad boulevard, except when the tides complicated matters. Winter was still young, and the ice had not yet reached its full thickness. Each flow of the tides lifted the ice and moved it away from the shores, making it impossible to reach the shore. I was forced to wait for the tide to ebb and push the ice back against the shore before I could reach dry land and pitch my tent.

In this part of the world, where a few inches of ice was all that stood between me and an ice-cold bath, everything seemed to be moving and shifting continuously.

"Everywhere you go around here, the ocean is alive," said Claude. "Never forget that you are walking on a living creature." He also warned me to be especially careful of every bulge or unusual rise in the frozen surface. "Sometimes it's ice, and sometimes it's snow. Put your foot on it, and down you go." This advice, which I took to heart, saved me more than once, even though it was hard to make out the level of the ice in the darkness, and the snow, which fell intermittently, made the night even darker.

I continued to travel on the frozen Admiralty Inlet, and not only because the flat frozen terrain provided me with a corridor leading in the right direction. In the winter on Baffin Island the temperatures are even harsher than at the North Pole, where the thirty-six or thirty-seven degree temperature of the water, radiating up through the ice field, makes the air a little milder. On Baffin Island's permafrost, forty degrees below zero really was forty below. On the frozen ice field of the Pole and of Admiralty Inlet, forty degrees below zero might moderate to, say, twenty-two degrees below zero due to the influence of the "warm" waters flowing beneath the ice.

In spring and summer it's the other way around, though. On the ice, the wind and the humidity drive the thermometer down, while dry land turns darker once the snow has melted and tends to absorb the heat of the sunlight. Thus, in the spring and summer I would try to stay on dry land as much as possible.

These nuances may bring a smile to the lips of experienced veterans of Nordic trekking, who claim that these minor effects are totally imperceptible. Personally, I believe that they make a substantial difference. For that matter, every time I got out of my tent I would play a little game. I'd try to guess the temperature before looking at the thermometer. I was rarely off by more than four or five degrees.

Every morning—so to speak, because sun never actually rose—I started my day by putting on a pair of heavy wool socks. Over the socks I slipped two plastic grocery bags, which in more technical terms I call anticondensation liners; they prevented my sweat from soaking through to my third layer, a pair of virgin-wool socks. The fourth layer was a pair of orange booties made of Polartec, a quick-drying fleece material that repelled moisture. When the temperature dropped below fifty degrees below zero, I added a fifth layer, a sort of large slipper made of polar wool. To facilitate circulation, none of these layers was very close-fitting.

Finally, I put on my boots—and all the layers that I just described should give you some idea of their size—and laced them only from the third hook up to give my toes plenty of room and not impede the blood flow.

These boots are the same as the ones that I wore to cross Greenland and to travel—almost—to the North Pole. They were custom-made for me out of Cordura, a material that would not break at sixty degrees below zero, and they were much lighter and more flexible than their bulky appearance might suggest. I had tried all sorts of footwear, and most of them, like modern ski boots, tended to restrict circulation in the ankles and force the knees to do all the work. Such boots might work for a few days of hiking, but no more than that. For long-distance trekking, they would be disastrous. In order to cover long distances, the whole body has to be working in unison. Plenty of trekkers, banged up or exhausted by excessively stiff boots, have been forced to give up in the middle of a trip.

I insisted that my footwear and clothing be as flexible and soft as possible, so as to help all of my joints to work together—ankles, knees, hips, shoulders. Moreover, they could not constrict any part of my body. These boots should allow me not only to hike, but also to ski, and even to climb.

They had only one shortcoming. After several thousand miles they would begin to crack where the toes flex, but I couldn't do anything about that. Any rigid structure must necessarily have a breaking point to allow the entire assembly to withstand strain. I would rather see my boots crack—I could always fill in the gaps—than come loose from the ski bindings.

Speaking of the bindings, I used three-point bindings that allowed my heel to rise with each step and at each turn, in accordance with the same telemarking principles that my skis are based on. Applying my three requirements of "solid, simple, and easy to repair," I chose these bindings because they are the least complicated model on the market. For that matter, they included a safety release, which, if I fell in the water, would allow me to get out of my skis in a single move. (The skis, unfortunately, would go straight to the bottom, dragged down by the weight of their edges and the metal bindings.) It was Børge Ousland who especially recommended adding the release. He knew all too well the mad-dog side of my personality that encouraged me to run risks.

The temperatures were soon flirting with forty degrees below zero, and they kept dropping.

+ ✦ ✦

Before setting out on each new day of trekking, I followed an old Eskimo custom. I blew my nose on my fingers and smeared the snot over my face. Don't be too grossed out. It's just a transparent liquid, and it froze to form an antifrostbite mask more effective than any creams available on the market. Moreover, it was one less item I had to carry in my sled because my nose was dripping constantly.

During each day's hike, I wore three layers of clothing on top: a long-sleeved mock-turtleneck pullover made of power-dry fabric; over that, an Eider wool-and-polyester jersey for its warmth and moisture absorption; and finally, a layer of power-stretch, a silk-based fabric whose ultratight weave held in a layer of warm air, preventing cold air from getting in. As the word *stretch* suggests, it hugged my body, following all my movements instead of hindering them. I had the shoulders reinforced, putting seams in the middle of the back and on the outside in order to keep the chafing from the sled's harness from rubbing my skin raw. I had openings placed at the armpits to allow perspiration to escape, and I added a breast pocket—a sort of bag—to hold the GPS that I wore around my neck. Last of all I cut a slit into the end of each sleeve with my knife. I stuck my thumbs into these slits, and my power-dry stretched out into an extra pair of mittens.

I could have opted for a single layer of clothing, three times as warm, enveloping and protective. But I preferred to be flexible and able to remove layers when the thermometer began to rise, which would happen often over the course of my trip.

The final and most important layer was my Gore-Tex parka. It had zipper openings under the arms to allow air circulation and pockets big enough to hold a meal . . . or my mittens, if I had to take them off. It hung down to my knees to provide an extra layer of insulation to my thighs and to the femoral arteries carrying blood down my legs to my feet.

The lining of my jacket hood was made of genuine wolverine fur, which protected my face against wind and had the special property of never freezing. Whatever ice formed on it could be removed by shaking it the same way that huskies—sled dogs—do. Under the hood I wore a fine polyester balaclava like the ones that race-car drivers wear, plus a wind-breaker cap that I designed and made myself. It was an especially adaptable device with a retractable visor to protect against bright sunlight, pull-down earflaps, and a shutter that I pulled down over my forehead on especially cold mornings to soften the stunning blow of the frigid air.

Beneath my parka but over my sports-wool underwear and my power-stretch tights (made of the same material as my top), I wore a pair of Gore-Tex ski overalls. In order to allow me to perform my "natural functions" while exposing me as little as possible to the cold, it had an opening in the front and a zippered flap in the rear. It was also equipped with special pockets for the following items: map, compass, camera, mittens, ice axes, knife, and so forth, each item had its own designated location so that I could find anything in a flash.

All of this equipment, including my boots, was to me an extension of my skin, a way of getting as close as possible to the elements, and not a protective shell, an image whose defensive connotations I especially disliked. In my mind, weapons were what you used to protect yourself. The day I needed protection from nature, I would just stay home.


Each evening, the ceremony of entering my tent followed the same ritual. While still outside, I removed my mittens so that I could rapidly doff my parka to clean off the ice that formed inside and the snow that covered it; then I put my mittens back on to scrub the parka with a normal housecleaning whiskbroom whose long handle was easy to grab. Taking off my clothes this way, at a temperature of forty to sixty degrees below zero, was the worst moment of the day! But I much preferred to go through this sort of ordeal than to have all that snow turn into ice on the inside of my tent. After all, when it was only ten degrees warmer inside than outside, I needed to preserve all the warmth I could.

For the second phase of disrobing, I sat in the tent with my feet in the vestibule, and I removed my boots, brushing them off to get rid of the snow and the icy film that my perspiration left inside them. I set my shoes down carefully—well opened, laces removed and stretched out without any knots, which would be impossible to undo the next day. (Once inside the sleeping bag, I would slip my large woolen socks under my undergarments, and my body heat would dry them out.) I took off my trousers—the other part of my outer layer—and left them in the vestibule as well. I didn't want to let even the tiniest snowflake get into my sleeping bag or on the walls of my tent where it would have immediately frozen and never thawed. Then, once inside, I continued to sweep out any snow that might have slipped in with me. All told, this procedure took about twenty minutes every night before I could close the zipper of my tent behind me.

When the temperature began to get close to sixty degrees below zero, I wore a large down jacket over everything else while I prepared and ate my evening meal. I only wore that garment in the tent.

While I melted snow and ice into potable water in the pan, I held my bare hands over the camp stove to keep them from freezing while I filled out my logbook for the day. Since my partial amputation after the North Pole expedition, frostbite returned quickly and much more easily, despite the warmth of my mittens. I could often barely use my hands, even to write in my little black notebook with a pencil. I used a pencil because ink would freeze at those temperatures.

My friend Pierre Morand made a one-of-a-kind camp stove for me, complete with a saucepan. Since I only used the stove inside my tent and had no desire to die of asphyxiation the burner was designed to release the smallest possible amount of carbon monoxide. As for the pan, it consisted of two separate layers of aluminum. This allowed the fire to first heat the intermediate layer of air, then the contents of the pan. The cover flipped over to become both a plate (so I didn't have to carry one) and a food warmer (which kept my meals from freezing again before I could finish eating them). I should point out that it took me two solid hours to eat the enormous amount of calories that I required because of my daily exertion. My spoon was made of plastic (freezing metal would have stuck to my tongue), as was my cup with a screw-on lid to prevent me from spilling the contents inside the tent.

When I turned the plate over, small openings released the heat contained between the two walls of the pan; and my little cooking set became a small radiator.

It had another use, I confess. At exceptionally cold temperatures, when using my trap-door toilet required a level of endurance that I couldn't stand, I sometimes heated up the pot, lined it with a plastic bag, and used it as a toilet. None too hygienic, I realize, but no one besides me ate out of this cook set.

My camp stove was, of course, designed for easy repair, because it would be unthinkable to be left without the tool that allowed me to thaw out my food, melt snow for drinking water, and heat up my tent a little—in short, to eat, drink, and keep from freezing to death.

Before getting into my sleeping bag, I slipped on a pair of heavy, padded knickers, a sort of knee-length down jacket for my butt. My own invention, it was meant to provide a little extra warmth and thus help the circulation of blood to my legs. I had to absolutely avoid crossing my legs in my sleep, or even laying one on top of the other. In this cold the slowed circulation would be enough to cause frostbite to my feet, and my heart could not beat fast enough to make up for it. Every half hour I changed position to keep my limbs from going numb, and my subconscious automatically woke me up every hour to make sure that everything was all right.

I was always, in any case, in a state of high alert. The hood of my sleeping bag would have made me deaf to any outside noises, such as an approaching bear, so instead I just used the insulating balaclava that by then I wore day and night; it had become a sort of second skin.

Once I was in my tent at night, I drank lots and lots of water—as much as three or four quarts before going to sleep. When a pressing need to urinate woke me back up, I relieved it immediately since holding it in was a waste of effort that would burn up calories and chill my entire body. Fortunately, I didn't need to get out of my sleeping bag. I had a portable urinal inside the bag. Once I filled it up, I placed it between my feet, which were thus warmed up by the heat of my own urine. The second time I felt the pressing urge, I needed only extend an arm out of my sleeping bag to empty the bag in the tent's vestibule before the contents could freeze; then I filled up my liquid foot-warmer again. This little portable radiator would become even more invaluable between the beginning of January and the middle of March when temperatures would drop even lower.

One night, I was suddenly jolted awake by a powerful and repeated nasal snuffling sound that resembled the breathing of an animal. The beast must be very close to my tent! Could it be that wolf that had been following me from a distance for two days now and that I spotted more than once out of the corner of my eye, even though it was cautiously keeping its distance? I was even more worried that it might be a bear. If it was, though, how did it make it past my bearwatch? I couldn't figure it out, but that question was no longer relevant. Seized by a wave of panic, I leaped up, forgetting the container of warm urine sitting between my feet. The "piss pot" overturned and spilled all over my sleeping bag. Nearly all the liquid remained inside the condensation-proof lining, which meant I would be able to get rid of it easily. But my clothing was soaked, and that's always dangerous when traveling in frigid temperatures. For the moment I had other priorities. I grabbed my rifle and my flashlight and rushed outside, ready to take on the monster, but there was no bear in sight. I took a hasty but careful look around and went back inside and got back into my sleeping bag. False alarm, it would seem. And yet I was certain that I heard the breathing of an animal.

Fear ate at me as my ears perked up, waiting for another suspicious sound. Suddenly, it began again! The same rough hissing, sharp and prolonged, that only an animal could have produced. It was coming from even closer this time, just the other side of the nylon wall. For the second time, I rushed out of my sleeping bag, without upsetting any liquids this time, and out of my tent. Yet I couldn't see even the shadow of a bear on the horizon! Could it be that solitude was beginning to un-hinge my mental faculties?

That was when I realized that I had pitched my tent right next to one of the holes that seals make in the ice so that they can surface and breathe! In the darkness, I never even saw it. It is true that the holes are tiny, and thin film of ice covers the holes back up very quickly.

It turned out that I had "pissed in my pants" for nothing!

My buddy, the wolf, continued to follow me at a distance. I skied over the tracks of a bear that was heading in the same direction as me. The natural dangers I faced were like a dormant volcano between eruptions.

But the volcano erupted suddenly about three weeks after my depar-ture from Arctic Bay, in the area around Bell Bay—in the form of a ma-jor Arctic storm. Luck would have it that at the very moment that the storm reached its peak of fury, I happened upon a shelter, a simple un-heated log cabin in which it was just as cold as outside—around fifty degrees below zero—but where I could at least pitch my tent without being exposed to the squalls of wind and thus warm up a little faster. I hunkered down there for a few days until the weather calmed down, and then I set off again.

Forty-eight hours later, I noticed the headlights of a snowmobile in the distance. The driver also noticed me and headed straight for me. His vehicle, equipped with Caterpillar treads and two skis, was pulling a covered sled.

When he stopped beside me, I saw that he was an Inuit wrapped in furs and caribou skins. He got off his snowmobile and stood before me, looking at my layers of Gore-Tex and Polartec. Once again, two worlds stood observing one another. The Inuit stared at me, his eyes buried in the folds and furrows of his face; then he opened his toothless mouth and yelled, "What the fuck are you doing here?"

I had been asked this question before. Without losing my compo-sure, I replied that I was heading for Alaska—on foot.

"Now?" he asked.

"Yes, now. Why?"

"And the night?" (The Inuit are unfailingly terse.)

"And so?" The dialogue was becoming surreal.

"So . . . we never travel when it is night."

I explained to him that I planned to cross the Bering Strait and could not afford to wait four months. Winter—the coming winter—would keep me from getting there in time.

The man just stood there, staring at me in astonishment for a few more moments, and then he burst out, "Incredible!"

He had no time to waste. They were waiting for him at Arctic Bay. It occurred to me that it would take him barely two days to make it back to a place that I had left three weeks ago. Since he was coming from Igloolik, which was right on my route, he told me what to expect: a few liquid gaps in the ice, a little drift ice, but nothing insurmountable.

When the time came for him to leave, he pulled back the tarp that covered his *kamutik* (sled in Inuktitut), took out a large Arctic char, frozen solid by the ambient temperature, and offered it to me as a gift. In winter such a difficult-to-obtain food takes on inestimable value for the Inuit. This gesture, which showed that he was not indifferent to my fate, touched me deeply. With the tip of my knife, I cut off a piece of fish and ate it, as raw as sushi.

Our conversation had not lasted any longer than seven minutes, and in that brief time this stranger who knew nothing about me had found the time to form an opinion of me, to give me advice, and to offer me some food. I forgot about the cold and the night. It was moments like this that made all the rest worth it.

December was approaching, snow was falling more heavily, and the thermometer was dropping. I crossed Easter Sound and began a long and grueling climb up to Saputing Lake, a body of freshwater a good thirty miles in length, perched high above sea level. I followed frozen rivers, crossed valleys. Snow replaced ice and then gave way to rock. I frequently had to stop, remove my skis, and push my sled. Sometimes I had to unload it to lighten it; it only weighed forty-five pounds less than when I had left Arctic Bay eighteen days ago. I would move the contents to a platform and pile it up there, then go back to find the sled and carry it on my back. The obstacle course was exhausting, and I only made a half mile of progress every twenty-four hours.

When I finally arrived at Saputing Lake, I was utterly spent. Until I could recover my strength, I would not be able to travel more than four or five hours a day.

Obviously it would take me more than one day to reach the fishing hut whose GPS position Claude had given me. It was the only hut on all of Saputing Lake, located halfway up the lake's length, on the shore.

There was a good reason that I was so eager to spend the night in the hut instead of camping on the frozen surface of the lake. Saputing Lake, wedged between rocky mountains and fed by mountain streams, acted as a trap for caribou. Once they imprudently wandered into this dead-end trap, the unfortunate creatures could no longer escape the wolves. And if I were to pitch my tent in the middle of the lake, I would be in the same situation.

I decided to camp just before the mouth of the lake, in the lee of the mountains, where I had some emergency escape routes in case of a surprise attack. That night, however, neither wolf nor human disturbed my sleep.

Anxious to reach the cabin and knowing that it would take me a full day's trek to reach it, I awoke and set out before what passed for dawn.

It wasn't long before I noticed the first wolves. They were few in number, admirably discreet, and they kept a respectful distance. But as the hours passed, their numbers grew and their distance diminished.

It didn't help that my silhouette with my sled was roughly similar to that of a caribou, and the speed at which I was able to haul it—no more than a mile per hour because of the wind and the irregular surface—was approximately the same speed a caribou normally traveled.

When I finally glimpsed the hut on the horizon, it was with a sense of relief equaled only by my feelings of gratitude toward the fisherman who built it. It was only a little bigger than an outhouse, and you could only enter it on your knees. However, I managed to pitch my tent inside and to pile up all around me my provisions, which I was not eager to share with the wolves.

I had barely fallen asleep when I was awakened by the sound of scraping on the cabin wall. I didn't need to wonder what the sound was—the wolf pack had found my hideaway. They had scented my dinner—or maybe me—and now the wolves were scratching feverishly at the thin walls that stood between us with a fury that was only increased by their hunger. In the total darkness I listened to the beasts' cries, their hoarse panting, and I imagined their emerald green eyes and their glittering fangs, just like in a cartoon. I could hear them scrabbling under rocks and blocks of ice in a frenzy to dig out even a tiny scrap of food. (The filthy beasts have the disgusting habit of urinating on their food to discourage anyone or anything else from touching it.) The immense emptiness surrounding us echoed this soundtrack from a horror film, and the cabin amplified the noises.

But I knew that the walls would keep them out. The owner of this tiny shelter built it to be wolf-proof. This confidence gave me a sense of invulnerability that I had not felt in quite a while. Despite the frenzy outside, I was actually quite happy.

When I emerged from the hut after a fitful sleep, nothing remained of the wolves but their paw prints in the snow and their claw marks in the wood. But my mind was already elsewhere: a long day's march still lay between me and the far end of Saputing Lake. After that, another mountain pass would lead me to Ivisarak Lake, and a last pass—where I would camp—would be followed by a gradual descent to Nyeboe Fjord. There I would not be far from Fury and Hecla Strait, which separates Baffin Island from mainland Canada.

I had been traveling on foot for a month and a half, and I had gone less than two miles westward, the direction I was actually heading!

I had been trying to keep my mind on other subjects and to stay motivated, and so I set myself the objective of getting off Baffin Island by Christmas. If I succeeded, I had decided to reward myself on December 25 with my first full day of rest. But Christmas was drawing near now, and I set off without wasting another second.

My forehead lamp was always on, but it seemed to me—unless it was just wishful thinking—that the night was ever so slightly less dark. The difference was approximately what you would get by pouring a thimbleful of white lacquer in a bucket of black paint.

Now I had a second reason for going into turbo power—the extreme cold. The cold was breaking records, but so was I. In less time than it takes to tell, I was pitching my tent on the pass between Saputing and Ivisarak lakes.

In the very middle of Ivisarak Lake, a white mass glittering in the shadows caught my attention. It was an igloo—perfectly made, at that—a compact hemisphere of snow built the way that only the Inuit know how to build them. This had to be the work of the people of Igloolik, who must have come out here to hunt caribou and wolves.

I soon discovered that, in compliance with Inuit tradition, the people who built this igloo left it open so that others could take shelter in it. They had also left some tea and biscuits as emergency provisions for them. And so once again I learned that it is in this part of the world, completely forsaken by the rest of humanity, that human beings are most deserving of the name.

At the far end of Ivisarak Lake the mountains forced me to climb again. And around noon, in a strange, diffused light, I first glimpsed the outlines of Nyeboe Fjord. My heart raced in my chest. In my eagerness to get down to the fjord, I set off skiing at a rapid clip. But skiing downhill here proved to be a lot less fun than on the slopes of Courchevel. My sled was heavy and moved faster than I could, hitting me in the back and knocking me down repeatedly. I had to let it run ahead of me and try to restrain it while moving forward, a struggle that made climbing look enjoyable. To make things even worse, the wind began to blow harder and harder, but Nyeboe Fjord was the Holy Grail to me, so it made everything well worthwhile.

When I finally got to the surface of the fjord, the wind was blowing so hard that it kept me from setting up my tent. It also kept me from getting anything to drink because it had swept away even the little bit of snow that had fallen so far this winter. I moved forward across the frozen salt water of the fjord, hunting in vain for even a tiny pile of snow. The gale, which was growing more intense by the minute, wasn't about to improve matters.

After struggling for two hours in the absolute darkness, fighting the wind the whole time at thirty degrees below zero, I finally managed to pitch my tent. I had food but not a drop to drink on the evening of December 24, 2002. Talk about a Christmas Eve dinner!

On Christmas I started the day by calling Cathy and my daughters on my satellite phone. We talked longer than usual as a way to make the most of this family holiday that brought us together—virtually, at least.

I left Nyeboe Fjord and made my way out onto the Gulf of Boothia, which had finally partially frozen over. In doing so, I left Baffin Island and was more or less on a line with the Fury and Hecla Strait. And so I had reached my goal! I had definitely earned this Christmas present.

The ice was passable, but I found myself on pack ice that reminded me of the North Pole, only more tumultuous. The frozen sheets of ice heaved, making it especially difficult for me to pitch my tent. When I finally found a campsite that was a little more stable, I enjoyed a big meal. I binged on freshwater, and I allowed myself a double ration of heating fuel, leaving the heater on longer than was customary. That night my nylon tent was a palace, and few men on earth could have been happier than me.

Because there was ice covering the Gulf of Boothia, there was a chance that I would be able to cross the gulf and then continue to the west! On the day after Christmas, I felt almost as if I could leap from slab to shifting slab of ice, all the way to the far shore. But first I needed to make a few preliminary checks. I contacted an icebreaker whose crew monitored the weather and the state of the ice on a regular basis. And I called Cathy and asked her to take a look at the most recent satellite photos of the region on the Internet site www.seaice.com.

From both sources I received the same answer. "Don't even try it!"

warned my friends from the icebreaker. Cathy confirmed the warning: "Cover 3/10, type 1 ice." Type 1 indicates fresh ice that's not very thick. As for cover, it is defined on a scale that ranges up to 10/10 when the surface is totally covered. At 9/10 I would have given it a try. But in the past fifty years the ice cover on the Gulf of Boothia had never been thicker than 8/10. And even at 8/10 the frozen surface could have been cut in half up the middle, forcing me to backtrack. In any case, with 3/10 cover there was no question of even trying. Crossing the Gulf of Boothia on foot was impossible. Period.

Waiting for the ice to firm up and the cover to spread would have taken at least three months. It appeared that my magical Christmas wasn't going to last.

I was determined to overcome this obstacle however I could and came up with the idea of taking a shortcut across a small island located at the southernmost edge of the gulf. However, upon investigation, it turned out that the ice was breaking up even more there, so this backup plan failed.

My worst fears had come to pass: I was going to have to walk all the way around the Gulf of Boothia via Committee Bay—the longest way around—before being able to head north again on a northwesterly course toward Kugaaruk, my next stop. The problem, to put it mildly, was that my provisions were running out, and I would be short of food before reaching Kugaaruk.

I decided to arrange for a complete resupply on the spot. I called Jean-Philippe Patthey, gave him my position on the Gulf of Boothia, and asked him to bring me not only new food supplies but also equipment with which to face the harshest months of the winter. I needed a new tent and lots of replacement gear.

Once he reached Arctic Bay, Jean-Philippe would be no farther than three days away from my campsite by snowmobile, and once he had dropped the material off, he would be traveling lighter, and it would only take two days to return to Arctic Bay. If everything went more or less according to plan, we would be together to celebrate New Year's Eve.

Claude Lavallée, whom I also called, was astonished and pleased to hear that I had made it this far. He decided to come visit me with Adam, his friend the photographer.

Jean-Philippe caught his plane in Switzerland, bringing with him a substantial shipment of equipment and food prepared by Cathy. But when he landed in Paris, where he was scheduled to catch the connecting flight, the airline had lost two of my bags! Since we always mixed provisions and equipment in different pieces of luggage because of precisely this sort of problem, I lost only part of my food and part of my equipment. Among the lost equipment were my new boots and skis, which I desperately needed. It was a catastrophe, but the Air France official with whom Jean-Philippe had a heated exchange appeared to be totally indifferent. Little did he care that my life might well depend upon the gear that had been lost due to his negligence or the carelessness of his colleagues! Cathy also got involved. Then so did I. Everyone lost their patience and wound up screaming at each another, in person or from thousands of miles away.

Jean-Philippe wanted to go back to Switzerland and reassemble the package of equipment and supplies that the airlines had lost. But if he did that, he would miss his connecting flight, and there were only two flights a week to Nanisivik and Arctic Bay. I asked him to travel on and bring me whatever the airlines hadn't lost. If by some miracle the lost luggage were to resurface, then it could be sent on directly to Igloolik. From there Johannessy, Lily's father, would be glad to bring it to me. It would take him only a short day's trip by snowmobile.

Two snowmobiles left Arctic Bay, heading in my direction: Claude Lavallée's snowmobile and another one carrying Adam and Jean-Philippe. Even though Jean-Philippe was in the prime of life, athletic and full of energy, this was the first time that he had ever traveled in an open vehicle at forty degrees below zero. Despite the "pope-mobile" attachment—a small protective glass enclosure—installed especially for him, his face and ears began to suffer from frostbite during the three-day trip. Each night when they stopped to camp, a little blood would begin to flow back into his extremities, but the next day they would begin to freeze all over again. What he endured was a terrible ordeal—I knew something about frostbite. All the same, he maintained a positive attitude that won everyone's respect.

As for me, a blizzard had forced me to get off the frozen surface of the bay—remaining in the same spot on the frozen water struck me as dangerous—and to turn back toward the frozen shores of Baffin Island, where I was of course reluctant to return. Falling snow gradually covered my tent, forcing me to clear it off several times a day with a shovel. That explained why Johannessy, who was bringing me my luggage, which had finally been found, passed right by my tent without seeing me. He shouted my name repeatedly, but his cries were lost in the raging storm. At the mouth of Nyeboe Fjord, he noticed the headlights of the two snowmobiles coming toward me, and Claude sent him back in the right direction. The blizzard was terrible, and the group was forced to cross a broad expanse of pack ice before it could reach me. I sat waiting like a blind man until I finally heard the roar of snowmobiles in the blizzard.

When my four friends finally joined me, it was exactly two hours before the beginning of the New Year.

Johannessy had to return immediately to Igloolik, and there was no way to persuade him to stay and take part in our New Year's feast. I gave him some money and fixed him a cup of tea. We shook hands and he was gone, heading back into the blizzard. He would wind up steering his snowmobile for forty-eight hours through an intense blizzard just to bring me my bags. This is the sort of amazing sacrifice that, up here, people don't even think twice about.

Claude, Adam, Jean-Philippe, and I all crowded into Claude's canvas tent, which was roomier than mine. The joy we felt at all being together made this a memorable moment. "Mike," said Jean-Philippe, whose cheeks were white with frost, "now I understand a little better." He didn't need to say anything more. He had brought a bottle of whisky to celebrate New Year's, but—and this was information worth remembering—it turns out that whisky freezes at forty degrees below zero. It wasn't whisky on the rocks, but rock whisky! Our other hard alcohol had also frozen solid. After a little while on the double boiler, our drinks were finally thawed and ready for the toasts.

We were thousands of miles from all civilization, in the middle of nowhere, buried in the depths of the Arctic night, four close friends huddled in a tent, spending the most unforgettable New Year's Eve of our lives.

We spent the three days that followed taking photographs, updating my Web site, sending information to my sponsors and notes to friends. Then the weather turned ugly. A blizzard and angry winds pinned down Claude, Adam, and Jean-Philippe for three more days before they were finally able to set out again for Arctic Bay. It was becoming more and more difficult to tear myself away from my friends. That is no doubt because there are few opportunities to make new friends in these parts.

Before heading back, Claude and Adam admitted to me that, despite my history and my reputation, they never thought that I would get this far, but now they were sure that I would achieve my goal. For the first time, nobody was urging me to give it all up. Now they were encouraging me to go all the way, to give it my all and succeed.

I no longer felt as if I were the only one who believed in myself. And that was what I needed most, even more than provisions and supplies. All the more because I was about to face the iciest months of the Arctic winter and the harshest terrain in this part of the globe, the Committee Bay region.

First, I would have to travel along the eastern shore of the Gulf of Boothia and cross the Fury and Hecla Strait to reach the Melville Peninsula on the Canadian mainland. There at least, whenever a body of water lay across my route, I would have lots of room to maneuver around it.

I would need to cross the Fury and Hecla Strait at its narrowest point. I wanted to spend as little time as possible in the danger zone where the islands caused turbulence in the water flowing beneath the ice, breaking up the icy surface and making it uneven. The smoother the surface, the faster I would be able to move.

I found an ideal passage at the mouth of the strait, the seventeen-mile stretch between Baffin Island and Nuvaluk Point, the northeastern cape of the Melville Peninsula. I had been told that there was a hunter's cabin there, a little larger than the hut on Saputing Lake.

Despite this new plan, I longed to shorten my route by crossing the Gulf of Boothia. I had been warned over and over that this would be impossible given the current state of the ice, but I had been on foot for two months now, and I had only made two miles of westward progress, so I had not completely accepted the idea that I would have to make a huge detour around Committee Bay.

They say that it's impossible? I wouldn't be able to sleep at night if I didn't go and see it with my own eyes.

Before I made it across the Fury and Hecla Strait, I cut off to the southwest. But after six or seven hours of hiking, I stood looking out over an immense expanse of moving pack ice. And on the horizon I could make out clouds that were a distinctive shade of gray. It was the gray shade of clouds that formed over water warmer than the air above it. If you know how to identify these clouds, you can change your course and skirt around the open water beneath them. But here, this foggy layer extended as far as I could see to the South and to the North.

I had wanted to see. Now I had seen.

I wasted no more time complaining, turned around, and set my course for the Melville Peninsula. I was now resigned to the idea that I would have to travel all the way around the Gulf of Boothia. At least after the resupply I now had all the food supplies I would need.

But over the satellite telephone Cathy told me that, ahead of me, the ice had broken away from the mainland, creating an impassable liquid barrier. So I was now trapped. The tides and currents had rendered the rocky shoreline inaccessible to me, and the pressure of the ice had lifted huge blocks of ice, giant dominoes that piled up into stacks towering as high as fifty feet in the air all around me.

There was nothing to be done. While I waited for conditions to become more favorable, I pitched my tent on the Gulf of Boothia, on the continental side of the Fury and Hecla Strait. From my campsite I enjoyed an incomparable view of the Melville Peninsula.

I had just lit my camp stove when it suddenly ran out of fuel—something that happens on average every two or three days. I left the tent to get a full bottle from my sled. I stepped back into the tent with the new bottle and separated the camp stove from the empty fuel bottle. Then I opened the new bottle before inserting it into the stove to replace the old one.

This routine procedure would not even be worth mentioning if I hadn't overlooked two details.

First, a tiny pilot light had remained lit on the camp stove, even though it was supposed to go out, in theory, as soon as the bottle of fuel was removed.

Second, my benzene bottles had been filled at a temperature of about fifty degrees below zero. However, for the past few days now, the thermometer had risen to a balmy temperature of ten degrees below zero, due to a completely unseasonable and inexplicable heat wave.

As a result of that forty degree rise in temperature, the gas inside the fuel bottle had doubled in volume. And despite the pressure valve, my fuel bottles had all become pressure cookers and were on the verge of bursting.

The instant I opened the new bottle, its contents exploded like a bottle of champagne shaken up by a winning team in the locker room.

The benzene expanded until it came into contact with the pilot light, and then . . . KABOOM! It caught fire instantly!

My face was covered with burning fuel. By smacking myself violently, I managed to put out the fire that had consumed my beard and my eyebrows, but my forehead was all one scorched blister, and the tip of my nose was an open wound.

But I had more serious worries. My survival instincts had led me to drop the bottle, and the quart of gas had spread everywhere. In a moment's flash I imagined my parka, my trousers, my boots, my satellite telephone, my GPS, my gun, my distress beacon, my mattress, and my sleeping bag—*all* burned to a crisp! All burned at the same time! I was surrounded by flames, and a wall of fire was crackling between me and the opening of the tent, preventing me from escaping. I thought of trying to get out the back of the tent by ripping open the nylon, but it was too strong to fight my way through it. I wanted to try to cut it, but in my panic, I could no longer find my knife.

The tent was fire resistant, so it was the only thing that didn't burn. Instead, it melted. Incandescent drops of liquid nylon rained down on me, setting my thermal underwear on fire, as well.

Suddenly, in place of the vestibule, which had melted from the blazing heat, there was nothing but a gaping hole. Instinctively, I plunged through the flames and leaped outside where I rolled in the snow to soothe the burns on my face and to put out the flames on my seared clothing. It looked like I would get away with minor injuries, but I had just narrowly escaped being roasted like a chicken.

At that instant I realized that unless I managed to save at least one GPS and my satellite phone, it would be impossible to contact Cathy to ask her to send new gear and give her my coordinates so that she could send help. I knew that the closest village, Igloolik, was at least ten days away on foot.

Without the slightest hesitation, I plunged back into my tent and plucked out of the flames a bag that held one of the GPSs, a battery, my satellite phone, and a gun. On my way through, I managed to snatch up a few other items, but I couldn't save my parka, my pants, or my mittens.

A few minutes later, standing in front of my campsite, now reduced to ashes, I took stock of the situation. It wasn't a very reassuring inventory. I stood on the ice field dressed in thermal underwear and socks; I had a spare pair of gloves and another cap in my sled; my boots were still usable. However, I no longer had a tent, no more sleeping bag, no more warm clothing, and no more heating stove because part of the stove had actually melted in the fire. Moreover, the rise in temperature that had been the cause of my catastrophe was not likely to last—these

Arctic "heat waves" are always short-lived. It had been pretty mild that day, but the weather forecast for that night was calling for a blizzard and a return to bad weather and more seasonable temperatures.

While I waited, I needed to find a way to stay alive.

To ward off the cold, I started to build the only conceivable type of shelter given the location and the circumstances: an igloo.

In contrast with what is commonly believed, igloos aren't built with slabs of ice but rather with bricks of compacted snow. But compacted snow, unfortunately, was still hard to find so early winter. Still, saw in hand (I had one in the sled), I went hunting for any small pile of snow on this piece of slowly drifting pack ice. Because of my lack of experience in building igloos, I took quite a while. And as I was feverishly working to build a shelter, the blizzard started blowing and the thermometer dropped back down to twenty-two degrees below zero. After many difficult and frigid hours, I was able to build my shelter.

Once I was in my igloo, I called Cathy to explain the situation—taking full responsibility for this incident. As a professional, I was expected to make sure that this sort of catastrophe didn't happen. I should have checked to see whether a pilot light was still burning on my stove, and since I knew perfectly well what effect a rise in temperature would have on the benzene, I should have checked the pressure in the fuel bottles. In short, I was guilty of a lack of vigilance.

I gave Cathy a long list of everything I had lost—luckily, back home I had replacements for everything—and asked her to bring it all to me at Igloolik.

In my sled, I found a packet of small round candles, known as nine-hour candles. I lit one, and fifteen minutes later it was as if central heating had been installed. I was still in my underclothes, but I was no longer cold. While the blizzard was howling outside, I used my candle to melt a little snow for drinking water.

I called Claude Lavallée and asked him to contact Johannessy in Igloolik. Lily's father, who had already done me one favor by bringing my gear and supplies out to me once, would certainly do me the favor of coming back out again. To keep anyone from panicking, I told him that

I could last for four or five days, or even reach a nearby cabin. "Okay," Claude replied, "call me back in an hour."

One hour later he had talked to Johannessy. The Royal Canadian Mounted Police—had asked Johanessy to find a teammate to come out and rescue me. A call from the authorities confirmed it, "Stay where you are; we will send a team to transport you to Igloolik, where you can wait for your supplies before starting off again."

In the Arctic even tiny incidents tend to take on the dimensions of affairs of state. I sensed a feverish quality bordering on panic in what had already become a large-scale rescue operation, a rescue that would result in my losing forty to sixty miles, since Igloolik was at the far end of the Fury and Hecla Strait! And to think how simple it would have been just to bring me my gear and provisions so that I could set off again from there.

I told the policeman that I would stay put for one day. Then I would start hiking toward Nuvaluk to move toward my rescuers and help them to find me, because in the pack ice where I was situated it would be hard for them to spot me. "That's out of the question!" shouted the policeman in a rage. "We organized this rescue operation, so we're telling you what to do! Don't move an inch!"

There was nothing left for me to do but make myself as comfortable as possible and wait. I had my nine-hour candles, enough food and fuel to withstand a siege, and all the time I needed to sit and relish the joys of meditation. While digging through the embers of my campsite, I found the fuel bottle that was responsible for the fire. I sawed it in half, I perforated it like a colander, and I stuffed the remains of a charred polo shirt, which I had soaked in benzene, into it. I lit it, and it provided a perfect burner to heat my coffee. It actually got too hot inside the igloo, and the snow started to melt. A little chimney, practically at the top of the igloo, let out the excess heat.

Back in Igloolik, Johannessy issued a call for help on his citizens band radio. He was looking for a volunteer, available and ready to start out immediately, for a nonemergency rescue mission on the Gulf of Boothia. Simon, an Inuit who lived in the village, answered the call.

He added that he had a family and dogs to feed, and that if there was no emergency, then he would take advantage of the trip to hunt seal. The two men purchased a number of heat-and-eat meals at the local co-op, hooked sleds up behind their snowmobiles, and loaded the sleds with extra fuel. The rescue office of the RCMP underwrote all the expenses.

Twenty-four hours after their first radio call, Simon and Johannessy set off into the night. Since they knew my GPS position and my condition, they took the time to stop occasionally along the way, searching for seal holes.

As for me, I sat listening for the slightest engine noise. The RCMP had told me that the rescue party would arrive the morning after setting out, but that evening arrived and no one had shown up.

The next morning I called the police in Igloolik again to tell them that I intended to set out for Nuvaluk. Once again, the policeman flew into a rage and ordered me to stay where I was. "The rescue party left twenty-four hours ago," he said. "If you leave your present location, they won't be able to find you!"

That wasn't completely true. They had a radio, too—even though they would have to stop and set up an antenna in order to use it. I could have easily radioed my new position to them. Once again, however, I obeyed his order.

Another twenty-four hours went by before snowmobile headlights began to dance in the distance. From the doorway of my igloo, I watched the firefly lights as they flickered on and off among the massive mountains of ice. In order to help them find me in the vast mosaic of pack ice, I shot off one of the flares from my "bearwatch" system. Simon saw it. Johannessy didn't, and he continued to wander around, lost, in huge, looping circles.

Simon—I only knew his name from having heard it over the radio—was the first to pull up and stop at the igloo. He was a fur-wrapped Inuit, dressed in caribou skin, with caribou gloves; on his feet were mukluks, the traditional Inuit boots. He was a true man of the Far North, like so many whom I had already met, but there was something distinctive and familiar about him.

When he took off his hood and showed me his face, his eyes buried in wrinkles, I was shocked.

"But . . . I know you!" he said.

"And I know you," I replied in astonishment.

Simon was the very same Inuit who, a month before near Bell Bay, had guided me and given me a fish. We hadn't spent more than a few minutes together, but we greeted each other like old friends.

His smile could have melted the polar ice cap. With enthusiastic sign language, he examined my igloo and asked me how long it had taken to build it. I answered proudly, "About six hours!"

"Much too long," he answered. "Next time die, if not faster."

Johannessy finally joined us. He and Simon had brought me a new sleeping bag and a heavy caribou-skin parka, which I quickly put on.

By the time I had piled what remained of my supplies on Johannessy's sled, attached my sled to Simon's harness, and climbed up on the seat behind him, we were starting off again for Igloolik.

Stung by the icy wind and battered by clumps of snow in my face, I began to literally freeze as we motored over the ice. Even the two Inuit, seated as they were on the hot engines of their snowmobiles, were forced to stop every two hours and dance around their vehicles to keep from freezing.

They were in no more of a hurry on the way back than they had been on the way out. What with the stops for seal hunting, the stops to fix Johannessy's old, broken-down sled, and the breaks to stock up on iceberg ice, which was the best tea-brewing water available, it was clear that we were going to have to camp a second night before we got back to Igloolik. We spent the night three hours away from the village, in a fishing shack that was abandoned for winter. Simon, who had never stopped observing me since chance had brought us back together, peppered me with questions. His black eyes shone with excitement as I described the various experiences of my long march thus far.

In turn, I learned a bit about Simon. He was about fifty years old and had always lived in the ways of his ancestors, making his living—and filling his belly—by fishing and hunting alone. He was also an artist and craftsman. He sculpted animals in motion out of marble,

ivory, and granite. He had even participated in international exhibitions
of Inuit art, traveling to Austria, Russia, and elsewhere.

In the time it took to get back to Igloolik, a tiny village of two hundred, Simon and I had become fast friends. When he asked me where I
planned to stay and I replied that I had no idea—especially because my
papers and my money had all burned up in the fire—I already knew
what he was going to say to me.

After I moved my things into Simon's house, he introduced me to his
girlfriend and the child that they had adopted. Life here was pretty basic, but the house was heated and we had plenty of caribou and Arctic
char to eat thanks to the hunting and fishing prowess of the master of
the house.

A few days after my arrival, someone announced on the radio that
he had killed three seals and two caribou, which was too much meat for
his family alone. Instead of building up a reserve of food, this Inuit did
what anyone in the community did whenever he or she had extra
food—he invited anyone who wanted to share his bounty to drop by.
Simon and his girlfriend brought an Arctic char to the feast. Sitting on
the ground in a strange kitchen, in the midst of a group of Inuit whose
sparse conversation amounted basically to the sound of chewing, I gobbled down the meat and raw fish and thought once again about how
much civilizations can differ.

My stay in Igloolik coincided with the big, traditional Inuit festival
held every year in honor of the sun, one week before the first sunrise of
the year. To call it a sunrise may be overstating things. When the sun
makes its first appearance after three months of darkness, it does nothing more than peep over the horizon for about five seconds. But that
mere cameo is quite sufficient to trigger great public celebrations.

During the course of the elaborate ceremony that was held, the Inuit
solemnly extinguished the sun of the previous year, symbolized by a
seal-oil lamp with a cotton wick that had once been used to heat igloos.

Then they lit a flame that represented the sun of the coming season, the sun of renewal.

This second sun also symbolized warmth and life flowing back into the bodies and souls worn down and left depressed by the interminable Arctic night. Those who endured the long winter often became depressed and, under the influence of alcohol, were sometimes rendered violent. Many suicides and killings resulted from cabin fever in the Far North, a violent neurosis triggered by the prolonged lack of sunlight and exacerbated by confinement.

I expelled these morbid thoughts from my mind when watching the spectacle of the traditional dances. The dance I witnessed that night had none of the flavor of the shows staged for tourists. This dance seemed to emerge straight from the mists of time; it was the absolute truth of a people whose spirit continues to burn like the age-old lamps burning in the igloos. The same igloos that the older residents still built and preserved in order to maintain ties to their roots, even if they, like everyone else, lived in prefab houses.

Cathy was supposed to have reached me by now with the supplies, but bad weather had grounded her plane for three days at Iqaluit, on Baffin Island, the administrative capital of Nunavut.

Once again I was stuck, unable to move. Simon, disturbed at the idea of seeing me waste precious time, decided to make the best of things by helping me complete my Arctic education.

"You learn to know bear!" he decreed when we found some tracks with claw marks near the village. He knew bears the way you might know members of your own family. He had killed an enormous bear once, and he often worked as a guide for hunters. In theory, polar bear hunting was illegal, but when the big beasts became too numerous in certain areas, then the local villages were each assigned a specific quota. Once these numbers were assigned, the Inuit had a choice. They could either hunt the bears themselves for their meat, lard, skins, and fur, or else they could sell their quotas—known as "tags"—to lucky hunters who have always dreamed of facing off with the biggest predator on the ice field. These tags often fetched prices equivalent to more than fifty thousand U.S. dollars.

"Look," Simon commanded, "paw prints far apart, snow comes inside. Bear walk this way." He started walking forward, swinging his posterior heavily from side to side, Baloo-style.

"Bear well fed," he said, "not hungry. Fat, big bottom. Not dangerous." He made a face that looked like the expression of the supposed bear with a contented snout and half-closed eyes, suggesting he was sleepy and ready for a nap. Then Simon changed his gait and his appearance, walking now with his legs rubbing each other and his bottom tucked in tight. Under his tanned leathery face, I could sense the quivering muzzle and the beast's fangs at the ready.

"Paw prints close together, not deep," he said, "no snow inside. Bear skinny, hungry. Dangerous." Now he stood on the tips of his toes, hands folded one over the other, depicting the bear's forepaws, muzzle pointing and eyes narrowed. I felt as if I could see the bear right in front of me.

"When bear like that, ears up," he said, "he looking, sniffing, just curious. Not attack. But when he like this"—he stretched his neck toward me and stared at me, glaring ferociously—"dangerous!" His whole body shook. He snarled and ground his teeth. He cupped his hands to describe the flattened ears of the beast.

"He attack," he said. "You die!" A shiver went through my body at the realistic performance. Simon leaned over the tracks and scraped carefully at the bottom of the prints.

"Bear pass by two days ago," he said.

"How can you tell?" He showed me the interior of the paw prints, where the ice was covered with a fine layer of wind-blown snow. The wind had been blowing for exactly two days.

A little farther along we found other tracks, free of snow, showing that a bear had passed by barely an hour before.

If the bear prints follow a zigzag pattern, Simon also taught me, then they belong to a bear looking for food. When a bear is out hunting for food, he often returns along his tracks. Better not camp along his path! It's also best to avoid the shores of any large body of water, which is where bears go to hunt seals.

On the other hand, straight tracks means that the bear, with its exceptional sense of smell, has scented a prey—or perhaps a female bear in heat—as much as forty miles away, sometimes farther! The bear will plunge straight ahead and completely ignore the presence of humans along the way. You can sleep where you find this sort of track because there is little chance that the bear will retrace its steps.

"Female . . . very bad!" Simon declared. The female bears, he explained to me, give birth only once every three years. Following the birth, they become fat and dig themselves a burrow in the snow, where they take refuge, doing nothing other than suckling their infant. When they finally emerge from their burrows, skinny and ravenous, then they have to battle their male mate who will do his best to kill the cubs so that he can mate with the mother again.

It's fair to say that with all of this conflict and hunger, the females are in a bit of a mood, and it's better not to meet up with one.

All the same, Simon added, such encounters are sometimes unavoidable. When confronted with one, he recommended not to shout, not to slow down, to keep on going, swinging your arms as wide as possible and trying to look as big as you can. If the female bear shifts direction, you should do the same, trying your utmost to wind up face-to-face with her. She will sniff at you, and once she figures out that you aren't edible, she'll let you go by. At least in most cases. If hunger wins out, then she'll kill you for want of prey better suited to her dietary requirements. After all, polar bears are at the top of the food chain, and we humans are much lower down.

In order to give me every tool for avoiding a face-to-face encounter with a bear, Simon also taught me to recognize the tracks of the Arctic fox. When you see those tracks, it means that a bear isn't far away because the foxes can scent the presence of seals on the edges of waterholes, and they feed on the remains abandoned by the polar bears. Ravens find this same banquet equally attractive, so if you see birds of prey circling in the sky, you can be certain that there is a bear nearby.

Last, Simon taught me to examine the stool left by bears. If the excrement contains hair (usually seal hair), it means that the animal has eaten and is therefore not a threat.

As for wolves, Simon went on, they fall into two categories. Solitary wolves with thick pelts have their own territory and their own family. They are only rarely hostile to humans. The wolf pack, on the other hand, can kill and devour anything it encounters and is much to be feared. Even when they are not in the pack, the individual wolves that make up a pack can be identified by their fur, which is usually rubbed away along their flanks because the pack tends to move in a close cluster, and the wolves rub against one other in order to stay warm. The wolf packs have their advance scouts that run ahead to sniff out potential prey. They come ahead of the others, and then the pack will circle around you for a while before rushing in for the kill. There is only one thing to do in this case, Simon warned me. Shoot.

He saved the best for last. The wolverine is the most ferocious animal in the Arctic. This squat, brown-and-yellow carnivore, almost never more than three feet in length, feeds on the carcasses left behind by wolves and bears but will also eat anything it can kill. It is as strong as it is aggressive, and it is considered the pit bull of the ice because it is impossible to get a wolverine to release its grip. It is known to attack elk and reindeer, but it also said that some wolverines have even killed bears.

The second phase of my apprenticeship with Simon was learning to build igloos.

"To survive in worst cold," Simon explained, "absolutely must finish igloo in twenty minutes. You say nothing, watch." He walked over to a long pile of snow pushed up by the wind behind a block of ice. That is "igloo snow," he said. He checked its consistency by probing it with his harpoon. The snow should be uniform, all in one block, and especially not in layers, otherwise the bricks will break when you cut them. When he finally found snow with the ideal level of compactness, he signaled me to draw closer, and he put my hand on his harpoon so that I could feel for myself the delicate balance between softness and strength.

"You see," he said, "this snow here what you need find." I could see perfectly. I was as excited as a little boy at this new discovery, which I already knew was going to transform my life—or at least my life in the next few months. I imagined myself building igloos as fast as I could pitch my tent.

With a shovel, Simon dug the beginning of a trench in the snowy ridge. Then, crouching on his knees in the trench, he began to cut out building blocks with a long wood saw, giving them beveled edges for a better grip. He continued cutting as he moved forward. The trench grew longer and wider and curved as the snow inside it was transformed into building blocks about two feet in length but never more than four inches thick. About eight of these blocks together created a platform on the floor where a person could lie down. Simon lined up the large blocks of snow along the edges of the trench as if he were laying bricks. Since the trench was already about three feet deep and the construction rose all around it, it was increasingly protected from the elements. Simon kept making blocks out of compacted snow, taking them from beneath the first line of blocks (that is to say, from the interior of the igloo-to-be). He gave them a trapezoidal shape, so that, once they were laid in place, they would lean toward the center and be pressed together, keeping the structure from collapsing in the middle. He arranged the blocks in a spiral, calculating that the quantity of compacted snow remaining on the interior of the igloo would be enough to complete its construction, and he ran out of snow just as he was laying the last brick.

Fascinated by the demonstration, I took in every detail, and I noted them down in my travel log. Once he was done with his little building, Simon invited me to have some tea with him inside before traveling back to the village.

The next day I got my second igloo-building lesson.

"This time," he said, "I build; you cut blocks." With considerable effort I managed to extract a block out of the compacted snow. I held it out to him. Simon barely looked at it and, without a word, broke it in two over his knee. The second block suffered the same fate. And then to the third. He tossed the fourth block over his shoulder.

I was furious—cutting out these blocks with a wood saw was

exhausting—and I was upset that I couldn't figure out what I was doing wrong. It wasn't until I had cut a sixth block that my work began to find favor with Simon, who said calmly, "Yes . . . that one, yes!" His teaching methods had paid off, and I learned how to cut a block of snow of the right shape and size to build an igloo.

On the third day, Simon decreed that he and I would each build an igloo of our own. I was still laying my first row of bricks while my teacher was sipping a cup of tea in his newly built shelter. Afterward, his air of disappointment as he stood inspecting my work made me ashamed to be such a bad student. When he dismissed me with the words, "No, definitely, you not survive," I felt my future looked dim.

On the fourth day, Simon sent me out alone on the ice to give me a head start. When he caught up with me, twenty-five minutes later, my igloo was finished. He inspected it closely and issued his verdict. "Now," he said, "you ready to go."


Unfortunately, my departure was still impossible. The weather was still horrible, and no one could say when Cathy's plane would be able to land in Igloolik. I would have to be patient a little longer.

But I couldn't bring myself to feel any regret over the dramatic chain of events that had forced me to spend these few days here in Simon's company. I might have lost most of my gear and provisions, true enough, and I might have been forced to backtrack sixty-two miles away from my goal, but it had certainly not been a waste of time. The lessons that my Inuit friend had taught me were a gift that no one else could have given to me.


When Cathy finally arrived with my replacement supplies, I left Simon's house and moved in with her in a little hut that the local chief of police had found for us. My relations with the police chief had started on a friendly footing, so I answered honestly and trustingly when he asked me during the course of a conversation what forms of self-defense I was carrying with me.

As innocently as could be, I pulled out the .357 Magnum that Cathy had very discreetly brought me from Switzerland to replace the one that had been lost in the fire.

The policeman practically choked.

"But that's completely illegal!" he yelled. "The possession of firearms for personal use is strictly forbidden anywhere in Canada!" He confiscated my revolver and arrested both of us, Cathy and me! My wife was sitting in a cell in the police station while the chief typed up his report. I pleaded with him that I was preparing to cross the polar bears' migratory route and that the gun he had confiscated was intended only to save my life if I happened to be attacked by wild animals.

"If you are stupid enough to trek through the Arctic on foot," the officer replied, "you are stupid enough to do it unarmed." I turned purple!

"Give me the gun," I said to the chief in an exasperated tone of voice. "I'll toss it into the ocean myself." He refused, and at this point I guess he felt as though he owed me an explanation.

"I'm just doing my job, you know." This was the ultimate argument of everyone who has a rulebook instead of a brain. I argued desperately that he was the only person on earth who knew about the gun, and I would give him my word of honor that if I was ever caught with it, I would never implicate anyone but myself.

But the representative of the law stuck to his position. He refused to give me back my gun, and he drove a nail into the coffin by informing his Swiss colleagues about this situation. As a result, not only were my wife and I treated like criminals during the three days that Cathy spent in Igloolik, but the Swiss police put her through all sorts of hassles when she got back home.

Eventually we were released, but this episode taught me to be much more careful where I placed my trust.

When he learned about my misadventure, Simon insisted on giving me his own revolver. Knowing the Arctic as he did, he considered it pure madness to venture out into the wilderness unarmed. In return, I gave him one of my new tents, as well as a GPS—he had dreamed of

owning one, and I showed him how it worked. It wasn't much considering everything that Simon had given me.

While a terrible blizzard delayed our departure (Simon wanted to
shuttle me back toward my route on his snowmobile), my Inuit friend
decided to channel his energy into sculpting something out of a little
block of gray-and-white marble, brought back from Arctic Bay where
my boat was still trapped in the ice. As we talked, and without taking
his eyes off me, he caressed and manipulated this tiny bit of rock patiently, as if he were trying to identify the link between me and this
stone. He worked on it later with an electric grinder. After two days of
work, he took my hand and placed in it the gray-and-white marble polar bear that he had sculpted just for me. The portrayal of the animal in
motion, neck stretched out, ears erect, was magnificent and stunningly
lifelike.

"Mike," he said to me, "you have the courage of this bear. Keep him
with you, so you always remember me." I noticed that on the base of
one of the paws he had engraved "Simon, Igloolik, 2003."

But even without the inscription, I was unlikely to forget this token's
creator.

We left Igloolik the next day, in a furious wind and a temperature of
fifty-three degrees below zero. Simon wanted to drive me on his snowmobile to the exact scene of the fire, at the end of the Fury and Hecla
Strait, but I asked him to drop me off somewhere along the way. It was
a shame if I had to march a little farther, but in this cold, I wanted him
to get back to his warm home as quickly as possible.

Along the way he taught me a great many things about seals, their
habits, and the holes where they surface to breathe. At one point we
stopped at one of these openings and Simon stood silent and motionless with harpoon in hand, moving nothing but his toes to keep them
from freezing. I stood over another hole nearby, making noise to push
the seals in his direction. According to Inuit tradition, eating the raw
liver of one of these animals symbolically (and literally) gave you its
strength and heat. Unfortunately, we caught nothing.

During my ride on Simon's sled, which he was pulling behind his
snowmobile, my nose and my lips began to freeze again. As I prepared

to put on my skis once more and return to endless days of slow and solitary progress, it felt as if the entire Igloolik experience and my meeting with Simon had only been a dream. However, my Inuit friend with a face furrowed like a Japanese garden, muffled in caribou hide, who practically suffocated me as he wrapped me in his arms with the strength of a bear, was very real indeed.

When he left, I carried in my mind the image of him that I had glimpsed while he hunted seals: a human silhouette, motionless against the ice, lost against the white immensity.

Simon disappeared over the horizon, and once again I was on my own. But I wasn't as alone as I had been before meeting Simon.

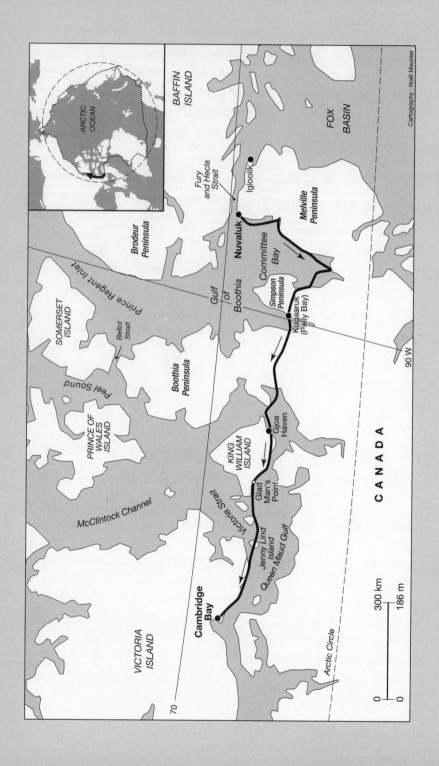

# The Big Chill

A T NUVALUK, ON THE NORTHWEST TIP of the Melville Peninsula, bad weather forced me to take shelter in a cabin used by bear hunters. Previous occupants had memorialized their exploits on the walls of the cabin. One Japanese hunter boasted that he had killed a beast that stood ten feet tall when rearing up on his hind legs. An American who came through in 1999 also claimed great bear-slaying prowess.

I added my own contribution to this hall of fame: "Mike Horn was here. He didn't kill any bears, and he hopes that no bears will kill him."

But all around the hut the countless fresh tracks were anything but reassuring. I was on the polar bear migratory route, the path frequented by female bears with their newborn cubs. Witnesses have seen polar bears knock down the thin plywood doors of cabins like this one with a single paw swipe—or even walk through the door.

After forty-eight hours in this flimsy shack, I couldn't stand waiting anymore. I needed to get moving on the way to Kugaaruk, my next destination. I headed for Committee Bay.

The snowy wind and the darkness reduced the visibility to zero and eliminated all contrast. The tallest mountains of ice were invisible until they materialized right before my face. Moreover, the high latitude confused any notion of distance and direction; even my sense of balance was muddled. I sometimes felt as if I were climbing when I was descending and vice versa. As for my GPS, it told me to go over the North Pole to reach North Cape. Of course it was just displaying the shortest route and by continuing along my predetermined route I was ignoring its advice. The gadget was hardly of use anyway. The liquid-crystal display was constantly freezing up.

Since I couldn't push all day on my ski poles with a compass in my hand, I had to rely on the wind to find my bearings and to keep from wandering around in circles on the ice in the starless winter night. Since I knew that the prevailing winds blow out of the Northwest in this part of the world, I kept track of the angle at which the wind hit my face. I also attached ribbons to my ski poles—"tell-tales," as sailors call them—and I regularly checked the angle that they made against the rear of my skis. When I pitched my tent I made sure that it was aligned with the wind, and the ribbon on my ski pole, planted in front of the entrance, confirmed the direction. If the wind direction had changed, it would be the first thing that I noticed in the morning, and I would mentally adjust the proper angle of my "tell-tales" against the skis to continue on my course.

If the wind shifted during the course of the day, I would be able to tell by making use of the piles of snow that built up behind any large object or hill. The largest piles were created by the prevailing northwesterly winds and would indicate that direction as reliably as a compass needle—a compass needle under normal conditions, that is. All I needed to do was ensure that my skis cut through the piles at the correct angle, and I could be sure I was on the right course. I even learned to read these angles blind—in the pitch black of night or the absolutely stark white of a blizzard—from the consistency of the snow and the way it was piled beneath my ski.

Mounds of snow and nylon strips: two navigational aids that were free, naturally occurring, and infallible—but which took quite a bit of training to master.

Despite my improving skills, I was constantly wasting time trying to find my way, and thus made an average daily distance of only seven miles. In this kind of cold every motion, every gesture had to be as economical as possible, measured out to the tenth of an inch. The greatest risk of dying under these conditions is not exhaustion but malnutrition or the irrational or erratic behavior caused by the panicked feeling of being lost.

The water along the shores of the Gulf of Boothia wasn't frozen, so I was obliged to stay on dry land and follow the shoreline. Bear tracks were increasingly numerous. Most of the tracks led down to the water where seals could be found and eaten. Day by day, more and more paw prints appeared—they were everywhere. I had never seen so many tracks in my life. But I still had not spotted a single polar bear. I knew that they were hidden in the darkness and in the cover of the rocky hills. The bears, on the other hand, had certainly spotted me.

Encouraged by a good strong wind that had been blowing in a favorable direction for several days now, I tried to use one of my kites, but the surface of the ice was too rough.

The next day a blizzard blew up. I knew I needed to pitch my tent quickly before the storm got too heavy. I didn't make more than five miles that day, and the thermometer was dropping.

The blizzard gave way to a rime fog, which soon turned into an icy fog, a pea soup with so much frozen water suspended in the air that I could practically feel it—so thick that I could taste it.

I couldn't see farther than six feet in any direction. Dry cold was tolerable, but this icy dampness penetrated beneath the skin and took hold of the muscles. While I skied along, my perspiration would freeze, forming a layer of ice between my jersey and my skin. I would begin to freeze, in the literal meaning of the word, and it got even worse when I stopped moving. To keep sweating to a minimum, I adapted my speed to the outside temperature and removed a layer of clothing once my body heat had risen. Whenever I started to feel beads of sweat forming, I would stop and bring my temperature down by removing my mittens or my hood for a few seconds. The heat would escape very quickly through my hands or my head.

**Forty degrees below zero.**

No matter how much energy I put into making forward progress, my body temperature kept dropping. In my journal I ranked the days in columns by good points and bad points: I had gained or lost this much ground in terms of distance from my goal; I had covered this much distance today; my last position and my new position. I needed to record this data in black and white and be able to interpret it all. This system helped me answer certain questions that I was curious about. What was the relationship between distance covered and wind speed? Or between my speed and the outside temperature? I could see that my aggressiveness would decline proportionally with the cold—in a sort of self-defensive reflex, no doubt. And the speed with which I completed everyday tasks followed the same curve.

**Fifty-eight degrees below zero.**

When I woke up, I found my nose frozen to my sleeping bag by the frozen vapor mist of my breath. The only way to extract myself was to tear the skin off the tip of my nose, skin that had already been burned in the fire.

**Sixty-nine degrees below zero.**

My blood was thickening, growing viscous in the cold. I was having a hard time bending my knees while I skied. I felt as if I were moving in slow motion. It was hard to breathe. The air was burning my lungs, and I was afraid that my tissue in my lungs was going to freeze. My fingers had already begun to succumb to frostbite again. They were swelling, and blisters resurfaced on my thumbs.

I had been told again and again that it was impossible to go anywhere in this region during the first two months of the year. Still, it was even worse than I had expected.

**Sixty-two degrees below zero.**

It was getting warmer—if the word can be used to describe such frigid temperatures. But now the wind veered around and began to blow hard out of the Southwest. The wind gusted straight into my face, and my abraded nose began to freeze. The blisters on my thumbs began to ooze.

I decided to spend a day in my tent.

+ + +

I started off the next day rested and with renewed determination, but my nose and my thumbs were painful, and I never really got warmed up. I kept moving forward, heading south, unfortunately, since it was still impossible to think about crossing the Gulf of Boothia. I began to wonder: would I ever be able turn west toward my ultimate goal?

Suddenly, I stopped short. I was face-to-face with a polar bear.

Fox tracks had already alerted me that there might be a bear nearby, and the crows flying overhead had confirmed the likelihood. But the birds were circling too widely to help me locate the beast with any accuracy, and so I had just charged ahead. The bear must have smelled me coming for some time—particularly with the wind at my back.

We stood about thirty feet apart on a strip of ice wedged between the open waters of the Gulf of Boothia—the bear was skirting the gulf, waiting to ambush the seals—and the cliffs of the coastline. It was impossible for me to go around.

All the same, I remembered seeing bear droppings earlier in the day that contained seal hair, and that memory reassured me. In fact, the animal was not looking too hungry or too aggressive. After ignoring me at first, it sat still, sniffing at my scent. That wasn't necessarily a bad sign. There seemed to be a good chance that it would leave me alone.

The bear wiggled its tiny ears (their small size keeps them from freezing), wrinkled its nose, opened its eyes wide, and gaped its mouth. This was its way of gathering information about me. Suddenly, the ears stood straight up! Questions crowded into my head: How was the bear walking? Paw prints—close together or far apart? Male or female? I couldn't see any cubs around.

I followed Claude's and Simon's advice. I walked straight toward the bear, swinging my arms to make me look as big as possible. The bear didn't move. Then, suddenly, it reared up on its hind legs. It still wasn't wearing the distinctive expression that warns of an imminent attack. Its stance was intended to frighten me, as well as to improve its vantage point, from which to get a better view of me. I knew that the bear was trying to make up its mind.

To attack or not to attack?

Just as I skied past it, the bear dropped back down onto all fours and looked back at me one last time before turning its back on me for good.

While the bear went on its way, swinging its big bottom heavily from side to side, I marched on confidently, not turning to look, and heaving a deep sigh of relief.

I was proud of having put into practice the things that Claude and Simon had taught me for the first time. After the police chief in Igloolik had taken my gun away, I needed to restore my self-confidence. This successful test helped me to reinforce it—the key to survival was my body of knowledge and experience more than my stock of weapons.

At the very bottom of Committee Bay there is a tiny island, Sabine Island, which I was planning to use as a sort of sidewalk to reach the western shore of Boothia. I set my course for it, but I soon realized from their tracks that countless bears were heading in the same direction. It's not hard to figure out that if the bears are heading in that direction, it's because there are seals there; if there are seals, it's because there is open water; and if there is open water, I won't be able to cross it on foot. So I turned south again.

**Sunday, January 16. Ninety-eight degrees below zero.**

The wind, blowing harder than usual, and the intensifying fog made this the coldest day of my expedition. This was the first time since my departure from North Cape that I experienced temperatures under the threshold of seventy-five degrees below zero. In fact, it wasn't just a milestone for me; it hadn't been this cold in the region in the past two decades.

That's what I call being in the right place at the right time.

I was constantly on the lookout for cracks, hollows, and openings in the ice where I might catch a ski or wedge a foot. Like anything else, bones break much more easily in extreme cold. But the hazards were all hidden under a fine layer of snow.

My thumbs were frostbitten once again. The blisters had reappeared under my fingernails, my fingertips were oozing the way they had on the way to the North Pole, and the prospect of amputation was jeering at me once again.

When I made camp, I was too exhausted to cook, eat, or drink. I fell asleep while I was taking my shoes off, my feet still in the vestibule. By the time I managed to restore a little warmth to my fingers, just enough to keep them from freezing a second time, the sensation that they were being pounded with a hammer began to torture me once again.

In any case, I couldn't risk staying in my tent. There was a real risk that I would freeze to death in my sleeping bag, which was only made for temperatures down to fifty degrees below zero.

There was only one way to survive—to get up and march through the cold, which is exactly what I did.

The bear that suddenly blocked my way was even bigger than the last one, at least ten feet tall. It was one of the most imposing bears I had ever seen. (Simon, on the other hand, had killed a bear once that stood eleven and a half feet tall.) Less curious but more aggressive than his cousin of the other day, he wasn't advancing with his paws close together (that was good news), but he wasn't very fat either (that was a little more worrisome). I didn't shift course by an inch and—according to the time-tested method—I swung my arms as high as I could.

The bear went by me without taking its eyes off me for a second. Then it turned around and started following me from a few yards back, walking a path roughly parallel to my mine, playing hide-and-seek behind the big blocks of ice. I knew that he was waiting for a chance to attack me from behind, because bears will almost never attack you face-to-face unless they are really hungry. I decided to seize the initiative, so I headed straight toward him, dogging him, following every turn he made. I wasn't trying to provoke him. I was just showing him that I was big and strong, too, and that I wasn't afraid of him at all— even if I was actually quaking in my boots. That failed to impress him, so I stopped and got my rifle out of my sled.

The Canadian authorities had warned me that it is strictly forbidden to shoot anything at a bear but firecrackers or rubber pellets. And that's only if the bear is acting in a very threatening manner. But I wasn't ready to run the risk.

Anyway, my rifle had been damaged in the fire. The breech was blocked solid with frozen snow, and the round refused to slip into the chamber. At these extremely cold temperatures, a weapon should be stored completely dry. Even lubricating oil would freeze, rendering a gun useless.

I had a sudden surge of ill feeling toward the policeman back in Igloolik who had confiscated my .357 Magnum with its very simple firing mechanism—trigger, hammer, bullet—that would withstand any climate.

Even so, it wouldn't have been easy to shoot wearing mittens, and without them my skin would freeze to the gun grip.

The bear came toward me. I unhooked my sled to give myself more freedom to move. I picked up my flare pistol. The phosphorus projectile that it fires would set the animal's fur on fire if I managed to hit him. But I only had one cartridge. If I missed him, he wouldn't miss me. I wasn't even carrying a knife. I guess I could have tried poking him in the eye with one of my ski poles, but I wasn't in much condition to try a stunt like that.

We stood there face-to-face, each with his weapons. One of us would have to give ground, and I'd prefer that it was him. The bear continued to approach. If I was still reluctant to fire, it was because my opponent wasn't yet showing the classic warning signs that usually precede an attack—the same ones that Simon had taught me. He stretched out his paws, flattened his ears, and snarled, his lip quivering, without really baring his fangs. I didn't have any idea what to do now.

Suddenly, as a sort of last resort, I started shouting, "Get out of here! Go on, beat it!"

I don't know what I was thinking, but it worked! As soon as he heard my voice, the beast stood still in his tracks and stared at me as if he had fallen into a trance. Then he turned and fled. My heart was racing at a hundred beats a minute. I refastened my harness and set off again, my flare gun in my pocket within easy reach. But I didn't think I'd see him again.


For several days running the temperature flirted with seventy-five degrees below zero, and then it modified a little. Scorched by the cold and covered with sores, the skin on my lips and my nose was coming off in strips and shreds. At these extreme temperatures, the slightest activity became difficult. I was exhausted by the time I pitched my tent, but because I was afraid of freezing to death in my sleep, I only took short naps. Every night I melted snow to make a gallon of water, which afforded me the luxury of an hour of relative warmth—during which time I would often fall asleep against my will—except on those nights when my fingers, paralyzed by the blisters from the frostbite, were unable to light my camp stove at all.

After eating, but before lying down for my series of short naps, I forced myself to stay awake to repair my most badly battered equipment. I used a special glue to fix the tip of one of my skis, which had split in two. For the umpteenth time, I reinforced the stitching of my mittens, socks, harness, etc., stitching that the extreme cold shatters like glass; I epoxied my thermos, which had cracked in the cold; and I refastened the grips on my ski poles, which came loose in the frigid conditions. There was no question of putting anything off till the next day. Tomorrow, there would be twice as much to do, and I would never be able to keep up with it. And I was constantly aware that the success of my expedition and my survival depended on keeping my equipment in good working order.

I was consuming my provisions at the rate of three and a half pounds per day, so my sled was that much lighter each morning when I clipped into my harness. (It had weighed 460 pounds when I left Baffin Island.) But I was having more and more difficulty hauling the load because of the normal exhaustion, coupled with my weight loss and psychological stress, both of which continued to drain my strength.

Not a day went by that I didn't collapse from exhaustion, repeatedly, falling like a sack, face down in the snow. Each time I would have to dig deep into my untapped reserves of energy and strength to get back on my feet and set out again.


On one of those days, after one of those falls, I reached the end of my rope. It might have been the hundredth time I had fallen. Or the thousandth. Who could say? Now it had become a sort of routine: fall, wake with a start, back on my feet, start off again. But this time, I was aware that the sensation of "kicking the bottom of the pool" was coming more and more slowly. My face was pressed into the snow as if into a pillow. A pleasant sensation of numbness swept over me, rapidly taking possession of my entire being. I felt a longing to slip down to the bottom and rest there. It would be so easy, so relaxing . . .

I remembered that on my trek through the Amazonian jungle I would collapse this same way, completely exhausted. But immediately, it seemed, the red ants would start biting me, and the intense pain would make me leap to my feet, as if a red hot iron were sizzling into my flesh. Here, to the contrary, all pain vanished, everything became comfortable. I knew perfectly well that I was freezing and in a few minutes would be dead, but I didn't care because I couldn't feel anything anymore. Irresistibly drawn by the other side, I was already beginning to cross over. It would have been so easy . . . if it weren't for a tiny voice that was ordering me to get up. The voice was faint and distant, but insistent: "Get up, Mike! Get up!" Then my subconscious took over, gradually bringing me out of that trance. The voice started up again, much louder this time, "Get up, Mike!" And now my mouth opened and I shouted out, joining the chorus, "Get up, Mike! Goddamn it, Mike, get on your feet!"

Before I had time to process what had happened, I was on my way again. Because I had been pushing my body's limits further and further, I had flirted dangerously with death without even realizing it. It was time for me to forget my obsession with the goal I was trying to achieve and refocus my attention on the absolute priority: survival.

I was constantly trying to grab just a few more moments of rest on the ice, like a child in the wintertime asking for five more minutes' sleep before getting out of bed. And because I was constantly pushing the limits further and further, I had come close to not getting up at all.

And yet I had gotten back up. And I knew what that meant in the final analysis—that I hadn't really wanted to die, not for a second. Dying meant giving up, and giving up amounted to shirking my responsibilities. It would be like throwing in the towel and saying, "It's harder than I expected, so I'm going home." Or else, "I'm dying," which amounted more or less to the same thing in these circumstances.

I thought back to the final expeditions of Greely, Nansen, Amundsen, and Franklin. After Franklin's ship was ground up by the ice, the entire crew set out on foot over the ice field. It was springtime, but the climate was still harsh and they all died of exposure. I had thought carefully about all those tragic deaths. While storms and other "fortunes of the sea" were the original cause of distress, there was one common trait linking all of these explorers' grim fates. It is soothing to die in the Arctic when you have reached the limits of suffering. The temptation to give up was almost irresistible. I knew something about that.

But man's determination to live is stronger than any other force. It is much stronger than anyone could imagine. And I also knew a little something about that.


By now I was beginning to understand why the people in Arctic Bay, and everyone that I had met since leaving there, had tried to persuade me not to venture into this icy hell. They were certainly right, but I couldn't say that I was sorry that I had ignored their advice. Little by little, I was beginning to get used to the suffering that this remarkable journey was forcing me to endure, to the point that I was starting to enjoy the sensation of overcoming the pain a little more each day. This agony was not a real agony for me, otherwise I wouldn't be there.

I was trekking through such inhospitable terrain not only to attain a goal, but also because I deeply loved the world through which I was traveling; because I love nature when it is at the peak of its violence and magnificence. When nature in all its grandeur forced me—in all my tiny insignificance—to endure the worst conditions imaginable, it was also accepting my presence into its fold, and that was a great honor. I had paid an extremely steep price for admission to this frigid theater, but I had the place to myself and could watch the action unfold on my own private stage.

Two foxes appeared out of the blue, practically at the tips of my skis, streaking across the landscape as if I weren't there at all. They were chasing after an Arctic hare in total silence. The two foxes, some of the fastest animals in all creation, barely touched the ice as they ran, churning up a cloud of powdery snow behind them. After they had caught and killed their prey, leaving nothing more than a small red stain on the infinite whiteness, one of the two hunters proudly held up the hare's head, as if to say, "I caught it!"

Later I saw two giant hares mating so enthusiastically that they were aware of nothing outside of themselves, not even me, though I was close enough to reach out and touch them.

One day, when I was struggling futilely to find enough wind to be pulled by my kite, a large red fox suddenly appeared just a yard away from me and sat calmly in the snow, observing first me, then my kite, with evident fascination. As soon as I uttered a sound, he vanished with an almost cartoonish "whoosh!"

Another fox stuck his head out of his den as I went by, then popped back into hiding. I could only make out the red tufts of his eartips, and his eyes, which seemed to be asking me, "And just what do you think you're doing here?"

Leaning over the edge of the ice, a polar bear waited patiently for its prey. The instant a seal's nose broke the surface to breathe, the bear sank its claws into the seal's throat with blinding speed, lifting it like a grouper on the tip of a harpoon and dropped it onto the ice at its feet. The bear placed one paw on the stunned seal's head to brace it and then sliced it open lengthwise with the tip of one of its razor-sharp claws. Several gallons of warm oil spilled out onto the ice. The bear repeatedly dipped its paw into the oil and licked it off until it had slurped up all of the seal's oil. The bear gobbled down the sealskin for dessert and with lordly nonchalance abandoned the seal meat for the foxes to devour.

I felt as if I had walked into the middle of a wildlife show on the Discovery Channel or National Geographic. But this was nothing more than everyday life, peaceable and cruel, funny and spectacular, flowing on uninterrupted around me, the uninvited guest. The native creatures of the Arctic and I shared one simple priority: survival.

On certain days when the snow was perfectly smooth, I would zip along over the white surface like a paintbrush over silk, with giant strides that would each move me forward the distance you might cover with a long jump on the moon. I would lengthen my gait, stretching out each lunge to the extreme limit, fully aware that inches lost now would add up over the course of a day to miles that I could have put behind me. If I extended each of my strides by four inches, the twelve thousand total miles of my journey would be covered a month and a half sooner.

The sense of euphoria I felt, which erased my exhaustion and seemed to lighten the weight of my sled and my body, came partly from the fact that I was finally getting close to Committee Bay. Soon, very soon, my interminable detour would be coming to an end. Soon I would be moving out of the path of the polar bears' migratory route, leaving the mother bears to suckle their young in peace deep in their snowy caverns. Soon I would be setting my course westward once again.

Until then, however, I would continue to have to be on the lookout for bears, and the blinding icy haze was not particularly reassuring.

My heart made a sudden leap in my chest when a huge shadow moved furtively through the mist a few feet away from me. Then there was another, and yet another.

In this pea soup it was impossible to tell what those shadowy shapes might be—but I had a nasty hunch. I wanted to stop so that I could watch silently and try to figure out exactly what I was dealing with and find a way to reach safety. But if I were to stand still, exposed to the elements at a temperature of eighty degrees below zero, I would quickly turn into a block of ice.

I could try to escape, but in what direction? The shadows grew in number, proliferating, racing by on all sides. This many polar bears traveling all together—it was impossible! This whole spectacle must be an illusion, the unfortunate result of collateral damage to my long-suffering nervous system caused by the extreme cold. After all, humans weren't meant to live in these conditions for extended periods of time, and perhaps there were secondary effects I knew nothing about. I had undergone just about every physical ordeal imaginable, but this was the first time that I felt as if I were losing my mind.

Finally, after several slow, terrifying minutes the silhouettes became a little sharper until I could finally see that they were ... caribou. A herd of caribou. A vast horde of caribou passing all around me and heading in the direction of Sabine Island.

The presence of caribou usually attracts wolves, but with this much choice meat on the hoof, I had no reason to fear that the wolves would pay any attention to me.

On February 14, back in Switzerland, Annika and Jessica picked up the receiver even before their mother could get to the phone, having seen the number of my satellite phone appear on their caller ID. "Don't forget to wish Mama a Happy Valentine's Day!" they whispered to me, in unison.

Committee Bay, at the far southern tip of the Gulf of Boothia, was well-known as a focus of ice field activity. This was ground zero, where the most significant currents of pack ice all converge and create impressive stacks of giant blocks of ice. Here you could see genuine eruptions of the ice pack with fissures spreading at terrifying speed, often in many directions at once, and with full-fledged ice quakes to go with them.

During a banquet of raw caribou meat and seal liver that we had eaten on his hut's dirt floor in Igloolik, an old Inuit friend of Simon's told me that one day, when he and his father were on their way to Kugaaruk on the same route that I was following now to Sabine Island, the ice they were crossing at Committee Bay had suddenly begun to shatter violently on all sides. They turned around and hurried back toward dry land, but the gaping crevasses opened and expanded faster than their dogs could run. Simon's friend made it to shore just in the nick of time, but his father was too slow and was swallowed up with his sled and dog team.

I had heard plenty of stories like that about many different places in the Arctic. But Committee Bay had an especially terrifying reputation among the local population.

I was especially happy and relieved to reach the end of the bay on February 17, 2003, in the midst of an ever-so-slight mild spell. I solemnly regarded the spot where a very small stream ran out from the mountains. It was an unremarkable place that held all of the significance in the world for me. Finally! Ever since the month of November I had done nothing but tramp south on a detour along the shores of the Gulf of Boothia. This was the exact spot where I would finally be able to start heading west again—toward my goal. That day would remain one of the most important days of the entire expedition, and possibly one of the more significant days in my life.

Making it this far during the Arctic winter had made me happier and prouder than if I had made it to the North Pole. I had crossed the most hostile region on earth, in the most challenging time of year, in the most inhuman conditions that could be found. Moreover, the only previous knowledge that I had of the Arctic winter was from tales of bygone expeditions.

That day I turned my course westward and did my best not to dwell on the fact that the ice blocking the Bellot Strait back in October had transformed a short, seven-day sail into a four-month-long detour.

The icy fog lightened slightly. The temperature was almost imperceptibly less harsh. After a few days, the pale winter sun skimmed just over the horizon, a little less timid with each day's appearance. Along my course, which ran north past Sabine Island, the ice was completely smooth and practically free of snow. A veritable freeway lay ahead of me across the frozen solid southern tip of Committee Bay.

But it was still a long, long way to Kugaaruk, and the route was full of potential hazards. I decided to stick to my old practice of relying upon the experience of my elders, and so I consulted one for guidance. Through the Royal Canadian Mounted Police I was able to reach Ron, a policeman in Kugaaruk, who made a special effort to help me out—thus making up for the bad impression that his colleague from Igloolik had made. He put me in touch with Makabi Nartok, a full-blooded Inuit familiar with travel in this area. I asked Makabi whether I could head north-by-northwest across Committee Bay to get to Kugaaruk along a more direct route.

"Every season Committee Bay is different," the Inuit elder said. "But one thing always true: further north you go, bigger risk meet bear, open water, ice mountains." In short, he recommended that I go to the south of Sabine Island and keep heading west until I reached the western shore of the bay. Only once I was over dry land should I head north.

I was having a hard time accepting this, despite my respect for those with local expertise. It's hard to change one's basic nature. Until I had bashed my own head against a wall, I couldn't accept on faith that the wall was there.

With the frustration that I had built up over the last few months and the certainty that, after the mountains of the Melville Peninsula, I was going to be traveling across flat terrain without any obstacles to block the wind, I decided to listen both to Makabi and my own instincts. I would continue north of Sabine Island and then cut over, heading slightly north of due west.

On the satin-smooth skating rink of southern Committee Bay, I zipped along at ten, even twelve miles a day with a dexterity and speed enhanced by the slight rise in temperature. It was dark out and visibility was low, but the icy fog had lifted. Twenty-four hours later, the weather had cleared up completely. The clear visibility allowed me to gaze out and see in great detail the immense clutter of giant ice obstructing the horizon—directly in my path.

There was still time to pay heed to the voice of wisdom—Makabi's voice, in this case—and to turn back to the South. I never considered it for a moment and continued toward the obstacle in my path.

I spent three full days in the midst of that giant's game of dominoes, sweating blood and water to haul my sled over ice blocks of all shapes and sizes. The clearing weather was accompanied by a plunge in temperature, which made the ice dry, rough, and as sticky as sandpaper soaked in resin. Like a stubborn mule, my sled refused to move forward. I pulled, I pushed, I shouted at it. I was painfully aware of all the time I was wasting in this labyrinth, and I cursed myself at the top of my lungs: "Makabi told you not to head northwest, didn't he? Next time you'll listen to people who have lived here their whole lives, instead of doing everything your way!"

But I couldn't bring myself to turn around. I would stick to my decision, even if it meant spending the next month climbing over huge blocks of ice, hauling my sled up behind me.

At last I made it to the other shore, and on February 22, five days after I finally turned west, it was with a feeling of triumph that I set foot on the peninsula that separates the Gulf of Boothia from the inlet of Pelly Bay, beside which stood the town of Kugaaruk. From here on, there would be no more obstacle courses through pack ice, just the terra firma of the Canadian continent and rolling expanses of tundra.

From this shore of Committee Bay, I was just fifty miles to Kugaaruk. With daily mileage of about ten to twelve miles, I would get there in about four or five days.

And only about six weeks from now, spring would timidly begin to emerge. If I could just keep going until then, I would have conquered the Arctic winter! In my eyes, this victory meant that I was clearly capable of completing my expedition.

A little cabin whose location Makabi had told me about was even more rudimentary than the cabins I had found along my route to this point. There were four sheets of plywood for walls, a fifth plywood sheet as a roof, and a door that had been shoved in by bears, so that I found the cabin full of snow. I cleaned it out with my shovel, pitched my tent inside, and enjoyed a well-deserved day of rest.

The frostbite-induced blisters that had grown under my fingernails had become so painful that I couldn't stand it any longer. I used a very fine drill bit to pierce my nails and drain the blisters, which gave me a modicum of relief.

An icy wind continued to blow, and I decided to extend my stay in the hut for another twenty-four hours. To warm myself up, I decided to stow my sled and the rest of my gear and take a little cross-country ski excursion through the surrounding countryside. It would also give me the opportunity to scout out the terrain on the route to Kugaaruk. As expected, the land was rolling, monotonous, and icy.

We are not there often," Makabi had told me. "But if you straight ahead with hills on your right, you arrive Kugaaruk for sure."

While climbing up one hill to get a better view of the surrounding landscape, I happened upon a magnificent snow-white wolf, majestically poised looking out over the landscape from a promontory, like the Lion King surveying its domain. The wolf's fur glittered silver with reflected light. I was fascinated and could not resist the temptation to try to get a little closer—just to see how close I could get. Step by step, I crept nearer to him in absolute silence. The wind blowing in my face reassured me that he hadn't scented my presence. I couldn't have been more than ten or fifteen feet away from him.

Suddenly it dawned on me that I was completely unarmed. What if the wolf attacked me? In a short fit of paranoia, I even imagined that the wolf might be rabid. After dispelling these wild notions, I stood still and admired the wolf for a long time, forgetting all else. Then I whistled very softly. The wolf turned its head in my direction and took off like a shot from a cannon. To my astonishment, he buried himself under the snow and—like a cat under a blanket—burrowed away from me, making his escape through a tunnel in the snow.

I started off again with my sled in tow. I was buffeted by a north wind, icier than before, blowing straight into my face. This was the main problem with the direction I had chosen for my journey; I was traveling against the winds and currents nearly the entire trip. The frigid breeze rendered me far more vulnerable to frostbite, especially when the squalls regularly drove the thermometer down below fifty-eight degrees below zero, as they regularly did between the Gulf of Boothia and Kugaaruk. Whenever the tip of my nose began to freeze, I would rub a little snow on it because the snow was much warmer than the ambient air.

Ice helped keep me warm, too. Whenever I encountered a shallow pond or running stream that was impossible to go around without a lengthy detour, I would simply wade across as quickly as possible. The layer of ice that quickly formed on my boots and the lower section of my clothing would serve as a windbreaker until evening—sort of like the snot that I smeared on my face every morning.

I was beginning to suffer profoundly from the physical fatigue this expedition had entailed. So it was with inexplicable joy that, about twenty-five miles away from Kugaaruk, I saw Jean-Philippe Patthey; Patrick, a Swiss-German journalist; Sebastian Devenish, my expedition photographer; and Makabi Nartok coming toward me. Of course, they weren't coming to help me trek or rescue me. Rather, like the first seagulls announce landfall after a long sea voyage, my friends and colleagues heralded my approach to the shore.

Since leaving Igloolik—that is, in the past five weeks—I had not glimpsed another living soul. I was somewhat shocked to realize how the planet could so easily do without our presence, just as it had for billions of years before us—and as it continued to in remote locations such as these.

Although I spotted my companions immediately and saw them as symbols of hope, they, on the other hand, failed to see me at all. Racing along on their snowmobiles, they sailed past me without noticing me and only found me afterward by following the instructions that I had given them—to follow my tracks from the coordinates of my last campsite.

Our reunion was one of those moments when words are inadequate to convey one's feelings. Jean-Philippe, Patrick, Sebastian, and Makabi were shocked to find themselves face-to-face with a sort of Yeti with a bandaged face covered in layers of snow and ice that almost obscured its eyes. In the course of a few weeks, the cold and the elements had turned me into an unrecognizable, mummified survivor, barely able to stand on my own two feet. My legs were still working, by a miracle of conditioned reflex, but I was on the verge of being totally frozen.

Makabi walked toward me, drawing so close that his face almost touched mine, and stared at me, intensely, interminably, to the point that I began to feel uneasy. He never said a word. When I stretched out my right hand to grip his in a handshake, he seized both of my hands, and then he tore off my mittens, replacing them with his own bearskin gloves. Encased in those sheaths of leather and fat, my hands felt as if they had been thrust over a wood fire. Makabi, in turn, slipped on my mittens. Once his own body heat had warmed them up, about twenty minutes later, he returned them to me, and he repeated this operation over and over, never saying a word, except, "You are very strong man." Embarrassed, I replied awkwardly. How could I explain to him the motives that were driving me?

Makabi returned to his village, and the others accompanied me at a temperature of forty degrees below zero for the last two days of my trek, as far as Kugaaruk. Even though they were perfectly well-equipped, Jean-Philippe, Sebastian, and especially Patrick, who had come straight from the well-heated offices of his magazine, suffered terribly from the cold. Sebastian took photographs and Jean-Philippe shot some video, which would keep me from having to backtrack later to reenact the various phases of the journey, as I had been forced to do after my trip around the equator.

Once again, I was marching along lakeshores, following rivers, and alternating level sections with occasional climbs up hilly and mountainous terrain. And from high atop one of those hills, in the glow of one of the first sunsets of the season, I finally caught a glimpse of the village that the Inuit call Kugaaruk and the Canadians call Pelly Bay, from the name of the inlet off the Gulf of Boothia on which the village is situated. Kugaaruk seemed to be on another planet, wedged between steep cliffs and a bay filled with craggy islands whose rocky faces concealed what lay beyond.

I descended to the village in the same time that it took the sun to set. By the time I found myself walking down the main street, most of the village's inhabitants—five hundred people, including three hundred children—were pouring out of their prefabricated homes to welcome me loudly and enthusiastically. They began rhythmically clapping, encouraging me on for the last few yards. My friends, who had traveled ahead on their snowmobiles, immortalized the scene, cameras in hand, as I was congratulated by many generations of Inuit, crowding around me. For four months, satellite phones, CB radios, and the like had all been reporting to every corner of the Far North: "There is a guy walking from Arctic Bay to Kugaaruk via Igloolik in the heart of winter! Inconceivable!" They had been anticipating my arrival as the main attraction of the year, and when they saw my freakish silhouette and my snow-white mask, they were not disappointed.

When I finally came to a stop, Makabi got right to work. He pulled off my skis, took my ski poles from me, and unharnessed me from my sled. With hands still stiff from the cold, I shook hands with nearly everyone in the village. The Inuit are not the sort of people to indulge in insincere compliments or acts of politeness—nor are they easily impressed. Their congratulations were heartfelt, and I took them to heart.

By making it this far, I knew that I had accomplished the hardest part. And so for me, the Arctic winter thawed for me right in this remote village, even if the calendar had a different opinion.

In the Far North, accommodations are extremely expensive, and Kugaaruk was no exception. Frequented primarily by construction workers, the Residence, an inn belonging to the the Co-op, a sort of Inuit authority, was not shy about posting rates of three hundred to four hundred Canadian dollars a night, per person! For that price, a visitor would be given a bedroom a few yards square, furnished with two beds. If another paying customer showed up, he would be given the second bed, whether you liked it or not, and there wouldn't be a discount, either.

I planned to spend three days with Sebastian, who hadn't been able to take any pictures of the expedition in four months, and three days with Patrick, the journalist who had spent time with me on several occasions during my expedition around the equator, and once already aboard my boat, the *Arktos*, on this expedition. His writing showed that he had grasped the true spirit of my adventures. His face, familiar to me now, was that of a friend—and a lucky charm.

I was going to have a chance to wash myself thoroughly for the first time in fifteen days, replace the sealskins on the bottom of my skis, get some treatment for the open blisters on my feet, and restore a little life to my cheeks, ears, nose, and lips, which were completely frozen, and my thumbs, which were in nearly the same condition as when I got back from the North Pole.

All things considered, I expected to spend about ten days or so in Kugaaruk. The total cost would come to two thousand dollars in hotel bills, which would completely blow my budget. But the members of the Native Corporation—whose respect I had won by accomplishing what no one in the memory of the oldest living member of the tribe had even done—decided to adopt me. Alex, the manager of the hotel, decided to let me stay as long as I liked in a mobile home adjoining his establishment. It might have been a mobile home, but to me, after all the nights I had spent on the ice, it was a three-star luxury accommodation. Sheltered from the cold and the elements, I would enjoy the calm and serenity I needed to recuperate.

Alex wasn't satisfied with just giving me a place to stay, either. He fed me soup, caribou steaks, Arctic char, pasta, and homemade bread. I got stronger but not any heavier. My stomach had become accustomed to processing the eight and ten thousand calories a day that I wolf down when I'm trekking cross-country, so my digestive system becomes a veritable reprocessing plant, continuing to operate even when my body was temporarily at rest. It would take time, and a lighter diet, before my metabolism would begin functioning "normally" again.

Ron, the policeman, continued to be immensely helpful, inviting me to dinner, helping me find or repair pieces of equipment, and gathering information that would be useful on my journey. Members of the community—especially the older ones—came in droves to ask me to teach them how to use their GPS devices, to read certain maps, etc. It felt like I was constantly holding court. Someone would come in, ask for my advice on this subject or that, share a mug of tea with me, and then leave as the next visitor entered. Others used their lunch breaks to come and sit in a circle around me—for no apparent reason. I became a real attraction for the town's residents, and not only because of my exploits. Kugaaruk is totally isolated for most of the year at the very end of its little frozen cul-de-sac, which even the icebreaker that links it to the rest of the world can't reach except for a few months of the year. So, in this place where life, based on subsistence hunting and fishing, hasn't changed in centuries, residents appreciated the infrequent visitor from the outside world.

Whenever I showed even the slightest inclination to start out again, my new friends would beg me to stay for just one more day. And I allowed myself to be persuaded by these people whom I found so immensely likable. After all, the time I spent here recharging my batteries was hardly a luxury.

Every day I explored the area around the village, and I pushed a little farther each time—to get new and more panoramic views of the bay and the mountains. I gradually became consumed by an ever stronger sense of longing, longing to go and see what was on the other side of those mountains—to pursue and experience the next stage of my adventure. I imagined myself battling for survival in a spectacular setting, bathed in the early sunlight of spring that was such a novelty after having walked in total darkness for so many weeks, staring at the narrow beam of light cast by my forehead lamp!

✦ ✦ ✦

One morning I woke up with a feeling of urgency mingled with guilt, which clearly indicated that the time had come. On the evening before I left, the people of Kugaaruk threw a party for me in the building that serves as city hall, school, and gymnasium. Knowing that my next destination would be Gjoa Haven, everyone I spoke to offered me advice on the best route to follow. We devoured a banquet of cookies and tea (alcohol was forbidden) while musicians dressed in caribou skins warmed up the crowd and played musical accompaniment for the Inuit dances. Children chased one another in all directions as I moved from one group to another, thanking everyone for their help, kindness, and generosity.

Pat, who ran a convenience store in town where you could rarely find what you were looking for but where you would always find the most unimaginable items, gave me pounds and pounds of Kit-Kats, Mars bars, and other chocolate candy bars. Someone else gave me a pair of sealskin gloves and a pair of reindeer-hide mittens. Makabi's wife, an Inuit artist, gave me a bearskin key chain and a card.

If I had not been forced to trek around the Gulf of Boothia, I would never have come to Kugaaruk, and I would have missed this very special town. I was happy here, and not only because I was emerging from four months of terrible privations and suffering. The people I met here had offered me everything they owned and had given me even more in human fellowship. I carried these treasures away with me when I left, and I promised myself that I would return to Kugaaruk someday.

One hundred and eighty-five miles from Kugaaruk, on the other side of Pelly Bay and the Boothia Peninsula, there was a little village on King William Island called Gjoa Haven. Like Upernavik in Greenland, the town was legendary because Roald Amundsen lived there for two years, hemmed in by the ice, before becoming the first man to explore the Northwest Passage. The name Gjoa Haven is Norwegian for Gjøa's Harbor, and was named by polar explorer Roald Amundsen after his ship, the *Gjøa*. The year I visited was the hundredth anniversary of Amundsen's expedition. But I must admit that if I was in a hurry to get to Gjoa Haven, it was only because Cathy and my daughters were going to meet me there.

I left Kugaaruk in a blizzard that reduced visibility practically to zero, with squalls and gusts of wind blowing straight into my face. Following my recuperation, it was a brutal reentry into the icy inferno. My nose began to refreeze immediately, and I was soon in the same physical state—without the fatigue—of ten days before.

I was in such a hurry to get to Gjoa Haven that, on the very first day, I froze my pulmonary alveoli by breathing too fast and deeply with the air temperature at fifty degrees below zero. The symptoms of this condition were painful and distressing; it became impossible to completely fill my lungs, thus producing a horrible and constant sensation of being asphyxiated.

In my medical bag I carried a drug specifically for this problem, but it was slow to take effect. The iron fist crushing my lungs was reluctant to release its grip easily. I tried to fight against it by a method I developed: I would take three of the deepest breaths I could manage, and then I would march forward for about ten yards, stand still for a moment, breathe again, march another ten yards, stop, and so on. In this laborious way I managed to cover seven miles in a single day, but I continued to suffer from severe shortness of breath. I would open my mouth, gasping in an effort to capture the smallest amount of oxygen. I felt a bit like a fish flopping on the deck of a trawler. I felt like ripping off my clothes to breathe a little more deeply. I was ready to do anything in order to fill my lungs with air.

When I settled in my tent for the night, the feeling that I was suffocating was made more intense by the onset of a wave of claustrophobia. Still, it never crossed my mind even for a second to turn back.

Three days after leaving Kugaaruk, I arrived at Simpson Lake, whose elongated shape reminded me a little of Saputing Lake, where the pack of wolves had given me a scare. Wedged between two relatively low mountain ranges, Simpson Lake offered me a flat track some twenty miles long, where I could ski comfortably between respiratory breaks. My frostbite was not improving, but the temperature rose to thirty degrees below zero. The wind died down, and the medications finally kicked in, which allowed my lungs to gradually recover their function.

I covered fourteen miles in one day. I went nineteen miles the next day. But the slight warming of the atmosphere also brought with it a snowfall that slowed me down and demanded a greater output of energy for each step I took.

According to Makabi, not far from this place was a valley that constituted the only known passage to Gjoa Haven. No one had traveled through the valley so far in the year, and no one could tell me its location in any detail. I would have to leave Simpson Lake to look for it, but in the darkness and with snow this deep, there was a good chance that I would tire myself out trying to find it. Since I couldn't run that risk, I decided to stay on course and keep going straight ahead, in what I believed was the right direction.

Suddenly I found myself atop a hill, and there stood an *inukchuk*, one of those mysterious rock piles that indicated the direction of the next village—just like the ones that Annika and Jessica had drawn on the backs of my skis. The *inukchuk* pointed toward Gjoa Haven, which meant that I had found the mysterious valley without even having really looked for it!

At the far end of the valley, the slopes grew flatter. I kept on marching forward, head down, stubbornly pushing ahead into a terrain of snow and ice where water and land blended together, where the snow that fell incessantly grew deeper each day, concealing the landmarks that would guide me to my destination. The wind blew straight into my face, and my body temperature began to drop again. The deep snow, my continued breathing troubles, and the frostbite on my face were all outweighing the advantages of the relatively flat topography. In theory it was supposed to be easier to make headway than before, but that was not proving to be the case yet.

Once the snow stopped falling, the wind weakened a bit and veered to the northeast. I got out my kite, which I had not been able to use even once since leaving Arctic Bay. I had only kept one kite with me—

the smallest one that harnessed the least amount of wind power. At frigid temperatures I had to be careful of my speed because traveling too fast would have a chilling effect on me that might well prove fatal.

I rejoiced that my kite and I would finally be able to make up some time in this heavy snow. And yet my kite had only been in the air for a moment when a sudden squall battered against it, gusting so hard that all the struts broke. To think that I had lugged this kite all the way from Arctic Bay for a day just like this one, and then the first gust of wind destroyed it, turning it back into deadweight on my sled. I would have it repaired on the next stop I made in civilization.

A slight downhill grade—I could tell because my sled suddenly felt much lighter—helped me to make progress. Soon I set out again on the frozen ocean to the east of King William Island. One day's march later, I could see in the distance the lights of Gjoa Haven, glittering faintly about thirty miles away. If all went well, Cathy and the girls would be landing at the village airport in just three days. But in the meantime, I spotted Jean-Philippe and Raphaël, the filmmaker, riding toward me on snowmobiles. They would accompany me for two days, which would give us a chance to get some more footage of the trip. Then they would leave me and head for Gjoa Haven to tell my wife when I would be arriving.

When I finally landed on King William Island, I climbed a gradual uphill slope about half a mile in length leading to the village. I looked everywhere for my daughters, whom I had not seen in six months. And then I caught sight of them, standing next to their mother by the airport runway. Their silhouettes became clearer as I got closer. I imagined that from the point of view of the little group that surrounded them, jumping up and down to stay warm (it was thirty-two degrees below zero), I was also just a dark spot against the frozen sea and then a shape growing larger as I climbed up the slope of the mainland.

Annika and Jessica hurried down the slope and through the snow in their haste to be the first to throw themselves into my arms. Their mother followed close behind them. The family was back together. My daughters climbed onto my sled—practically empty by the end of the stage—to enjoy a ride to the "finish line" on a sleigh pulled by their father instead of a team of horses.

Surrounded by the locals who had been alerted by the townsfolk of Kugaaruk to the arrival of "the hiker," I recognized my friend Vincent Borde and a few journalists. There were also two representatives from one of my chief sponsors, the private bank Mirabaud. Every month or two, a lottery was held to choose two bank employees—the entire bank staff was following my progress with enthusiasm—to travel to "cheer on Mike at one of his supply points." These two must have been this month's happy winners.

I planned to spend five days in Gjoa Haven, and I had plenty to do. I needed to get my equipment back into shape, restock my supplies of benzene and other provisions, and recover my strength before setting off for Cambridge Bay. Since it had taken me eleven days instead of fifteen to get to Gjoa Haven from Kugaaruk, I was ahead of schedule. I would be able to rest up and take advantage of the extra time.

I helped the Mirabaud bankers put together a slide show that they would present to their colleagues when they got back home. Between interviews and photo sessions, I went out on long snowmobile outings with my family. I taught my daughters to build an igloo and took them to visit three old women who still lived in igloos. These Inuit spent their time softening the animal hides from which they made their clothing by chewing on them interminably. My daughters could scarcely believe their eyes. They had played hooky from school to be able to come visit, but cultural encounters like this one were rich experiences that no school could ever have taught them.

"Rich" experiences were required to justify the cost of this visit, since our family's hotel room cost eight hundred dollars a night! The only hotel in Gjoa Haven was run by a married couple—a Canadian woman and an Englishman—who took advantage of their monopoly to charge scandalously high prices for a tiny, bare room with two beds and a television set, where my daughters slept on a mattress on the floor. And looking for hospitality in town was out of the question, since the Inuit were already crowding ten or fifteen people into each room of their tiny houses.

After just five days, our hotel bill had soared to almost twelve thousand dollars for me, my family, and my team! When I asked the owner of the hotel for a discount, she very graciously agreed to deduct the two hundred dollars for the children's meals.

There was clearly no way of avoiding this pendulum that swung wildly from brotherly love to outright swindles, from generosity to extortion, from my hosts in Kugaaruk to the innkeepers of Gjoa Haven.

Just before my family was scheduled to leave, the village organized a drum dance for us, an event that was certainly the most remarkable ceremony that I witnessed in my time in the Arctic. The drum dance was at the same time the Inuit's only form of public entertainment and the demonstrative language of their storytelling ancestors.

We watched in fascination as the men beat on sealskin drums strapped to their bellies, while telling stories in strange guttural chants of the invasion of the village by a bear, a famine during which their shaman demanded the expulsion of one of the tribe in order to remove a curse and bring back the caribou, and many other legends as well. Then they turned to me, asking me to tell the story of the journey that had taken me all the way from Arctic Bay to this town. With the drum on my hip, I walked around the town square, beating away and chanting into the night. Variously walking bent over or upright, legs spread wide or standing as tall as I could, I imitated the loping gait of the caribou, mimed the menacing silhouette of a bear rearing up on its haunches and the pack of wolves that were following close at my heels. I recounted how I had climbed over mountain passes and crossed lakes. I let loose the performer and child within me, and I had a fantastic time. The Inuit applauded, shouting with joy. I was a hit!

The warm enthusiasm of the inhabitants of Gjoa Haven helped me forget about the greed of its hoteliers. When I moved on I would take with me not only the friendship of the people of this village but also the memory of the wonderful moments I was able to spend with Annika and Jessica. When you spend only five days every six months with your children, every minute needs to be extraordinary. And every minute was.

When I put Cathy and my daughters on the airplane home, I had a very atypical bout of depression. The accumulation of fatigue, no doubt, had something to do with it, but the main reason was the harsh awareness that I wouldn't be seeing my family again until I reached Point Hope, Alaska, more than twelve hundred miles from here, a distance twice as far as the direct path to Russia across the North Pole. I was gripped with terrible longing to return home with them. Then I thought again of the incredible moments when, after months of separation, they ran toward me to leap into my arms. Moments like that, days like the ones we had just spent together, were worth all the sacrifices. I just needed to hang on, and there would be another reunion to reward me for my trouble. My case of the blues vanished as quickly as it had arrived.

After my family left, I became friends with Ron, an Australian teacher, and Sari, a nurse from New Zealand, who invited me stay with them even though they had barely enough room for the two of them. In any case, I planned to stay only a couple of days, but on the day before my scheduled departure, I suddenly fell ill, which almost never happens to me—my bout of the blues might very well have been a warning sign. The illness put me completely out of commission with a throbbing headache and waves of nausea, and it was as if my batteries had been drained to zero. Could this have been a belated side effect of my frozen lungs? At the town clinic where Sari worked, I met Roger, a physician from Cambridge Bay who served all the villages of the region. After getting me back on my feet, Roger also offered to act as my "post office box" in Cambridge Bay. I could stay with him when I arrived, and Cathy could send my provisions for the next stage of my journey to his address. I accepted with pleasure.

On the next day, May 2, I left without looking back—like a cowboy in an old Western. Despite the weight of my sled, loaded to the gun-wales, and the nearly flat terrain that allowed a strong northwesterly wind to blow straight into my face unimpeded, I made nineteen miles that first day. That evening I had the happy surprise of seeing Ron and Sari pull up; they had decided to follow my tracks by snowmobile to come and wish me good luck and urge me to keep up my courage. To be welcomed by friends and family after a long trip in the wilderness is a wonderful thing. But friends who come to wish you luck on your journey is a great comfort, as well.

Over the past five months I had made almost no westward progress. Starting now, I absolutely had to make up for lost time. After Cambridge Bay, which was about 250 miles away as the crow flies, I had set myself a little challenge: to cover nonstop the eight hundred miles between Cambridge Bay and Paulatuk, on Amundsen Gulf.

The season that was beginning was ideal for travel. As the Arctic spring was beginning, the cold was dry, and temperatures rarely dropped under twenty degrees below zero, except during rare plunges to forty degrees below zero caused by strong frontal systems. In comparison with what I had suffered, it was practically balmy. It was ideal for traveling. I would sweat less while marching along, and I would have a few more minutes of grace time in which to pitch my tent. After the long winter night that had undermined my strength and deprived me of vitamin D, the more prevalent sunlight gave me a new surge of energy. And with it came optimism. I felt certain that now I would enjoy the good weather that I never experienced between Arctic Bay and Gjoa Haven.

According to the Inuit elders, the best route to Cambridge Bay was to hug the south coast of King William Island, then climb back onto the island to avoid an area prone to open water before crossing back down to the mainland and heading south and west along the edge of the Queen Maud Gulf and the Barren Lands. Then I would head back north to Victoria Island and Cambridge Bay. I had no time to waste. The route that I was planning to follow was 125 miles shorter and

meant going to the west point of King William Island, then—since the
shortest distance between two points is a straight line—crossing directly over to Victoria Island through the Royal Geographical Society
Islands. The currents around these islands are so rough that the pack
ice piles up into insurmountable barriers. This was where Sir John
Franklin's boat was crushed in the ice and where his entire crew died
trying to reach dry land.

I followed the coast to Glad Man's Point, a promontory on the westernmost point of the island. Like so many other locations in the area
the place was named by Franklin, Amundsen, and their men after
episodes (often tragic) that had taken place there.

In this icy wasteland there were no signposts, so I made use of Inuit
"signage." According to Makabi, the route to Gjoa Haven had passed
over "the mountain that looks like the two breasts of a woman," past the
peak "shaped like a bear's teeth," and, one day's march further on, the
hill "that looks like the back of a humpback whale." Such descriptors
made it that much more necessary to know how to observe subtle
shapes, something which I had been slowly learning to do. And so I recognized the "woman's breasts," the "bear's teeth," and the "back of the
humpback whale." This time, on the westernmost edge of King William
Island, I was looking for a cove shaped like the egg of a snow goose,
longer than the average egg. When I came upon it, the resemblance was
striking. I was on the right path.

At Glad Man's Point, a radar station on the Distant Early Warning
(DEW) Line, a solitary outpost, continues to stand guard against the
nuclear threat. In contrast with what you might think, this spot isn't actually very far from Russia. You need only travel to the far side of the Pole.

The interior of the station looked like an abandoned hut on a construction site. I decided to pitch my tent in the second room, next to the
generator that continued to provide power for the automated radar.
There I would be sheltered from the wind and close to a heat source
that would keep me a few degrees warmer.

As soon as the metal door closed behind me, I realized I was under surveillance by the lenses of a number of security cameras. I was shocked to hear a voice out of nowhere: "You are in a high-security military building. Please pick up the receiver, call the following number, and identify yourself." I realized that a soldier on duty in an office somewhere, perhaps in the Pentagon or on some American military base located thousands of miles away, was watching me.

It was certainly in my interest to comply with the order. After all, the station also had remote-controlled weapons. I called the guard and explained to him briefly who I was and what I was doing. I told him he could check out my Web site if he didn't believe me.

I assured him that I was just passing through and that I wanted nothing more than a shelter for the night.

"Okay," answered the voice. "You can stay the night. But we're keeping an eye on you." In the morning, as soon as I woke up, I broke camp and packed my bags in haste. I had no desire to spend any more time under the watchful eye of Big Brother.

Sir John Franklin and his men passed through Glad Man's Point in June 1847, just prior to the last leg of their fateful journey. My imagination was attuned to this fact and, here and there, led me to glimpse a pile of stones, identify a cross carved into a rock, or hear what sounded like cries for help.

At this point along the route, I was supposed to listen to the voice of reason and head south across Queen Maud Gulf to the Barren Lands and follow the coast west from there. But I was more determined than ever to keep heading west, traveling via the Royal Geographical Society Islands, and then Jenny Lind Island, which would be my last landfall until Cambridge Bay, which I would reach by crossing Icebreaker Channel and hugging the southern coast of Victoria Island. This alternate route of mine was theoretically impossible because of the enormous blocks of pack ice that rendered the way impassable. They had told me the same thing about Committee Bay.

As was my way, I didn't resist the temptation to go take a look for myself. If I couldn't get through, I would just make a detour to the South. It wouldn't be the first detour of my trip.

At first, the frozen ocean was like a speedway underneath my skis, and I was setting distance records every day: fifteen, sixteen, seventeen miles. At this time of year, each day was between eight and twelve minutes longer than the day before.

I was in the middle of the area where Franklin and his men wandered at length, searching for Glad Man's Point and King William Island, which they hoped would be their way back to civilization. Armed with rifles and animal traps, they tried to hunt bear and caribou for sustenance. I hadn't seen any bear tracks for a while, but otherwise, game seemed abundant. Why would they have starved to death? As I moved through these haunting, magnificent landscapes that once enveloped Franklin and his men, I pondered the other factors that might have contributed to their deaths. I could think of only two good reasons: the inadequacy of their equipment, intended for navigation rather than traveling over ice fields; and the rigid chain of command of the time, when a captain was all-powerful and his orders could never be questioned, even if those orders threatened to condemn the entire crew to death. These same two reasons were likely the cause of nearly all the maritime tragedies in the Arctic during the nineteenth century.

When no messages were forthcoming from her husband, Lady Franklin financed numerous rescue missions. The missions went on for years and managed to produce only one piece of information: the "Eskimos" had named a small island in the area Floating Boat Island. This suggested that Franklin's ship, once freed by melting ice, had not sunk immediately but had drifted until it reached the island in question and then finally settled to the bottom nearby. In the year I ventured into the region, new sonar surveys were being done in an attempt to locate the wreck.

Franklin's body was never found. We know that his men wouldn't have performed a burial at sea because naval regulations of the period required that the body of a dead captain should be carried home with his ship except in case of shipwreck. The crew would certainly have warehoused his body in a shallow trench carved in the ice, or in the earth's surface just above the permafrost, with a pile of rocks heaped above it to mark the spot. The sailors probably expected to be able to come back to recover the body after they themselves had been rescued. But that was not how events unfolded.

In the years and decades that followed, explorers continued to search for that "temporary" grave—now more than 150 years old—and for the body that the cold would have preserved virtually intact.

The story of Sir John Franklin and his men has been handed down from generation to generation among the Inuit of the region, becoming one of the countless legends of the Arctic. I imagined the phantom ship and the mysterious corpse lying undiscovered below my ski tracks as I traveled over the frozen straits and barren terrain of that unforgiving region.

I pitched my tent just before the Royal Geographical Society Islands and their daunting pack ice. I was in a hurry to start climbing these huge, supposedly insurmountable piles of ice. To my eyes, they were more of an exciting challenge than a daunting obstacle. The challenge was primarily physical—it takes more time to haul a sled up while climbing than it does to pull it behind you while skiing on flat terrain. Then came the strategic challenges of picking a route. Should I try to go to the right around this or that block of ice, or to the left? Should I try to climb this giant block, which looked like it led to an easier passage beyond, or this other smaller block, in which case I might have to unload my sled in order to get over the wall that stood behind it? The days were filled with decisions of this sort, each of which influenced the chain of decisions that followed. The strategic component was like a chess match, while the stakes were like a high-rollers' game of poker. The wins and losses were collected on the spot—payable in blood and sweat. There was no cheating. There were no loopholes. It was a language that I understood.

I wasn't disappointed by the challenge posed by these ice blocks. The battle was as tough as I had expected, and my average distance dropped drastically. But the smooth sailing had been getting a little dull anyway. I was calculating, evaluating, negotiating, and the fight was stimulating and exciting. With a single-minded focus on my task, and watching foxes and birds out of the corner of my eye, I felt a kind of happiness in giving it my all.

During the night, both guarded and surrounded by those thousands of colossal sentinels of ice, I thought to myself that this would be an ideal spot to leave a letter to my daughters. This idea, which had been buzzing in my head since Arctic Bay, sprang from my desire to have Annika and Jessica see everything that I had seen. But to get them to come up here, it wouldn't be enough to tell them that the landscape is worth seeing. I would need to give them a specific goal. To find a letter that had been left for them would be a sort of treasure hunt that might motivate them many years from now, if and when I was no longer around.

This area was so difficult to reach that the mere achievement of getting there would help them understand my line of work. Although, who knows, ten or twenty years from now, global warming might have melted all the ice, and people might travel this coastline in cruise ships!

In the middle of the night I wrote a letter to my daughters that began with a few statistics—position, daytime temperatures, and so on—and then went on in an attempt to explain the emotions that I experienced while I was there. I tried to re-create some of the more exceptional moments that I had experienced during this adventure, and finally, I tried to justify, in my own words, both my dreams and my long absences. In short, I told my daughters everything that I had long wanted to be able to say to them but that they were still too young to be able to understand.

I slipped the letter into a plastic bag, which I planned to hide under the rocks on the next island I encountered along my route.

The island I found the next day was about the size of a pickup truck. My letter in one hand, my camera in the other, I searched for the ideal place to hide my message. Noticing a small jutting ridge, I decided that it would make the perfect hiding place, and I began to excavate the frozen earth beneath it with great difficulty. Suddenly, as I was moving some rocks, I uncovered a wolf trap! The trap was still attached to its rock with a chain. The powerful jaws, still pried open, would never snap shut on anything because the spring, like the rest of the trap, was badly corroded. The rust had literally fused the whole mechanism into the stone, but not so completely that I couldn't break it away with a little effort. Scientists and historians would have some fun with this item, which must be at least a century old—roughly from the period of the Franklin expedition. I could see them, him and his starving men, setting that trap with feverish hopes.

I am one of those people who believe in a "Leave No Trace" ethic, meaning that even when chance brings us face-to-face with this sort of treasure, the only alteration we dare make to the scene is leaving footprints in the snow.

I put the plastic bag containing the letters for my daughters on top of the trap, and then I placed the stones on top of them. I noted the exact GPS location of the spot, which I then photographed for my records. Then I continued on my way.

After fourteen hours of struggling through the pack ice, I pitched camp on Jenny Lind Island. Before slipping into my sleeping bag, I repaired a tear that I had made in my tent with the tip of one of my skis. Because temperatures had fallen again to forty degrees below zero, I couldn't leave a hole in the tent. I stitched it up and "welded" the stitching with a special heated silicone gel.

When I emerged from the tent in the morning, I found myself nose to muzzle with the only animal still missing from my Arctic bestiary: a musk ox. This amazing animal is reminiscent of the bison and the extinct wooly mammoth, with its rounded tusks and its coat of thick, matted fur dangling to the ground like a heavy mattress. The musk ox can calmly withstand the most intense cold and dig up its food even under the snow. I wondered if it was aggressive, and whether there was much chance of being trampled by stampeding herds, as is the case with the African buffalo. Makabi had already answered this question of mine by telling me about hunters that had been charged and fatally injured by herds of musk oxen.

Jenny Lind Island boasts the highest density of these animals in the surrounding region. It is a veritable musk ox preserve! It is believed that the animals are trapped here by the pack ice. They have less and less living space as they continue to reproduce, but plans were under discussion to move part of the herd to Victoria Island to make room for them.

When I climbed onto the island's elevated plateau, the sight took my breath away! Hundreds, even thousands of musk oxen and their curly-haired, thick-set silhouettes as far as the eye could see! And I was in their midst, zigzagging politely, doing my best not to disturb them. Up close, despite their relatively small size, these animals gave off an impression of power that demanded admiration and respect. And to think that they were members of the sheep family. Instead of attacking me when I got a little too close for comfort (and I couldn't help getting up close to take pictures of them), they lined up in a semicircle and stared at me with a dull gaze. This demonstration of force was a warning: "Don't come any closer." If I did get closer, the chief of the herd would begin to swing his head from side to side. It was the equivalent of a bear grinding its teeth—it was the last warning I would get. After that, the musk oxen would begin stamping their hoofs, and a gland located behind their ear would send a signal to their brains to attack.

While avoiding any sudden movements, I continued to photograph them. One of them began to swing its head and I suddenly realized that, harnessed to my sled, I wouldn't be able to run very fast. I immediately started inching away, and just then the herd began to charge at me. A few yards closer, the herd came to a halt. They had been bluffing just to throw a scare into me. It had worked perfectly.

Since I preferred not to pitch camp among the musk oxen, I left the island and set up my next camp on Icebreaker Channel. The next morning I began to trek along the eastern and southern coast of Victoria Island. According to my information, I shouldn't expect to run into any more serious obstacles between here and Cambridge Bay.

It was the beginning of summer, the season when Arctic explorers and other adventurers come north to launch their assaults on the ice. Cathy told me there were even two Norwegians retracing Amundsen's route. They had started off from Copper Mine River and they were heading for Bellot Island. Since they had left Cambridge Bay three days ago, they were now in the Jenny Lind Island area and were more or less heading in my direction. They had told her that they would love to meet up, and I shared their enthusiasm. They were about sixty miles from Jenny Lind Island; I was north of it. They were making twelve and a half miles a day, and I was making almost nineteen miles. I suggested that we meet up in two days on Icebreaker Channel.

Two days later, the Norwegians were just twelve miles away. We called one another constantly on our satellite phones to check our positions. And then at some point, two tiny dots appeared against the vastness. So slowly that it seemed as if time were standing still, their specks grew larger and took on human form. At last I could see their faces, as white with hoarfrost as my own.

When we were finally face-to-face, one of the two men held out his hand solemnly.

"Mike Horn, I presume?" he Livingstoned.

"How ever did you guess," I answered, in the same spirit.

The meeting was dizzying, euphoric, and exciting. Their eyes glittered with the thrill of the adventure and the almost unbelievable joy that they were actually there in the Arctic—it was the special glow that belongs only to those who are living their dreams. I felt an immediate burst of fraternal feeling toward these men, the first Europeans and fellow explorers that I had met since the beginning of my journey.

We pitched our tents close to one another, and Brent and Randolf insisted on preparing our first meal. I agreed, on the condition that I host them for the second meal. Since I had been making better time than expected, and I knew that I would be resupplied at Cambridge Bay, I calculated that I could spare fifteen days of rations. We could afford to feast and agreed to do so—until we had bellyaches. In their tent, which was bigger than mine, heated as if by a fireside with my extra fuel reserves, we shared our first banquet and then washed it all down with a bottle of cognac that they had brought all the way just for this occasion. The meal lasted the whole day, and the conversation never lagged.

We exchanged contacts and tales of our adventures. Our discussions were the diametric opposite of those superficial conversations that you can hardly escape these days.

Brent and Randolf planned to head toward Bellot Island, Gjoa Haven, and Igloolik, following a route close to the one that I had been unable to follow in the opposite direction. I recommended that they follow my course in reverse, and I gave them the various positions of my campsites, as recorded in my GPS. Moreover, I advised that they detour around Committee Bay and the Gulf of Boothia because their sleds weren't designed for pack ice.

Friendships develop very quickly in the Arctic, along with a sense of mutual assistance and fraternity. Brent, Randolf, and I might not be pursuing the same objective, and our paths might be leading in different directions, but we had in common the fact that we were all here at the same time. That was enough.

After a final breakfast of coffee and muesli, a few souvenir photographs, and my promise to write an introduction to their planned book, we set off again in our respective directions. Two hours later I turned around and looked behind me. Their silhouettes had become specks on the horizon once again, and I felt a strange sense of sadness to be separated from these men. I had spent just twenty-four hours with them, but I felt as if I had known them for years.

It was still thirty degrees below zero, but in just a month the snow and the ice would begin to melt. I was now in a race against the spring thaw; I marched all night long to cover as many miles as possible. Heavy snowfalls slowed me down, but the favorable winds and terrain allowed me to use my kite—for the first time in quite a while—on the last sixteen miles before Victoria Island.

One Saturday evening, three days after parting company with Brent and Randolf and thirty days after leaving Kugaaruk, I set foot on the island at last and pitched camp within sight of Cambridge Bay. I lined up the opening of my tent with the village, three miles away, so that I wouldn't have to take my eyes off it. I had been dreaming of this place for six months; I had planned to arrive here by boat, but I was forced to come on foot. It was safe to say that I had earned my passage.

If everything had gone according to the original plan, by now I would be somewhere in Siberia, about four months from the finish line. But I couldn't say that I regretted anything about having taken that immense detour, which offered me an invaluable array of experiences and which allowed me to meet amazing men like Simon, Claude, Makabi, Brent, and Randolf.

On my satellite phone I called Simon, and then Makabi, to tell them that, thanks to their help, I had finally reached Cambridge Bay. They shouted with joy like sports fans whose team has finally scored a goal after a long and hard-fought struggle. There I stood, all alone in a stadium all my own, champion of the world.

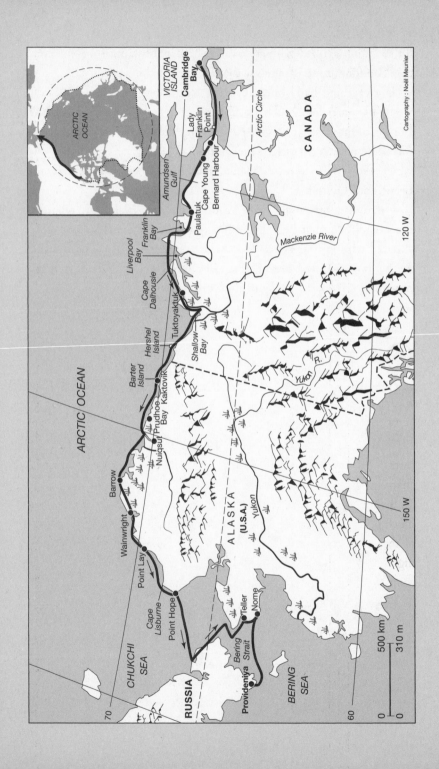

( 5 )

# The End of the Earth

O N A SNOWY SUNDAY MORNING, I entered the empty streets of "Cam" as if I were walking into a ghost town. One building served as a hotel, but it was closed, so I pitched my tent outside the front door. A policeman finally showed up and asked me what I was doing there.

"I'm waiting for the hotel to open."

"That won't be for three weeks." The policeman called the owner, a certain Angela, who—when I offered to pay—gave me a suite free of charge as long as I wanted to stay.

If I had listened to my own gut, which was urging me on to cover as much distance as possible before the thaw, I would have taken possession of the DHL package being held for me by Roger—and I would have high-tailed it out of town without wasting another moment. But I couldn't come to Cambridge Bay without spending an evening with Peter.

Peter was a fifty-five-year-old American engineer who specialized in radar and weather stations and worked for the DEW Line. A few months ago he had contacted me by e-mail and offered to help me out with my expedition in whatever capacity he could. After that we had been in regular contact, and he had proved invaluable in reporting on the condition of the ice, the strength and direction of the winds, suggesting routes, and so on.

I had called him the day before I arrived in town to invite him out to dinner. Actually—since there was no restaurant in town—I prepared a meal for him myself. As soon as I was settled in town, I ransacked the local superette and prepared a small banquet for him, a fitting recognition of his help and his friendship.

The next morning, while Peter saw to a few small repairs to my electronic equipment, I went to see Roger, the doctor. He was surprised to see me so soon, and he told me that my package had not been delivered yet—even though it had been shipped about fifteen days ago and DHL had promised to have it there on time. They told me it would certainly come in any day now, and I just needed to be patient.

Days passed, and the food rations and the detailed maps that were supposed to take me all the way to Paulatuk still hadn't arrived. And yet, Cambridge Bay wasn't exactly cut off from the rest of the world. Supplies and freight came into the village on two weekly flights!

At the end of my rope and running low on time, I needed to get off Victoria Island and back to the Canadian mainland before the thaw. I decided to do without the services of my courier. Combining the provisions I still had in my sled with what I was able to obtain there, I figured I should be able to stock up for the eight hundred miles between Cambridge Bay and Paulatuk. At Peter's request, the directors of the DEW Line gave me a substantial supply of chocolate cookies. Chantal, Roger's wife, worked in a plant where they made dried musk ox meat and smoked Arctic char, and she got me several pounds of each. And I finished obtaining my supplies with powdered mashed potatoes, chocolate, walnuts, and dried fruit from the corner grocery store. In any case, I wouldn't be needing as many calories once the temperature started rising again. My metabolism would simply have to become accustomed to my change in diet.

Peter and one of his friends, Anton, a military helicopter pilot who transported the engineers from one radar surveillance station to another, managed to obtain maps of the region for me. A relative of Makabi's who also lived in town gave me a few tips for the next stage of my journey. Everything fell into place once again, thanks to the amazing kindness of the men and women I met along the way.

I arranged for an additional supply rendezvous with Jean-Philippe Patthey at Paulatuk. We had originally been scheduled to hook up at Tuktoyaktuk, five hundred miles away at the mouth of the Mackenzie River, where the warm waters from the spring thaw would by then have partially melted the ice, turning the immense and unavoidable delta into a swamp—hence the need to replace my winter equipment with summer equipment, trading my skis and my sled for a kayak, my snow boots for neoprene boots.

I asked Cathy to send some gifts to my friends in Cambridge Bay to thank them for all that they had done for me, and I set out once again, this time with the goal of reaching Paulatuk in one month. The thermometer had risen to about thirteen degrees below zero, and it felt as if I could see the ice melting beneath my skis. Now it was a race against the clock. If I wanted to be able to follow the southern coast of Victoria Island to its western end, cross Dolphin and Union Strait, and reach Cape Bathurst as early as possible while staying on the ice of Amundsen Gulf, I would have to maintain a daily average of twenty-five miles. It worked out to nearly a marathon a day.

The immediate question at hand was whether to move forward on the dry land of Victoria Island or venture down immediately onto the ice of Coronation Gulf. On the ice I would be forced to take a longer route, but on the island, which was flat as a pancake, the blizzards would blind me and slow me down by burying me in spring snow.

I decided to go back to the ice. The temperatures—around thirty degrees below zero—were tolerable, and my daily mileage was often higher than the allotted twenty-five miles. As the days passed, I noticed the daylight increasing and the temperature rising. The prevailing winds were no longer coming from the northwest but now began to blow from the south. I was ready for it, and all I needed to do was to adapt my methods of navigation—tell-tales on my ski poles and snow mounds—to take this into account. By this point, since the Arctic sun was visible almost twenty-four hours a day, it also served as my compass. I only traveled when the sun was visible above the horizon, though it never rose very high in the sky. At any given moment of the day, the sun was rotating around me as if I were its axis. Since fifteen degrees of angle corresponded to one hour of time, it was clear that the sun—wherever I happened to be—would always be due north at midnight, at fifteen degrees east of due north at 1:00 A.M., thirty degrees east of due north at 2:00 A.M., due south at noon, and so on. I divided up the sky into pie wedges of fifteen degrees, and then into subsections of one degree each in order to obtain the most accurate bearing possible. Imagining that I was at the center of a clock or a sundial, I would check my shadow to determine my course.

This natural compass was more effective and more reliable than any other navigational tool at my disposal. At these very high latitudes, even my GPS indicated a distance to North Cape that was always approximately the same.

During my long days, which had extended to more than eleven hours, I never stopped discovering and learning new things. My daily observation of ice crystals, their size and shape, indicated the slightest temperature variations, and the shape of the clouds warned me of upcoming shifts in wind. My brain never stopped processing all of this available information. I spent part of these long stretches of time examining questions of course and navigation from every angle. I spent the remainder of the time thinking about things I had never had the leisure to consider in such depth in my daily life. Freed from the madding crowd, undisturbed by any distracting movement or visual stimuli, unhampered by material concerns other than my daily slog, my mind was completely open, and I used it to dissect or ruminate on this or that aspect of my life. Or else I became absorbed in more general reflection. My imagination was churning incessantly, and it kept me from losing my mind in the solitude and silence.

If I could keep up this pace, it might be possible for me to reach Tuktoyaktuk before the delta of the Mackenzie River became a marsh. If so, I might be able to traverse it on skis and put off my change of equipment until later. This would keep me from getting bogged down in a situation where the breakup of the ice makes cross-country skiing dangerous and where my kayak would risk being wedged and crushed between the surviving blocks of ice. This intermediate season is the hardest time to travel in the Arctic. For that reason, no one bothers to do so—no one but me, that is.

Spurred by the prospect of crossing the Mackenzie Delta before the full-blown thaw, I put the pedal to the metal and really covered some distance—as much as thirty miles a day. One day, when I was able to use my kite, I beat my daily distance record for the Canadian segment of my trip—with fifty-six miles in a single day! That was in spite of visibility of almost zero and wind-induced spills that pulled me across the ice on my rear end.

I wasn't the only creature anxious about the change of seasons. This was also the time of year when the caribou hurried to cross Coronation Gulf to reach their summer grazing grounds on Victoria Island before the thaw. Their long, single-file lines would run across my path until I got close, and then they would scatter in all directions. Thanks to my kite, which allowed me to move as fast as they did, I could follow them, catch up with them, and slide along next to them. I heard the clattering of their hoofs on the ice and their rapid panting, and I could see the uneasy gleam that danced in their round eyes and the effects of the breeze that played in the silky sheen of their hair. I was one of them. It was magical and exciting.

But I stayed focused. In soft snow, with my heel not fastened to my ski, using a kite is a dangerous exercise—not recommended when traveling solo. If I slipped into a hole or hit a block of ice and dislocated my knee, it would be a catastrophe. So I decided to give up using my kite on days when the wind was favorable but visibility was low. The farther I advanced, the less willing I was to run risks that weren't absolutely necessary.

As I drew closer to Lady Franklin Point, the southwestern extremity of Victoria Island, the coughing noise of an engine announced the unexpected arrival of a helicopter. When the pilot spotted me, he veered toward me and set down a few yards away. It was Anton, my supplier of military maps.

"I'm just coming back from the DEW Line station at Bernard Harbor," he told me. "There is plenty of open water over there, and I don't even know how far it extends."

I sighed unhappily. Bernard Harbor was very close, right across my route.

But then Anton added, "There is a slim chance you can get through if you travel along the far southern edge of the strait. Unfortunately, the ice is very rough there." I didn't care. There was hope.

The Bernard Harbor station lay a mile or two inland. It was one of the unmanned DEW Line monitoring stations that also serve as refuges and usually contain food supplies for those awaiting rescue. In order to encourage me to go that way, which I hadn't planned to do, Anton had left extra provisions there just for me.

"Have yourself a little feast and a good night's sleep on me," he said.

The closer I got to open water, the more worried I became. If I couldn't get through, I would have to retrace my steps and head south until I reached the mainland, an enormous detour that would ruin all my plans for Tuktoyaktuk and the Mackenzie Delta. And God only knew what would happen after that.

To keep these worries at bay, I continued to cover my daily marathon distance—and even more on certain days. I continued past Lady Franklin Point, and the route still looked fine. Pushing on, I camped right in the middle of Dolphin and Union Strait.

At daybreak the seals had transformed the ice into a solarium. I had fun seeing how close I could get to them; it was difficult, because seals are highly suspicious. A quick inspection of the openings that they had made in the ice confirmed my suspicion: the ice was thin, which was how they had penetrated it so easily and probably meant that it ended not far away. Prudence suggested that I head south, but I couldn't help being drawn northward.

I continued on my way. Visibility dropped from hour to hour. Suddenly, when I was still two and a half miles from dry land, I felt that my skis were not supporting me as well, that they were strangely sinking beneath me. An instant later, chills of horror ran up my spine as I realized that I was no longer marching on ice—I was on a layer of snow "floating" on the water! At low temperatures a thick layer of snow doesn't fully melt when it hits the ocean.

I had fallen into one of the most treacherous traps of the Arctic! The transition from ice to snow was nearly unnoticeable—so subtle is the difference between the two. Usually, in fact, you don't even notice that you're standing on mushy snow until it is too late.

Should I turn south? But how far would I have to go before I found a more solid surface?

Should I turn back? But marching back over the same snow would amount to tempting fate.

I decided to keep on going toward dry land and pray that the gods of the Far North would be on my side. I moved forward, trying to tread as lightly as possible. But I hadn't gone fifty yards before, with a muffled crunch, the ground gave way beneath me. I was falling.

If I fell in, I would have nothing to grab onto to haul myself out of the water, only soft snow. I would be stuck in the water, and that would be the end of me.

In the fraction of a second during which I felt the snow open up beneath my feet, I had the reflexes of a parachutist. I curled up and began to roll, but on my side, so that I landed, skis in the air, on a surface that was still solid. But it began to crumble beneath my weight, too, so that the opening in the snow quickly expanded. I tried to spread out my weight as much as possible by continuing to roll, haphazardly and as quickly as possible, despite my skis and my sled. The snow continued to open beneath me until I clambered onto a pile that was a little thicker and stronger. At last, I was on solid ground. Saved!

However, my sled was in the water, and the sea was rapidly transforming the snow all around me into a gooey slush, and I was stuck on a little island about the size of a dinner table. To make things worse, I was soaked through. Luckily, it was "only" thirteen degrees below zero, and the snow that stuck to me when I rolled through it absorbed the moisture, which kept me from freezing to death on the spot.

Should I turn back? Continue on toward dry land? Should I veer north where, according to Anton, there would be nothing but open water? Regardless of my choice, I would be almost certain to fall in. So, I might as well stay on the same course and push on. And that's just what I did, walking on eggshells the whole time, trying to distribute my weight as evenly as possible. I did my best to find a rhythm—a completely fluid stride with no bumping or stumbling—trying to be as light as a feather.

I employed a tactic used by polar bears, which picked up only one leg at a time to spread their weight out over three points of support. I spread my legs and moved forward gingerly, as if my private parts were hurting me badly, without picking up my skis or moving them too far apart, which could have made me lose my balance. My three-hundred-pound sled followed me at its own distinct pace, floating on the water I left in my wake, sparing the spider web of snow below me any further burden.

One thing was certain. If I fell in the water—for good this time—I would toss my fuel and my food into the sea and I would use my sled as a boat—even if it meant paddling for twenty hours with my shovel to reach dry land.

From snow pile to snow pile, excruciatingly slowly, I inched my way closer to the mainland. It took four hours: half-a-mile per hour. And the last fifty feet, walking a tightrope as I weaved my way among the ice blocks bobbing against the shore, took a full half hour. I was wearing a jacket of ice, but the exercise had warmed me up. And Bernard Harbor was just twelve and a half miles away.

I wouldn't be reaching it that evening, though. After four miles, my body failed me. I barely had the strength to pitch my tent. And yet, once I was inside the tent, I wrote another letter to my daughters. I felt the need to talk to them because, once again, I had come very close to never returning home at all.

More than anything, I was angry at my own stupidity. I couldn't forgive myself the lack of judgment that had come so close to costing me my life. I shouldn't make that sort of mistake, not at my level of experience. Nevertheless, beneath the sense of frustration there was a vague but growing sense of confidence that now there was nothing that could keep me from succeeding.

The next day I woke up to one of the worst blizzards I had experienced since the beginning of the expedition. I skied forward, practically lying flat on my belly as I went because of how far I had to lean forward against the power of the gusting winds. I couldn't see the tips of my skis, and I was navigating by the angle of the wind hitting my face. Pressing my nose against my GPS in order to make out its indicator, I read, "Destination reached." I raised my head and looked around. Total whiteness. Then the curtain of snow parted briefly, and Bernard Harbor materialized right in front of me.

It was strictly a military outpost and operated like all the stations along the DEW Line, without any personnel on site. The station consisted of a building topped by a white radar dish. The structure, roughly the size of a small house, could be seen on a clear day from sixteen miles away. Peter and Anton had given me not only the exact location of the outpost but also the security code to open the door and the telephone number to call once I was inside to report my presence—all confidential information.

"Hello, Mike," said the voice of the soldier at the other end of the line. "Anton told us you would be coming. He left you something to eat. Enjoy your meal. Give us a call back, just to let us know when you leave."

The noise of the generator kept me from sleeping, so I camped outside at the base of the radar tower, where I waited a day and a half for the blizzard to die down. I enjoyed the break and toasted the health of Peter and Anton.

Once the weather improved, I set out to traverse the eighty-seven miles to another station on the DEW Line: Cape Young, at the foot of Mount Davy on Amundsen Gulf. Just as I was leaving the peninsula to climb down to the ice again, Anton's helicopter, bringing American military personnel and engineers to inspect Cape Young, flew overhead once again. Camera flashes went off as the aircraft hovered around me and set down nearby. Four uniformed men burst out of the chopper and came running toward me, exclaiming, "Unbelievable! It can't be true! You told us about him, but we didn't believe you!" and so on. They all offered me their lunch boxes, without worrying about the fact that they would be feeling hunger themselves in a few hours.

Soda, bananas, apples, chocolate, freshly made ham-and-cheese sandwiches—in short, these lunches had everything I had been missing most since leaving Cambridge Bay a month before. It seemed as if the entire population of Arctic Canada was taking turns feeding me and making up for the shortcomings of my courier service.

Before taking off, Anton warned me that enormous quantities of pack ice had formed along the coastline. I didn't let it worry me much. From now on, I knew that I would get through, whether on dry land or on ice.

There was a danger more formidable than pack ice: grizzlies. Global warming was pushing their habitat farther and farther north, where they were starting to encroach on polar bear territory, causing some serious tensions between the two species. Anton had seen some in the Cape Young sector. Because the ice was starting to melt, they were moving along what is known as the flow edge, whether that meant following the coastline or the banks of a river, wherever their prey might be likely to come to play or breathe. To make things worse, this was the season when mother bears and their cubs were emerging from their dens. Because of all of this, I would have to be on the lookout.

After leaving Bernard Harbor, I made excellent progress along the coast, covering average daily distances of twenty-eight to thirty-two miles without even making use of my kite because the wind was in my face. The pack ice wasn't bad, and I got around the obstacles I encountered without too much trouble.

One day, when the wind shifted a little, I hoisted my kite. Moving along at a good clip among barriers and obstacles as hard as concrete was no simple matter. As I was zigzagging along, I occasionally found myself with one ski in the air, trying to regain my balance. More than once, my sled got caught behind me, causing some hard falls. I improvised some nice jumps off of snowpiles and bumps in the ice, using them as springboards.

I narrowly avoided one catastrophe after the other. I knew the slightest mistake could have proved fatal, but I just couldn't bring myself to stop. I was intoxicated with the adrenaline rush. When evening came, I had traveled forty miles, but I chided myself for running risks that were quite unnecessary. I would be in a lot of trouble if someone up there stopped watching over me. As I folded up my kite, I swore I would never use it in pack ice again. I had a complete change of attitude. My goal from now on was no longer to get to Tuktoyaktuk as quickly as possible, rather just to get there at all. The farther I went on this expedition, the less of a right I had to compromise its success by running pointless risks.

The landscapes I was traveling through were some of the most beautiful places I had ever had an opportunity to see. This Far North, where land, sea, and sky are all different facets of the same diamond, where the mountains look as if they had burst through the ice, made me think more than ever about the fragility of our earth.

By the time I came even with Cape Young, I saw no remaining signs of the grizzly bears except for their tracks through the snow that headed toward Banks Island on the north side of Amundsen Gulf. It snowed periodically, which was the natural companion of the warmer temperatures. The thermometer no longer dropped below fifteen degrees below zero, and the ice would partly thaw during the day and then freeze up again during the night, which gave it an unpleasant, cardboard-like consistency. This "damp cardboard" stuck to my skis and slowed me down. But I was like an athlete in midseason condition, and I approached Paulatuk on schedule to meet up with Jean-Philippe and his basketful of provisions.

Jean-Philippe had also brought his closest friend, Pierre-Alain, a

Swiss restaurateur who closely followed all of my expeditions. Jean-Philippe brought him along to this reprovisioning point as a present for his fortieth birthday. All of Pierre-Alain's friends had chipped in to pay his way, and so there the two of them were, traveling from Paulatuk to meet me, on their rented snowmobiles and accompanied by their Inuit guide. We met at the exact spot where I climbed onto dry land. The trip from Paulatuk had taken them four hours. It would take me three days to retrace their brief journey.

During those three days we camped together, but while I made progress toward Paulatuk, Jean-Philippe and Pierre-Alain set out to explore the region's amazing landscapes and wild fauna. Thanks to the mobility that their snowmobiles gave them, they could rejoin me from time to time to check on my progress or to bring me a snack, vanishing into the distance and then reappearing unexpectedly, chasing me down by following my tracks, or going on ahead to set up their camp. Pierre-Alain had brought supplies of fondue and other Swiss delicacies, so that the three days we traveled together turned into a jolly excursion. Despite that conviviality, and even though we weren't very far from Paulatuk by this point, I didn't waste the tiniest scrap of food or ounce of fuel. I never wasted food or fuel, both out of a sense of principle and superstition. Even if I had an extra forty-five pounds of surplus food to haul, I could never bring myself to abandon any of it on the ice field. There was no question of letting my friends carry part of my load either—for safety reasons. If for any reason we were unable to meet up again, I had to be self-sufficient.

On the last day I told Jean-Philippe and Pierre-Alain to go on ahead to wait for me in Paulatuk. Arriving at the end of a stage is a gift that I like to enjoy greedily, all by myself. I like to be alone so that I can gradually slow down to a stroll, taking my time to watch as the village grows larger and closer, considering what I went through to get there, savoring the small victory while allowing myself to think ahead to the next stage.

I had taken thirty-three days—only two of which were sunny—to reach Paulatuk from Cambridge Bay with daily distances of about twenty-five miles. That distance might not seem like much when plotted out on a map, but it had taken me four months to cover the same distance under harsher conditions from Arctic Bay to Committee Bay.

If there was a reason I had made it this far, I think it was first and foremost because I believed in myself, and also because I had never let disappointments diminish my sense of hope. The other ingredients of the magic potion were a blend of experience and wisdom. The wisdom was the product of the terrible errors and hubris that had come close to costing me my life. I would need wisdom and experience, in spades, to cross Siberia in winter.

I had crossed into the Northwest Territories, which lies between Nunavut and the Yukon, and I was on schedule to cross the Bering Strait in August. I would hoist sail at Point Hope to cross the Chukotka Sea to Vankarem on the Russian side. From there I would set out to cross Siberia. The timing was perfect, as long as I didn't waste a single day—as long as everything went smoothly until I reached Point Hope.

Paulatuk, the smallest town in all of the Far North, is just a cluster of prefabricated houses near an airstrip. The place was empty because the few inhabitants had left to hunt snow geese, which were migrating from Banks Island. Each family had a goose quota to contribute to its supply of meat for the coming winter.

We were housed comfortably as guests of Christian Buchère, a Swiss biologist who had been living here for the past two years, working on a Canadian government project to monitor and study wildlife. Christian was surprised when Jean-Philippe told him a few days prior that I would be arriving. His shock was partially due to the fact he hadn't heard from us for a year, but mostly because he had heard that I had died on my aborted attempt to reach the North Pole!

The snow was melting, and I wasted little time, leaving Paulatuk after two days. Before departing, I consulted a village elder, John, about the best route to follow, as was my custom. It is no accident that at regular intervals, I sought out men who were close to nature, in whom knowl-edge and wisdom had traced rings, like the rings of an oak tree. More and more each day, I understood that my journey was much more than a physical or athletic challenge; it was an expedition of discovery—into the remotest territory of humanity and my own human nature. My ex-ploration of this remarkable terrain was taking me farther and farther afield, which is certainly why my adventures were relatively short early in my career and now take years.

I set out at four in the morning, under a heavy snowfall that clumped to my skis and slowed down my progress. The snow was partly melted, and it spread out across the ground in a black-and-white patch-work that was soon quite impassable with a sled. I climbed back down to the ice on Amundsen Gulf, but the ice, because the snow wasn't freezing anymore, was covered with a liquid film.

The Paulatuk Peninsula proved to be sufficiently snow-covered for me to cross it on skis, so I did so, following the tracks left by the goose hunters.

I had almost reached the other shore when I met an Inuit family of five—including an old man who looked like he was at least one hundred—returning from a hunting expedition. Green was their sur-name, inherited from a family of Boston whalers, and they offered me the hospitality of their traditional encampment for the night, which they had already set up near their snowmobiles. I accepted with pleas-ure, and once again I was treated as an honored guest. Seated around a banquet of caribou and goose, with Eskimo fritters made from flour and seal oil for dessert, the Greens explained that no one had traveled by snowmobile from Paulatuk to Tuktoyaktuk in at least eight years. And as for on foot, well, according to them, it would be impossible for me to cut across Cape Bathurst Peninsula because of the cliffs on the east coast, which were two- to three-hundred feet high. These cliffs were called the Smoking Hills because at regular intervals they emitted roaring jets of steam, as if a dragon were breathing deep within their black flanks. As for the river whose mouth lay a few miles ahead, the ice covering it was very likely to be flooded already. I would certainly drown if I fell through and was swept under by the current.

The Greens recommended that I skirt around Cape Bathurst and Baley Island, directly west, before crossing Liverpool Bay, which should present no problems at this time of the year. On the other hand, the marshes at the estuary of the Mackenzie River would prevent me from reaching Tuktoyaktuk with my sled if I took a straight line. They recommended that I go north around the Tuktoyaktuk Peninsula and cut down at a gentle southwest angle toward the village itself, staying on the ice the whole time. The ice would certainly be covered with river water. But my new friends figured that I still had five days to get through safely before it became impossible.

Finally, they warned me that there would be a high risk of encountering grizzly bears and polar bears, which were attracted to the Smoking Hills by the openings made in the ice by the crosscurrents near Baley Island.

I set off again after a breakfast consisting of rice, snow goose, and fritters, following the route that they had suggested. A little past Franklin Bay, I happened upon polar bear tracks. Soon after, I saw the grizzly paw prints in the snow. The bears were following the river that flows out into the sea midway up the Cape Bathurst Peninsula, where it gushes out onto the surface of the ice. I continued toward the cape after making an enormous detour to avoid being swept away by the river water.

Just to make things more difficult, the temperature rose several degrees, and the heavy, wet snow that had been falling ever since I left Paulatuk had now changed to rain! There is nothing worse in the Arctic. You can get rid of snow by brushing it off, but rain soaks you. It gets into your clothes, and it freezes as soon as a little wind starts blowing. In any case, the rain would change to something else very soon. The weather changes from one minute to the next in this part of the world. It shifts almost undetectably from snow to sunshine, from heat (relatively speaking) to cold, from calm winds to squall. "If you don't like the weather here, just wait fifteen minutes," they say in Arctic Canada.

The farther I climbed along the peninsula that leads to Cape Bathurst, the less ice there was. Soon, the waves were practically pounding against the rocks. The blocks of ice—crashing against one another like ice cubes in a glass—pushed me against the Smoking

Hills, and soon I was wedged onto a beach two yards wide, where rocks were poking through the snow.

Something made me look up. A good fifty yards above me stood the first grizzly I had encountered. The animal was looking down at me with interest but had no way of getting down to me. At least I hoped he didn't.

Two hours later, still wedged between the cliffs and the blocks of ice, my skis weighed down by sticky snow, I felt like I was moving through a fantastic film set. The snow was falling through fog, the mountain next to me seemed to be panting as it belched out its jets of steam. Locked one against the other, the icebergs seemed to be struggling near me, like a bunch of unsettling monsters.

Suddenly, thirty yards away from me on the beach, there appeared a mother grizzly with her two cubs. Snouts sniffing the air, they were all looking for their next meal. The wind was blowing toward me, which prevented them from noticing me for the moment. That was not necessarily a good thing. If the mother saw me too late to turn and run, she would have no choice but to attack. I stopped, but I was reluctant to turn around because it would take me four solid hours of skiing to retrace my steps off that beach—four hours during which I would be easy prey.

I decided to squeeze as close to the cliff as possible, hoping they would just walk right by me. But the mother bear and her cubs saw me and froze. The mother reared up on her hind legs, but the cubs began to gallop toward me! That was the worst thing that could have happened. My rifle, packed on the sled, was out of reach. The only thing that I could think to do was to keep on going, swinging my arms as high in the air as I could, according to a trusted old polar bear method that I was praying would work for grizzly bears, too.

The cubs kept on coming. If they got too close to me, their mother would necessarily consider me a threat; she would rush to their rescue and turn me into hamburger.

The cubs raced past me, continuing on their way as if they hadn't seen me at all. I continued to ski toward their mother, swinging my arms. She dropped down onto all fours. By now we were practically face-to-face. When she moved over toward the water, I squeezed as tight against the cliff wall as I could.

All at once, she broke into a run. As she went by me, she turned her head toward me and took a final look at me. She then caught up with her brood, and the whole family continued on its way. Mechanically, I continued to swing my arms while continuing on my way as quickly as I could. I was so frightened that I was still trembling.

I would need to get off this grizzly bear highway; the traffic was too heavy for my liking, and I couldn't always count on getting so lucky. I tried to find the easiest possible way up the cliff face, but as I got closer to the tip of the cape, my options narrowed. I opted for a cliff face about two hundred feet high. Once I was up there, I could cross the mountains to Liverpool Bay. In a snowy wind that pressed me against the wall, I climbed up and drove in a piton. I used a pulley system to haul up, one after another, my bags, then my empty sled, and finally I climbed up myself.

After six and a half hours of hard work, I reached the summit of the Smoking Hills, where I found an expanse of perfectly passable snow-covered tundra, which only made me regret not having climbed up much earlier.


Across rivers and valleys, I gradually descended back down toward Liverpool Bay. The weather cleared up, as if a curtain had been raised on the blooming of an Arctic spring. The magnificent landscape extended farther and farther into the distance, with silhouettes etched in diamond, colorful flora emerging from the snow, and light growing more vivid with each day.

As soon as I set foot on the Beaufort Sea, the sun, which was up twenty-four hours a day by now, began to melt the fresh snow and covered the ice with lakes. All of this water melted through the frozen surface, opening up enormous dark holes, which became treacherous traps. The entire surface would gradually break up and shift, then be pushed northward by the winds and currents.

It's not only because seawater is so harmful to snowmobiles that the locals stop traveling on the ice once spring has arrived. The Far North has many tragic stories, like the story of the man who set out one day from Tuktoyaktuk with his sled and his dogs and who suddenly found himself on a drifting ice floe, separated from his team. They found the sled and the dogs floating out beyond Cape Bathurst. He was never found.

With my feet and legs constantly soaked, and an unrelenting fear that I would fall into a fissure concealed beneath the layer of water, I progressed with difficulty toward Cape Dalhousie. And then chance came to my aid in the form of an ideal wind for breaking out my kite. Under a perfect blue sky, I found myself sailing along on the ice—or rather, on the water. I was practically waterskiing along that sparkling mirror whose surface my skis barely grazed!

I rounded Cape Dalhousie and was beginning my descent along the Tuktoyaktuk Peninsula, when I chanced upon the most impressive polar bear tracks I had ever seen. To judge from their size, it must have been a real monster. Frankly, by this point I had had my fill of bears. I had come within a hair's width of being mauled and eaten, and I wasn't eager to enjoy that experience again.

The tracks zigzagged between the ocean and dry land, indicating that the beast was hunting for food. The tracks headed south toward Tuktoyaktuk, just like I was, but the bear wouldn't venture close to a human settlement unless it was overwhelmed by hunger. Instead, I figured the bear had scented open water at the mouth of the Mackenzie River, and it knew there was a good chance of finding seals there.

Tiny snow crystals, still visible in its tracks, proved that it wasn't far ahead of me. It was unlikely to turn around and head back toward me, but between its wandering path and the speed of my kite, I was certain to catch up with it. I decided that it would be a better idea to pitch my tent and let the bear get ahead of me. Twenty-four hours from now, it would have covered over a hundred miles and would have disappeared safely into the delta.

I wasn't more than twenty or so miles from "Tuk" when Jean-

Philippe Patthey arrived, accompanied by Sebastian Devenish and Raphaël Blanc, my cameramen.

The thaw had begun early that year, and the area around Tuktoyaktuk was flooded. The ice had broken away from the mainland, and the sea was flowing between ice and land, creating a liquid corridor about fifty feet across. I covered the last miles over ice covered with lakes, knee-deep in water. The skin on my feet, constantly drenched for more than a week, peeled away in strips the same way it had in the swamps of the Amazon jungle. When I ventured to use the kite, the shifts in wind direction regularly dumped me headfirst into the water, dragging me for fifty feet at a time.

In some areas a fine layer of ice had formed on top of the water that pooled on top of the main ice layer. This thin floating ice was too fragile to support my weight, so I walked along, shattering it as I went, playing the human icebreaker with my shins.

Sometimes I would fall and find myself up to my neck in water, with my sled floating behind me. Luckily, the water temperature was thirty-six or thirty-seven degrees, and the air temperature was just below freezing, which saved me from hypothermia.

Sebastian and Raphaël were impressed with the spectacle.

At the end of the day I was so exhausted that I pitched my tent on the first reasonably dry spot I found. The Lord only knew when I would find another.

After Cape Bathurst all the territory I traversed, or nearly all of it, proved unknown and unexpected. I had planned for the beginning of the thaw and changes to the terrain, but I had no idea that these factors would cause me so many problems. I had foolishly held onto the notion that springtime could only bring good things—sunlight, warmth—and make my progress easier. In reality, my difficulties had only changed in nature.

When I first glimpsed Tuktoyaktuk on June 2, 2003, I immediately nicknamed it "brown town" for the color the melting snow gave to the land around it, its few streets, and its houses. It was a striking contrast with the completely white universe in which I had been living since I had set foot on the North American continent.

The appearance of "Tuk" had been shaped by the great number of floating fir and larch logs carried down by the Mackenzie River and used by the native population to build what they called sod houses. These were wooden houses, completely covered with large blocks of peat moss or sod, a material with exceptional insulating properties. Nowadays, the sod houses still stand next to prefab huts and trailer homes—among them the Tuk Inn, where I moved in with my team. The owner, Paul, was an Inuit who purchased the property after retiring as a ranger in the nearby Mackenzie Reindeer Grazing Preserve. He and his wife, Norma, presided over a collection of rooms and added capacity when they could afford to.

The stopover at Tuktoyaktuk was an important one, because here I was going to switch over from winter equipment to summer equipment. This almost solemn transition attracted some of my sponsors and numerous representatives of the European media—including an editor from German *Playboy*—as well as my first American journalists, whose interest in me and my story increased as I got closer to Alaska.

I explained to them that over the next few days, since the mouth of the Mackenzie River was becoming a patchwork of floating ice and swampland, I would wait for most of the ice to float out to sea, and then I would paddle up the river in a kayak against the current and then cut westward to get across the delta. Because of the lakes that would have formed on the ice that remained, my kayak would need to serve, variously, as both boat and sled. That was why I had selected a polyurethane kayak from Prijon. Fiberglass or Kevlar kayaks would be lighter—a distinct advantage when hauling the boat across the ice—but the polyurethane plastic kayak would withstand wear and tear and impacts better, plus it would be easier to patch in case of leaks.

The kayak was about fifteen feet long and contained two waterproof compartments that would hold my provisions and fuel. The rest of my equipment would be stored in waterproof bags and fastened to the rear of the kayak with the weight distributed evenly. In order to keep the excess weight from sinking the boat, Steve Ravussin and I had transformed the kayak into a sort of trimaran by adding two short floats or "shoes," each about a foot and a half long, to improve the boat's stability. The shortcoming of this system was that the aluminum arm that joined the floats together prevented double-paddling, forcing me to use a simple, less effective, "Indian-style" paddle. I made up for that, when the wind was favorable, by hoisting a removable aluminum mast with a sail; the mast was stored in my backpack.

The rudder at the stem was controlled by a double rudder assembly that I operated with my feet. There was a centerboard fastened to the arm of the floats, so that it was within reach and easily maneuverable. The cockpit, which featured a built-in compass, was enclosed by a waterproof neoprene sprayskirt, which fastened around my waist to keep icy water from getting in. Finally, a spare double paddle was fastened in two parts on either side of the bow.


My friends and the journalists left after filling up on anecdotes and interviews. Jean-Philippe went back to Europe with my sled, my skis, and the rest of my winter equipment. I was alone again, content with the four days that we had spent together and ready to resume my journey on June 7. By that date, according to statistics based on annual satellite analyses, the river should be clear.

But the thermometer dropped suddenly again, and the ice stopped breaking up at the river's mouth. On the eighth, I was still in Tuktoyaktuk. Norma and Paul insisted on giving me a place to stay as long as necessary. They also continued to refuse to accept a penny from me.

On June 16, ice was still covering the Mackenzie Delta, and I no longer had the right gear to cross it on foot. I would be forced to haul my kayak over the slushy late season snow. Yet a miracle occurred during that night, as if, while I lay sleeping, a huge broom had swept all of the ice away. There was hardly a speck of ice anywhere on the delta, but the wind blowing between thirty and forty knots that had "swept up" was still keeping me from leaving.

There were two schools of thought about the best way to leave Tuktoyaktuk by kayak: either paddle around the Mackenzie estuary via the Beaufort Sea, or paddle upstream to reach the Reindeer Channel and follow it to Shallow Bay on the far shore of the estuary.

The next morning, the three-foot waves surging across the estuary made me choose the second option.

For the first time during the expedition, I was dressed in summer clothing. I wore wool socks and sneakers that would dry easily and fast (I also had a pair of insulated neoprene slippers), and long underwear beneath my Gore-Tex trousers. Same thing on top: an insulating stretch shirt and Gore-Tex wind-breaker, a hood covering my baseball cap, and neoprene gloves.

I said good-bye to Paul and Norma and climbed into the cockpit of my kayak. I set out into the mouth of the river. Another leg of my expedition was beginning. A new challenge and the excitement made me forget about the winter entirely.

My bottle of drinking water was tucked under my sprayskirt and my trail snacks were in the pockets of my parka—once I started out, I wouldn't stop until the end of the day. I hoisted the sail with the crank, I dropped my centerboard into the water, and I was off.

Paddling is less a matter of pulling the paddle toward yourself than of hauling your boat toward the paddle, using it as a point of support. In other words, it's the kayak that goes toward the paddle and not the other way around. Extending the stroke behind you and pulling the paddle out of the water too late actually pulls the kayak downward, thus slowing it down. The stroke should follow a straight line, and the paddle should be planted in the water as far forward as possible to extend the distance covered. Finally, the straighter the paddle is when it enters the water, and the more of the paddle's surface is immersed, the more effective the stroke will be.

To keep from wasting energy, I used my whole body—feet, legs, hips, shoulders, and so on—in each stroke. I tried to be as connected as possible to the kayak, whose rigidity constitutes an especially effective transmitter of energy. In order to minimize my effort and prolong my endurance, I created a lever effect between the lower hand, which pulled, and the upper hand, which pushed.

I changed sides every hundred—or two hundred—strokes of the paddle. Since that tended to cause the kayak to veer in one direction, I used the rudder to compensate for it. The rudder's role became even more crucial when the boat approached the shoreline, to keep the kayak from turning sideways and being capsized by the waves. I had a cable that allowed me to lift the rudder, to keep it from breaking on impact with the rocky bottom. Kayakers know that to reduce the wear and tear on the rudder caused by the constant pressure of water, it is important to use the rudder deftly, delicately, and as sparingly as possible.

Despite the wind, when it was blowing in my favor, and my razor-sharp stern (considering the distances I would have to cover, I wanted to reduce the water resistance as much as possible), I noticed that my kayak was answering only flabbily to my strokes. However hard I paddled, I couldn't get any forward motion—at least, not as much as I should have. If it was a matter of weight, my food rations would become much lighter with the passage of time; if it was because I wasn't in very good shape, that was a different matter. In a few days my upper body, which hadn't gotten very much exercise since the beginning of the expedition, would regain much of its strength.

On the first day, facing into the wind and fighting a four-knot current that pushed me downstream whenever I stopped paddling, I spent my time slaloming between residual ice floes and trying to find my way through the labyrinth of braided channels of the Mackenzie River. It was cold and plenty of water was making its way into the kayak, but the hard work of paddling often made me feel uncomfortably warm. So I took off my wind-breaker, keeping only the fast-drying insulating layer on my upper body.

In twenty hours of nonstop paddling, I had covered only twenty-three miles. Soaked and exhausted, I spent the first night along the East

Channel (the Mackenzie has three channels—the East, Middle, and West Channels) on a small rocky beach.

I began to wonder if it had been a good idea to go up the river against the current, but there was no time to waste on second-guessing.

When I woke up, the wind had died down, and the river was smooth as glass. I decided to take advantage of the lull and try to reach the Reindeer Channel. Since the river was still running very fast, I hugged the banks. The problem was that the thaw had made the river overflow those banks, and the shoreline was difficult to make out. I would repeatedly find myself scraping bottom in water that was barely a foot deep. When I returned to the middle of the river, I had better clearance, but the current became a problem again. I stopped after twelve hours and nineteen miles covered. In order to reach the Bering Strait before September, the beginning of storm season, I would need to cover at least twenty-eight miles a day.

The next day I got lost in the maze before finding Reindeer Channel. After another few hours of hard work, I was in the West Channel. Finally, I could stop fighting the river's current! Now my kayak was shooting forward like an arrow with each stroke of the paddle.

But the West Channel was also flooded. Its banks were impossible to find, or else so boggy that it was impossible to find a dry spot where I could pitch my tent. I wound up sleeping sitting up in my kayak.

The estuary of the Mackenzie River was changing its appearance every day. The river now meandered through curves lined with beaches of sediment. When I landed on the beach that I had chosen as a place to spend the night, I discovered that it had a muddy surface where I got stuck with my kayak. The beach was covered with grizzly tracks to boot—which made sense since this was where they crossed the river.

Nonetheless, I was completely exhausted, and I couldn't paddle another foot. To hell with the bears! I pitched my tent, wolfed down a little food and collapsed. If a grizzly bear had come sniffing around my campsite, it wouldn't even have woken me up from my deep slumber.

I wound up emerging from the river channel into Shallow Bay on the Beaufort Sea. Shallow Bay takes its name from the great quantities of sediment that are pushed out into the sea by the river and which have built up its bed. From here, the land was nothing more than a narrow, slightly dark line along the horizon. There was no more current to deal with, but there were waves, pushed by a north wind, which battered against the right side of my boat in an endless succession of rollers. My floats kept me from capsizing under this repeated assault, but it certainly wasn't pleasant traveling.

I was even more focused on observing my surroundings than when I was traveling overland, and I was even more at their mercy. I had to be more attentive than ever. Whatever might happen, I was glad to be out of the estuary, and I paddled optimistically and vigorously.

Nine miles of ocean lay between me and Tent Island, so-called because the Inuit always pitched their tents there before setting out to hunt beluga (they eat its blubber). In fact, I noticed that these orca-sized albino whales were all around me, spouting their geysers skyward and letting the sun reflect off their rubbery curves. There were hundreds of them! Their sheer numbers gave the general impression of an optical illusion, or a giant impressionist canvas. Overwhelmed, I stopped paddling and paused to take in this unique spectacle.

The whales swam toward my kayak, and I could touch them by just reaching out my hand. They could have overturned my boat with a stroke of their tails, or by surfacing underneath it, but their ultrasensitive sonar allowed them to avoid all obstacles with the grace of ballet dancers.

In the foreground of a horizon line now barely punctuated by the first foothills of the Brooks Range, the waves rolled forward and died with scarcely a whimper as they washed over the tundra that barely rose above the water and disappeared behind the ocean swells. The absence of a sharp-sloped shoreline made it difficult to find a suitable campsite. Moreover, the absence of ice and snow would have deprived me of drinking water, if it weren't for the fact that the ocean water was practically desalinated by the vast quantities of freshwater that the Mackenzie River Delta washed out to sea, even at this distance.

The next day, not far from Hershel Island, two- or two-and-a-half miles from the coast, I saw foaming waves crashing on the sandbars along the coast. The waves that break over the sandbars are higher when the wind is rougher and the bottom shallower, and I realized that I needed to venture out into deeper waters. I tried to sail out to sea, but a gust of wind that was too strong to fight drove me toward the breaking waves. One of the waves lifted me up and capsized my kayak despite the floats; it tossed me facedown onto the sandbar! My mast was driven into the sand, and the kayak righted slightly onto its side. The next wave hurled me once again, and although the mast kept me from capsizing completely, I was lying in the icy water, twisting desperately to keep my head above water. I was afraid I would lose the equipment fastened to the rear deck. Moreover, I wanted to get out of the kayak to right the vessel, but if I opened up my sprayskirt, the seawater might well soak my provisions and my fuel supplies. I tried pushing down on my paddle, but the waves that continued to break over me were too powerful.

There was no choice. I got out of the boat and by hauling on the fore mooring line, I was able to pull it farther up onto the sandbar. I did my best to drain the boat of seawater, but the waves continued to fill it. I hauled it a little higher onto the shoal, which allowed me to bail it out completely. I finished drying it with a sponge, and I could now see that the waterproof compartments had remained pretty well dry but that I had lost a few food rations and a water can.

I had just had an icy bath, and I was shivering from the cold, but I needed to plunge back into the rollers, to get back out into the open sea. The waves were coming in a series, and I counted them to identify the sequences and figure out when there would be a lull during which I could try to make it through. If I guessed wrong, the huge waves would toss me back onto the shore.

By paddling like a madman, I managed to get through the barrier of the rollers. The wind died down, and I took advantage of the calm to paddle as far as possible from the sandbars.

Soon, I couldn't even see the land except when the massive swells lifted me high. I was drenched, but paddling warmed me up.

Heading due west, I coasted along the shore at a safe distance. And when the wind began blowing offshore, I took care not to get too far out. If a squall were to push me out to sea, I wasn't sure I'd be able to make it back in.

Suddenly, the wind started veering madly in all directions. It was time to head back in to dry land. I barely had time to turn the kayak landward when the wind started to blow again, this time from the shore. I paddled hard, but not too hard, to save the reserves of strength that I would need in order to make a final effort. I had been paddling long days for nine days straight, and I could feel a fatigue coming on, caused both by the overloaded kayak and the fact that my arms weren't in shape for the workout they were now getting.

As I got closer to the coast, I realized that the currents had pushed a number of small icebergs between me and it. The waves, many feet high, partly obscured them, but their sharp ridges came into view periodically, pointing up menacingly.

The waves were likely to hurl me full onto them, and the impact might well be fatal.

At this point, I had a difficult choice to make: either allow myself to be pulled out to sea by the wind, with slim odds of making it back in to land, or else allow the waves to shatter me on the icebergs.

As if things weren't uncomfortable enough, I suddenly felt a pressing urge that—after twenty hours on the water—soon became irresistible. The sea was choppy, and the wind was blowing furiously: there was no chance of undoing my sprayskirt to urinate overboard. Overwhelmed and exhausted, I peed on myself like a baby. I was drenched with seawater on the outside and with urine on the inside, and all day long all that I had eaten was a chocolate bar and some peanuts. Exhaustion swept over me.

I had only one aspiration: to sleep. However, access to the land was blocked off by a barrier of ice floes and icebergs three football fields wide. And there was no question of falling asleep sitting in my kayak. The minute I failed to pay close attention, the waves would toss my little craft to its destruction on the ice. And if I found myself upside down in the water, wedged between blocks of ice, it would be impossible to right myself. My kayak would wind up broken in two; my equipment would sink to the seabed; and I, without even a life jacket to help me, would drown.

Staying as focused as fatigue would allow, I paddled in to where the waves were breaking. Constantly pushed back out to sea, I worked my way back in, trying repeatedly to find a way through. But the ice was growing thicker and thicker around me.

Paddling constantly against the offshore wind, I could only think of one solution—to wait for the smallest in a series of waves, surf over it with my kayak, plunge down among the blocks of ice, and then jump out onto the ice and haul my boat behind me, climbing up until I reached a surface where I could rest safely.

Only the first half of the icy wall was moving, the part where the waves were breaking. The second part of the wall was fixed to the shoreline. So I didn't need to get all the way across to reach safety. But if I fell down between the icebergs before I made it across, I wouldn't be getting back up.

The consequences were clear: succeed or die.

I positioned myself just outside a gap that looked clear enough to paddle through. I waited for the last in a series of waves—the smallest one—and launched myself forward. The wave took me in, among the icebergs, and dropped me . . . with the bow of the kayak on the ice. I was repeatedly raised, then shoved down, lifted up on one side while the other side plunged under, and I attempted to regain my balance by pushing my paddle against everything within reach. It wasn't easy, in a giant ice shaker filled with ice cubes each the size of a truck.

When a series of large waves came in, I felt sure that they were going to turn me over like a pancake and snap my kayak like a twig! I didn't have time to get out of the kayak. The first wave lifted me up and sent me crashing against the ice. My rudder splintered, and the kayak cracked all over. The second wave smashed me against an iceberg, and the bow of my kayak was wedged against it. Another slab of ice bobbed up beside me, and ripped off one of my float arms. My kayak was going down. The third wave lifted the rear of the kayak and drove me bow first into the water, but the functioning float arm was wedged between two blocks of ice, so I couldn't get clear. The next wave tore me away from the iceberg and spun me around forty-five degrees so I was facing the waves now.

The next wave hoisted me higher, higher . . . and then broke just after I made it over the crest. The trough in its wake pulled me back, and I was still looking out to the open sea. With one twisted float arm pointing uselessly at the sky, I saw the next series of massive waves approaching. The first one crashed down with full force onto the front of my kayak and took me down. This time, I was completely underwater. I shot to the surface on the other side, but the next roller swallowed me up again. Since I no longer had a rudder to steer with, I paddled forward furiously on the side of the broken float. So it was the missing float that saved me, by allowing me to make longer strokes and to come up fast on the next wave, which lifted me up and crashed down on the stern of my kayak. After I floated over the next wave, I saw with a sigh that I had done it! I had escaped from the icebergs and made it back out to sea through the barrier of the rollers!

I had really thought that I wouldn't make it out alive this time. Sure, I could have abandoned my kayak to give myself a better chance of reaching dry land. But without food or shelter, and no way of calling for rescue, I would have died anyway.

Still in a state of shock, I resolved not to try to make it through the ice floes again until I could find a safe and reliable opening. If the wind was dragging me out to sea, I could at least nap, following the swell, and recover my strength for a while as I drifted. But I wasn't very comfortable with the idea of sleeping aboard a kayak with a float on just one side, especially since my kayak was still weighed down with a month's supply of fuel and provisions.

I kept on paddling along the iced-in border of the shoreline, until all of a sudden I saw coming toward me an immense ice floe, which in short order had wedged me against the icebergs clustered along the shore. If the ice floe continued on its course, I would be crushed.

But this huge expanse of ice actually formed a floating breakwater, behind the shelter of which the ocean was suddenly smoother than a marina. I took advantage of the calm to accelerate, and caught up with another large chunk of pack ice, drifting near the shore. It would still be impossible to get in to dry land unless I was willing to take on the challenge of another fifteen-hour battle, and I definitely wasn't up to it. I could easily commit a fatal mistake in my fatigued state. It would be a better idea to get some rest before charging off to the attack again.

I pitched my tent on this second floating chunk of ice field, which was also drifting in toward shore and breaking apart with resounding cracks. But it would take more than that to keep me from sleeping—I had been operating in overdrive since that morning. I would wake up every two or three hours all the same, just to make sure that the ice wasn't cracking apart beneath me. Aside from that, I slept like a baby.

When I woke up, the sky was blue, and a beautiful day was dawning. The weather was balmy enough for sunbathing, but that would not have been advisable. The ice on which I had been sleeping had been busy melting and cracking apart while I slept, like an ice cube in a bathtub. My tent was practically in the water.

I was racked with aches and stiffness for the first time in a long while, but otherwise I was in excellent shape. I patched up my rudder with epoxy adhesive, improvised a repair of the broken arm of my float with a piece of driftwood, and set course for dry land once again.

My route was blocked by a labyrinth of ice and water, where my kayak had to serve alternately as a boat and as a sled. Sometimes I would take a running leap from one floe to the next and then haul my kayak toward me. Or else I might use the kayak as a bridge between floes, if the gap were sufficiently narrow. But when there was a gap of fifty feet or so of water, my tactic was to run as fast as possible, pushing the kayak right up to the edge of the ice, and then leap into it as it went into the water. The momentum was usually enough to take me and my boat to the other floe.

Paddling, jumping, hauling, and surfing, I improvised my way toward Hershel Island, where the ice had absorbed the slushy melting snow until it had become passable once again. Wearing sneakers and using a makeshift harness, I was dragging a boat that was certainly not built for the purpose, much less to carry a load of 240 pounds. When a wide fissure in the ice allowed me to drop my kayak into the water, I hauled it from the water as if I were some kind of ancient slave laborer. When along the coast, where the ice always melts first, a broader gap of open water allowed me to use the kayak for its intended function, I was forced to maneuver along the jagged trajectory of the shore.

In short, I was negotiating terrain for which my equipment was no longer suitable. I thought of calling Jean-Philippe and asking him to bring back my winter equipment, but I decided to wait. I wanted to make some forward progress, in the hope that the ocean water would clear up a little farther along. Even when Cathy informed me that the ice was compact and solid all the way to Cape Barrow—including along the shoreline—I still hesitated. The ice breaks up rapidly during this season. The ice "rots" invisibly, and it might very well break away from the mainland from one week to another, or one month to the next, or just about any day now. It was impossible to say for sure.

In the end, I kept the kayak. It looked like that was the right decision because the currents had broken the ice up in places around Hershel Island, opening a passageway along the coastline. Thanks to the breakwater effect of the ice farther out, the sea was smooth as glass to the immense joy of this paddler. I had no idea how long or how far these ideal conditions were likely to continue, but they only encouraged me in my decision to remain in summer mode.

After Hershel Island I began to see sandbars just breaking the surface. Beyond them the ice was still solid, but between these sandbars and the coastline, the water from the mouths of two large rivers a bit farther ahead had melted the ice. I zipped along as if I was paddling across a swimming pool. That day I covered about forty miles.

The sandbars generally extended the length from one cape to the next, running along the coast at a constant distance—except when the navigable corridor was only a few yards across or when there was a break in the coastline, forming a lagoon between coastline and sandbar that might be many miles wide.

When the sandbars and shallows began to encroach on the mainland, I was increasingly obliged to haul my kayak up onto the shore and drag it over the ice for a way before I could find another passable stretch of water. This was exhausting work, and it usually cut my mileage back down to about twelve and a half per day.

The water itself was sometimes so slushy that I couldn't drag my paddle through it, but not yet sufficiently frozen over for me to be able to hike over it. In such situations I would have to beach my kayak again to get past the obstacles. When I was forced onto the shore, I would bog down in a mushy liquid snow. I began to truly understand that I was here at the worst time of the year.

Nevertheless I made progress, at the price of fewer and fewer hours of sleep, alternating between paddling, trekking, climbing, and jumping in this seemingly endless labyrinth of ice and water. On the morning of June 28, at exactly eight in the morning, I got out of my kayak to climb to the copper marker that marked the boundary between the Yukon province of Canada and the state of Alaska. I photographed this solitary monument, built in the middle of nowhere, from every angle. In the small symbolic turret next to the benchmark, a family of seabirds had built a nest and were crying out in alarm as I drew near them.

Canada was behind me. I had done it, I had crossed it!

Since there was no one there to congratulate me, I decided I might as well press on. I climbed back down to my kayak and, with a triumphant paddle stroke, I entered Alaska by sea. Nothing could stop me now. Not even the fragments of ice and the slushy summer snow that were doing their best to slow me down.

I hugged the coastline of the North Slope, an immense swampy tundra that extended more or less the length of Alaska's northern coastline. This time of the year, all the birds of the Far North and beyond met up there for a symphony of chirps and warbles. The snow geese streaked across the sky in long lines in close formation, flocks of thousands of Arctic ducks sailed overhead like banners in the sky, and families of swans crowded the shores. This was the season of courting dances and mating, of the great congregation of the species with a spectacular backdrop and not a single human disturbing the vista except for me.

When suddenly it seemed as if the earth was moving, I realized that I was witnessing the annual migration of the Porcupine Herd, the largest herd of caribou ever observed—120,000 animals all heading together to Canada. The procession extended from one end of the horizon to the other. I had never seen anything like it!

The North Slope is like that—a never-ending spectacle, insanely beautiful.

I hurried on toward the village of Kaktovik, which lies a little farther along the coast on Barter Island. I had not planned to stop there, but I hoped I would have a chance to repair my rudder and my float arm there. Moreover, since I had not seen a living soul since Tuktoyaktuk, I wouldn't mind catching a glimpse of a few human faces.

I raised my sail again and made twenty-five miles in one day. The wind grew stronger, and my daily distances climbed to thirty miles, which I achieved by paddling and sailing from twelve to sixteen hours a day under a sun that never set.

Four days after entering Alaska, I fought one last battle against the ice that continued to surround Kaktovik, and I finally hauled my kayak up the little beach that serves the village as a harbor. Facilities were rudimentary in this tiny village where, for lack of running water, residents still used buckets for toilets.

"Where you come from, like that?" yelled a man who was busy hauling a boat up onto the beach.

"From Tuktoyaktuk!"

"Impossible, with all that ice!" he replied. So I gave him a brief account of my most recent adventures, and I asked him if he could show me the way to the house of a friend of the Norwegians I had met near Cambridge Bay. I hoped to ask their friend for a place to stay. Unfortunately, the house was locked up, and the owner had left on an expedition along the Colville River.

Leonard, the man I met on the beach, and his girlfriend, Caroline, generously offered to take me in. The next morning, a little repair shop that fixed road-maintenance vehicles helped me to get my kayak back into shape. The owner, a master handyman, carved me a new rudder out of a piece of sheet metal and made me a new float arm out of a length of pipe.

On the fourth of July I celebrated Independence Day with residents who were handing out Coca-Cola and hot dogs in the streets of Kaktovik.

The next day, forty-eight hours after I arrived in town, I picked up my refurbished kayak and went back to sea after informing local authorities that I had entered American territory.


To the west of Barter Island, the water was partly clear for about twenty miles, and then it was frozen again. I set up camp on the ice after a day wending my way among the blocks of ice. The next day things looked bad because the fragments of pack ice were too small to walk over, too big to push aside. I retreated to the beach and shifted back and forth between sand and ice, depending on the state of the terrain. Most of the time I used my kayak as a sled, which didn't help the rudder any. When I was able to cut over dry land, I would roll my boat over lengths of driftwood, much like the builders of the Egyptian pyramids. It was daunting labor, and it didn't yield much speed. I was progressing at a rate of less than one mile per hour.

When I was fifty miles from Prudhoe Bay, I noticed a pair of barracklike tents, surrounded by tools and oil-exploration equipment, evidently the property of an oil company. I arrived, soaked, at two in the morning after a lengthy battle with the pack ice that resulted in numerous plunges into the water. Despite the midnight sun, there was a light on inside.

I yelled, "Is anyone there?"

Three round-eyed, tousled heads poked out of the tent.

"Who are you? What are you doing here?"

The three men were ornithologists who were studying the effects of oil exploration on the nesting of birds. Their names were Eric, Craig, and Craig. They helped me repair my rudder and offered me a camp cot for the night.

When I opened one eye in the middle of the night, a violent wind blowing out of the north had shoved a veritable ice field against the shoreline. It would be impossible to make it all the way to Prudhoe Bay hauling my kayak over those blocks of ice.

The next day nothing had changed. I took advantage of the opportunity to go for a hike on the tundra. My three guides, excited by my accounts of my adventures, reciprocated by showing me all the secrets of Arctic birds, including the habits and customs of each species.

I was especially astonished by the amazing habits of the eider ducks. I knew that in summer eider ducks migrated to the Far North to lay their eggs. I also knew that the female eider ducks shed their feathers and used them to keep their young warm—hence the trademark Eider for my ultraprotective insulating winter suits. But no one seemed to know where the mysterious eiders traveled for the winter. Only recently had someone attached homing devices to a few individual ducks and discovered their incredible secret. When winter comes, they do not fly south. Instead they settle on the water, right in the middle of the Bering Strait! There, millions of them cluster together side by side in a compact mass, and they prevent the ocean from freezing over with their own body heat and the incessant paddling of their webbed feet. They dive to the ocean bottom—they are capable of descending to depths of one-hundred feet—to catch shrimp and mollusks. And this goes on all winter long! During that whole time, the enormous quantity of duck droppings enriches the seabed, and thus helped to nourish their marine food sources—a perfect natural cycle!

✦  ✦  ✦

The ice was showing no signs at all of opening up, so I decided to start off again despite everything. Eric and the two Craigs recommended that I warn British Petroleum that I would be arriving in Prudhoe Bay, where the company had built a huge car-accessible causeway jutting out into the ocean about five miles. That jetty, whose pipelines hooked up with the main Alaskan pipeline, was called Endicott, and access to the area around it was strictly prohibited without special authorization.

I was determined to get a permit for myself. So I called a certain "Joe," who was in charge of security for the oil company in Anchorage. He refused my request brusquely. I told him that my kayak was damaged, that it needed urgent repairs, and that I needed supplies. If I was forced to choose between the danger of dying at sea and the risk of arrest, I would land on Endicott property, with or without his permission. I added that my crew was going to meet me in Prudhoe Bay and that it needed to have authorization to meet me on the jetty. I also mentioned that I was planning to alert the press to my arrival, which I thought might give him a little extra incentive.

"Joe" wound up authorizing me to come in. His men would pick me up at the end of the jetty, and they would take me back to the same place when I was ready to leave. However, my crew was forbidden to approach. I asked again, but he wouldn't budge. This obstructionist cop put up a wall of stupidity and treated me like garbage.


I continued to grapple with the pack ice, and the gusty winds made my progress even more difficult. Finally, though, I saw on the horizon the characteristic flame of deep-sea drilling platforms. I had reached the famous causeway.

I climbed up onto it and walked calmly between the pipelines. There was no one in view in any direction. I had just entered a supposedly high-security area, and there wasn't a guard anywhere in sight to ask me who I was.

INSET PHOTO: After the helicopter deposits me, Cathy, and the kids on the ice field, I take my first steps toward the North Pole and discover the terrible weight of my sled. On this training mission for my *Arktos* expedition, I don't make it to the top of the world, but I gain invaluable experience with the cold and ice. *Photo by Sebastian Devenish*

ABOVE: As the Arctic night comes to an end, nearly five hundred miles of barren ice stand between me and the North Pole. At that moment I understand the true meaning of the word *solitude*. *Photo by Sebastian Devenish*

The moment comes to test the tent and the rest of the equipment that will allow me to survive at extreme temperatures colder than seventy-five degrees below zero.

*Photo by Sebastian Devenish*

My logistics team, family, and friends join me for a photo in front of the globe monument that stands atop the cliffs of North Cape, Norway. My departure on the grand expedition draws near. *Photo by Sebastian Devenish*

LEFT: August 4, 2002. At last, my departure! I set my course for Greenland on the other side of the Atlantic Ocean. *Photo by Sebastian Devenish*

BELOW: I struggle to moor my tent to the ice with my ski poles before it's blown away in a gale. Despite the poor conditions, I cross Greenland in fifteen days and eight hours, a record time for the route I chose. *Photo by Sebastian Devenish*

In Nanisivik, the hut that serves as the airport terminal is temporary, just like all the other buildings. Just a few days after this photo was taken, the building was demolished and renaturalized along with the rest of the town. *Photo by D.R. *

RIGHT: An Inuit friend offers me this traditional outfit to wear for a photo. Despite its warmth, this clothing would not meet the functional requirements of an expedition like mine. *Photo by D.R. *

Just as I arrive in Nanisivik in Arctic Canada, the mining town is shutting down operations for good. The smiles on the faces of the miners show their relief, but also conceal feelings of nostalgia and even anguish. *Photo by Sebastian Devenish*

In Nanisivik, Cathy and my daughters, Annika and Jessica, spend a few days with me as I wait to depart on the next stage of my journey. *Photo by D.R. *

Circumstances force me to travel on foot between Arctic Bay and Pelly Bay around the southern end of the Gulf of Boothia. I am the first one ever to complete this route in the dead of winter. *Photo by Sebastian Devenish*

Within a few weeks, the Arctic winter turns me into a Yeti-like creature. My face is so plastered with ice that my eyes are barely visible. *Photo by Sebastian Devenish*

After testing my kites during my Greenland traverse, I break them out again to help me cover more daily mileage en route to Alaska. *Photo by Sebastian Devenish*

My sleeping bag is designed to keep me warm at temperatures as cold as forty degrees below zero. I have to keep my head on the outside so that the moisture of my breath doesn't form ice in my sleeping bag and cause me to freeze to death. *Photo by Sebastian Devenish*

Come summer, I struggle in my kayak to avoid being thrown ashore by the surf or swept out to sea by strong currents. *Photo by Sebastian Devenish*

The Russian bureaucracy earns its fearsome reputation, but after four months of administrative delays, I venture out into uncharted terrain. When I pass through the rare small town, relics like this monument of Lenin remain as evidence of the fallen Soviet Empire.

*Photo by Sebastian Devenish*

Few men have ever seen the wild terrain I crossed in Eastern Siberia.
*Photo by Sebastian Devenish*

Vasya, the only remaining resident of the abandoned Russian town of Tobseda, grew to be a true friend of mine during my three-week stay with him. Although the Russian bureaucracy foiled my plans at every turn, I found the Russian people to be amazingly warm and generous wherever I went. *Photo by Sebastian Devenish*

October 21, 2004. After two years and three months, I return full circle to North Cape and celebrate my expedition's success—and more important, being reunited with my family. *Photo by Sebastian Devenish*

Finally, I chanced upon a panel with a number to call in case of an emergency, so I got out my satellite phone: "Hi, this is Mike Horn. I'm on the causeway. What are you waiting for? Come on out and arrest me."

There was panic at the other end of the line: "What? Where are you, exactly? How long have you been there?"

A few minutes later, a team arrived in a truck and picked us up—me and my kayak—and took us back to Prudhoe Bay.

The town was not a town at all, not even a village, but rather a cluster of barracks where about thirty Inuit lived, surrounded by employees of the oil company. A hotel had been built to lodge them, and an airport, served by Alaska Airlines, to bring them in and out. The place was vaguely sinister, and its second name seemed to suit it well: Deadhorse.

There I met up with Jean-Philippe, Sebastian, and Raphaël, who had arrived before me to bring supplies of equipment and food, and to film me as I arrived and left. Sebastian had called the notorious "Joe" to request authorization to travel with the guards who had been sent to pick me up at the end of the causeway. Just long enough to take a few pictures. "No!" the head of security had answered, brusquely. Could he go back with them when they took me back out onto the jetty? Same answer. Sebastian asked if they could meet me somewhere else along the coast. "No!" yelled Joe before hanging up on him.

It was very obviously prohibited to access the sea where the petroleum facilities were located! As for sneaking past security and reaching shore, that was out of the question. There were surveillance cameras and guards all along the coast. If I had managed to slip through the net on the causeway, it was only because I had arrived by sea.

Frustration and anger reigned with my team members. After looking at the matter from every angle imaginable, we finally decided that my three teammates would fly to Nuiqsut, a small village located farther south on the Colville River, and there they would hire an Inuit who would take them in his boat around Prudhoe Bay, and then return along the same path as me. It would take a day. And then they could at least film my arrival . . . or my virtual arrival.

I carefully "forgot" to report this project to the guy in charge of secu-rity at Prudhoe Bay—a warm and understanding fellow, unlike his boss—when he accompanied me back to the end of the jetty.

When I got out to the causeway, though, it was impossible to leave. The wind blew so hard it would have driven my kayak back against the rocks.

Wrapped in my sleeping bag, I waited in the lee of the causeway for the squall to die down. Without having planned to do so, I gave Jean-Philippe, Sebastian, and Raphaël, who had already left Nuiqsut, enough time to catch up with me. Via satellite phone, we arranged to meet up. The next day, without any difficulties, they arrived from the sea at the same place that they had been forbidden to enter, and were thus able to film my "arrival" and follow me for two days.

I spent a last night in the cabin where we had all camped together on the banks of the Colville River (also off limits, by the way), and then I headed back out to sea. The ice had all melted at last, and despite a slightly stronger wind, I sailed straight for Cape Barrow. I camped on the tundra not far from the shore, near streams that had become, along with the rain, my sole source of potable water. The sky was clear, the sea was calm, and the summer temperatures—between fifty and sixty degrees—allowed me to wear shorts and a T-shirt. In these conditions kayaking was a picnic, an outing that I could have shared with my daughters.

The next day, July 16, I would turn thirty-seven.

"Mike, what would you like most for your birthday? A day of rest, when you wouldn't have to do anything but sleep, eat, drink, and stroll around to restore the circulation in your legs, all cramped from being in the kayak?"

I answered myself that this was certainly a tempting offer but that I would hate myself the next day for having failed to make any progress.

I had a better idea. I had been born on July 16, so I would paddle for sixteen hours on my birthday. I was born in 1966, So I would cover at least sixty-six kilometers, or forty-one miles, that day. It would be a practical, superstitious birthday gift to myself.

The next day at dawn I wished myself a happy birthday, gobbled down my breakfast, and hopped into my kayak. In a state of euphoria, I put my pedal to the metal, taking risks by crossing bays on a straight line from one cape to the other, which sometimes took me as far as sixteen miles from the shore. I was fortunate enough to escape the wind's punishment. After sixteen hours, I angled in to the mainland. When I finally reached shore, my GPS told me that I had covered forty-two and a half miles, which worked out to sixty-eight and a half kilometers! My personal best in the kayak, and a birthday present that I had really earned.

I fell asleep, exhausted, with a smile on my lips.

Obsessed with the fear of arriving too late and having to wait until the end of winter to cross the Bering Sea, I slept less and only ate when I was hungry. I paddled with all the energy that came from being in shape again. My kayak was lighter and lighter, and the wind sometimes helped by allowing me to hoist sail. Without repeating my birthday record on a daily basis, I still managed to make an average distance of about thirty miles.

The nights were filled with caribou silhouettes. One of them woke me up with a start when it slipped its head into my tent. Then we posed together for a photograph.

Less amiable were the clouds of mosquitoes, so dense that you couldn't open your mouth without swallowing a handful. It was a relief to escape them each morning when I paddled out onto the water.

To save time I would sometimes sleep in the kayak. Lulled by the immense peace of the ocean, I would set down my paddle when I felt sleep coming on. The Beaufort Sea is muddy and shallow. You can even sometimes touch bottom three miles away from shore. The currents are weak, too, so only a violent storm could blow me out to sea, but the gales would wake me up from my drifting sleep before that could happen.

On July 21, two days away from Cape Barrow, my GPS indicated that I was exactly midway through my trip. I had covered 6,200 miles, out of the 12,400-mile distance of my complete circumnavigation of the Arctic Circle. It had taken me nearly a year to get this far, and it might take me that long again to finish the trip. The only thing that I knew for sure was that starting from this point and this moment, I would be on my way home the rest of the time.

I memorialized the moment by taking a picture of my kayak resting on a sandbar. While taking the picture, I noticed two eider ducklings about to be attacked by a bird of prey. I couldn't help myself. I hurried over to scare the predator away and to get the ducklings to shelter. Let's just say that I saved two little lives to celebrate my triumph.

The thirty- and forty-knot winds blowing west for the next two days would normally have prevented small craft from venturing out to sea. But my kayak was so light that it just went faster, and my sail worked perfectly. Pushed along by the tailwind, I had the time of my life surfing over the waves. I wouldn't have traded those days for anything in the world. When I thought back on the winter months I had just endured, I felt as if I were on vacation.

Located on Cape Barrow, the little town of Barrow is a typical Arctic cluster of boxy houses, whipped by high winds and snow squalls. At seventy-one degrees north latitude, Cape Barrow is the northernmost point on the mainland of the continent, America's North Cape.

I reached Barrow at one in the morning. The first two inhabitants that I met were Inuit, and they were both falling-down drunk, but that didn't keep them from generously offering me the hospitality of their sofa for the rest of the night. Just before collapsing into sleep, we celebrated my arrival by opening a bottle of wine.

The next day Cathy reported a wonderful coincidence: *Vagabond* was in Barrow! *Vagabond* was the sailboat on which my friend Éric Boissier had, just the year before, navigated the Northeast Passage, which was the water route along the northern coast of Europe and Asia between the Atlantic and Pacific oceans. This year he was attempting to complete what he had already started and become the first man to sail around the Arctic Circle in two seasons by sailing the length of the Northwest Passage.

For the past two years we had known that, since both our expeditions were planned for the same period of time, we might be able to meet up somewhere in Alaska—without knowing where, of course.

Éric and his girlfriend, France, introduced me to Christine Lambert, who was in charge of the housing construction program for the entire North Slope. When *Vagabond* tied up in Barrow, Christine got in touch with the sailboat's occupants and offered them a place to stay. With the same spirit of generosity, she offered me accommodation as well. And so I left the sofa of my Inuit friends and moved into her house. Her older children had moved out some time before, and she adopted me immediately. She fed me, helped me with my laundry, and took me to see the only dentist in town to have a molar taken care of that had been bothering me ever since I cracked it on a frozen chocolate bar four months earlier. While I was there, I asked the dentist to take a look at an old crown that had come loose a few weeks before. I had stuck it back into place with superglue.

Truly a guardian angel, Christine Lambert even called up the governor of Alaska and asked him to intervene with the Russian authorities to try to facilitate my passage through Chukotka. When I told her about how important it was for me to have a weapon when crossing the Russian steppe and how much trouble I had had in procuring one, she promised me that she would look into the problem.

◆ ◆ ◆

I had hoped to swap my kayak for my sailboat in Barrow. It was clear that I would need a boat because I would reach the Bering Strait in August, and therefore would not be able to cross it on foot. My boat was finally freed of the ice north of Baffin Island, but I couldn't arrange to get it transported to the west coast of Alaska in time for my departure. Threrefore I was in the market for a new boat. Since I was already familiar with the Corsair Marine trimaran, I purchased a twenty-four-foot model at the recommendation of the company representative. I had it built in San Diego, taken by trailer as far as Seattle, and then loaded onto a barge run by the Bowhead Transport Company, which was supposed to deliver it to Point Hope on the west coast of Alaska on the first of August.

However, because of the bad weather that was causing all sorts of problems with cargo routes, Bowhead was running late. I could have them transfer my trimaran onto one of their barges running the sea lift, which is the annual resupply of all the villages along the north coast. The sea lift would arrive in a month. Since I was ahead of schedule, I could afford the delay. But I had ants in my pants, and the urge to get across the Bering Strait was driving me crazy.

I would pick up my boat as scheduled at Point Hope.


A series of bad storms blowing out of Russia battered Barrow for eight days running, and the weather forecasts predicted that there would be weeks of this. There was no chance of setting out in my kayak in sea conditions this rough.

But if I couldn't go by boat, I could still go on foot. A fan of my adventures, the local manager of an air-freight company, Hagland Air, offered to ship my kayak anywhere I asked free of charge. I told him that I would be very grateful and assured him that Wainwright, a village located 125 miles away, would be more than sufficient. I should be there in four or five days. If the weather improved, I could pick up my kayak and proceed by water from there.

I shipped most of my gear and supplies with the kayak, and I carried with me a sleeping bag that a friend of Christine had sent me from Anchorage. I marched along the Skull Cliffs, behind which stretched a marshy tundra crisscrossed by streams and rivers and studded with lakes that were hard to cross. Ocean inlets regularly forced me to take detours around them, and there were plenty of large bays that lengthened my route. It was easy to understand why people preferred to travel by boat and by plane around here.

I was making reasonable progress—about twenty or so miles a day—until I reached a large, boggy peninsula. At the edge of the peninsula were a number of hunting and fishing huts, and nearby I met an Inuit named Hopkins. When I explained to him that I was planning to swim across the bay that extended from the other side of the peninsula, Hopkins told me that the bay was too big. Moreover, it was infested with spotted seals, which could be dangerous to humans. He offered me a cup of tea in his cabin and recommended that I climb down to the bay, hike to the river that emptied into it, and then follow it upstream until I reached a narrow stretch where I could easily wade across.

On the other side of the peninsula, though, I was met with a grim surprise. The shores of the bay were lined with walrus cadavers, swollen and decapitated. This was the work of poachers, ivory traffickers, who hunt the walrus with rifles and then dump their dead bodies into the ocean. The corpses had washed up on shore and lay there rotting. I also found beluga corpses with bear tracks around them.

This appeared to be the work of locals, and if so, there was no doubt that Western greed had infected their hearts and had undermined their traditional respect for the environment and the tenuous balance of nature.

I hiked all the way to the river. According to my map, the river didn't narrow for a good sixteen miles upstream, so I decided to try to cross it right there where it must have been about 150 feet across.

Sheathed in Gore-Tex from head to foot, my backpack wrapped in a plastic trash bag, I waded into the water. It only took a couple of seconds for it to seep through my clothing, which was not waterproof under such conditions. All at once, the cold literally took my breath away.

All around me bobbed ugly heads with the distinctive drooping whiskers of the spotted seal. The unsettling little beasts, covered with white patches as if they suffered from some skin disease, were observing me, perplexed.

I sensed that I wouldn't make it across, so I turned around and climbed back onto the near bank. Soaking wet, walking as fast as I could to restore a little body heat, I went in search of a narrower stretch of river. But the river was flowing west, and if I followed it upstream, I would be losing ground. One way or another, I would have to get across.

Carrying my backpack on my head, I waded into the water for a second time, holding my breath as the icy chill clamped down onto my skin. Once I was chin-deep in the water, I began to dog-paddle, pushing my bag ahead of me, struggling at the same time against the current that was sweeping me out to sea and against the cold paralysis that was spreading through my limbs. I was so cold—probably a result of the fatigue that I had built up during all those hours of hiking—that I might as well have been swimming naked. I nearly gave up a second time, but I hung on, knowing that I probably wouldn't have the strength to make a third attempt. At least not today, anyway. Hobbled by cramps, I finally reached the far shore.

There was no question of stopping to catch my breath, unless I was willing to freeze on the spot. I pushed on in order to warm up. About twenty-five miles of tundra and a few smallish lakes still lay between me and Wainwright. I moved forward through marshland, up to my knees in water. At the end of the day, I looked around in vain for someplace dry to camp, and I finally took shelter on a hummock not much bigger than my tent. It felt as if I were camping on a tiny island. I spent a damp night in my soaking wet sleeping bag. It was impossible to get any sleep until I could get it dry. I would have to reach Wainwright by the next evening.

On the uneven terrain of the tundra, weighed down and thrown off balance by my backpack, I nearly sprained my ankle repeatedly. The damp vegetation drenched me up to my chest, and I hiked bent over to withstand the gusting wind. After fifteen hours of slogging, I allowed myself my first break. The second halt came five hours later. And at ten in the evening, after twenty-five hours of nonstop hiking, I arrived in Wainwright, overjoyed and completely overcome by exhaustion.

My kayak was waiting for me there, and the forecast was calling for a forty-eight-hour window of good weather in two days. I decided to take advantage of the opportunity since the price of a sandwich in Wainwright—twelve dollars—wasn't encouraging me to linger there.

My trimaran was also getting closer to Point Hope, where we had arranged to rendezvous. I thought it over and called my brother Martin to ask him to take delivery of the sailboat and then sail it 110 miles north to Point Lay. I would meet him there.

I was paddling against wind and waves that occasionally kept me from making any headway at all. Battered by rough currents on the approach to Icy Cape, I took shelter between the coastline and the sandbars. Wading through coastal lagoons where the water level fell once the wind veered, I pulled my kayak behind me, two miles from the shore. From the beach, which I could barely make out, I must have looked as if I were walking on water. Once the water got a little deeper, spotted seals started to cluster around my kayak, diving beneath it, leaping over it, orchestrating a spectacular show in an apparent attempt to make me capsize and fall into the water.

On August 10, I reached Point Lay after traveling 140 miles in four days. I got there at dawn on foot, hauling my kayak behind me through the lagoon. Far off on the horizon, I could make out a white spot that I immediately identified. It was my sailboat! Martin had arrived the night before and had called to assure me that I wouldn't be able to miss it. Its presence symbolized the end of the North American portion of my journey.

I had not seen my brother for more than a year. Our reunion was deeply emotional, and we set sail together on a course for Point Hope. It gave us a chance to talk, and he brought me news about our mother and the rest of our family.

In a few days I would experience another joyous reunion because my wife and my daughters were waiting for me at Point Hope; I hadn't seen them since Gjoa Haven six months before.

Cape Lisburne and the squalls blowing down out of the Brooks Range were living up to their reputation. After some trying moments at the helm, Martin and I drew close to Point Hope. The big swells seemed to be trying to warn me that I needed to hurry up and get across to Russia. Autumn would be upon me soon enough, and conditions were going to deteriorate fast in the Bering Sea.

We reached Point Hope around three in the morning. Because it wasn't possible to pull the trimaran out of the water at that time of night, I dropped Martin off on the beach and anchored off shore.

A few hours later, Cathy, Annika, and Jessica appeared on the shore. I sailed toward them, and I held in my arms the three people who mean the most to me on this earth. Once again, my daughters had grown while I had my back turned.

In the blink of an eye, people were crowding all around us, ready to help haul my boat out of the water and onto its trailer. One kind Inuit moved his entire family into his grandmother's house so that we could stay in his house.

Jean Baligand, the president of Groupama; many of the company's executives; the mayor of Château d'Oex, the village in Switzerland where I live and sponsor of this next phase in which I would leave the American continent and start across Russia; along with all the inhabitants of the village and friends who had decided to make the trip up to Point Hope, came to greet me. A local resident named Steve Umatuk was there, too.

When Martin came here to pick up my trimaran and sail it up to

Point Lay, he had contacted Steve, whose number I had gotten from Christine Lambert in Barrow. Steve was the captain of the fire brigade there, and he had given Martin a place to stay in the firehouse. He had fed him and helped him to unload my sailboat from the barge that brought it. In short, he had helped Martin in every way possible.

During our stay in Point Hope, an old whaling town with a population of four hundred, Steve took us to see the cemetery where whale bones served as headstones for the captains of whaling vessels.

Like all North Slope Inuit villages, he explained to us, Point Hope lives off its annual quota of whale. According to the philosophy of the people of the Far North, it is the whale that offers itself up to the hunter in order to provide sustenance to the village. Legend has it that a whale possesses three lives, and so it can offer itself up three times before dying completely. The hunters set out after the whales in dugout canoes covered in oiled walrus skin. Sometimes the whale, three times the size of the boat, will dive and pull the hunters down into the depths. But when the hunters are victorious, they carry the whale's body back to the village before returning its soul to the ocean. Thus the whale will be able to be reborn and offer itself up during the following season, ensuring the community's survival.

As he described this vital bond between men and the giants of the sea, Steve illuminated an important spiritual concept. From that day forward, whales would be more to me than just majestic sea mammals.

We were treated to performances of traditional dances and a special display of Inuit culture. The mayor of Château d'Oex, Jean-Jacques Mottier, handed out Swiss chocolates and cheeses to everyone in the village. An artist who specialized in decoupage, a Swiss specialty, taught her art to schoolchildren and presented the mayor of Point Hope with a tableau that featured me, standing between depictions of the town of Point Hope and the village of Château d'Oex.

The mayor of my hometown christened my sailboat by shattering a bottle of champagne against its hull before the startled eyes of Inuit bystanders, who lived in a "dry" town devoid of alcoholic beverages. I had a difficult time explaining to them that in our culture, this was a libation offered to Neptune, the god of the sea. In the end, they remained skeptical.

At Point Hope, Martin met up with Ronan le Goff, also known as Ronnie, a French skipper who had come to help him to take my boat back once I left it in Providentiya, Russia, on the western shore of the Bering Strait. Ronan le Goff is a noteworthy individual in the adventure world since he was a member of Ellen MacArthur's sailing crew when she tried to break the record for the Jules Verne Trophy in February 2002. My trimaran would be in good hands with him.

I had originally planned to cross the Bering Strait by kayak and then continue along the Russian coastline until the East Siberian Sea forced me to continue on foot. But I was only authorized to enter Russia through the official portal of Providentiya, which forced me to cross the Bering Sea, waters much too rough for a mere kayak. So I would bring the kayak with me aboard the trimaran, and I would embark from Providentiya in my kayak.

Since there were no flights between Providentiya and Point Hope, Martin and Ronnie flew to Nome, at the southern end of the Seward Peninsula. They planned to reach Providentiya by Bering Air, a small airline that was the only one to provide service but whose flights were not regularly scheduled.


Just as I was getting ready to set sail, I was surprised to run into Christine Lambert, my guardian angel from Barrow. She had brought me a special package containing a .45 Magnum.

"It's from one of my girlfriends," she said. "It belonged to her late husband. She is happy for you to have it."


I left Point Hope in good weather, heading west by southwest toward the Chukotka Peninsula. Soon I was within sight of the two Diomede Islands—Little Diomede and Big Diomede—which lie squarely in the middle of the Bering Strait. The border between the United States and Russia runs right between the two of them, and so, during the Cold War, each had served as an advance observation outpost.

As I sailed by, I found myself in the middle of a school of about fifty humpback whales—the first of that species that I had ever seen. Summer was the season when they migrated from the south, passing through the Bering Strait on their way to the Chukotka Sea and the Arctic Ocean—they would retrace their route come autumn. These sixty-foot-long mammals were frolicking all around my sailboat, which was only twenty-four feet long. As I stood admiring them, I thought back to Steve Umatuk's words.

Off of Cape Prince of Wales, where the waters of the Bering Sea rush through the narrowest part of the strait, the wind whipped up short, choppy waves. When the Ice Age ended millions of years ago, it brought about a rise in sea level and the separation of the two continents. It also created this "muddy pond," a relatively shallow stretch of sea that is said to be one of the coldest and most treacherous places on earth to sail. When the wind blows over the Bering Sea, the currents flow more rapidly and the chaotic waves crash in every direction, rushing into the funnel of the strait and triggering whirlpools in the Chukotka Sea. One Frenchman who tried to windsurf across the strait vanished, never to be seen again.

On my satellite phone, my brother was telling me that, because there was no flight available to Provideniya, he and Ronnie were stuck in Nome. They would have to charter a plane and wait three days for authorization to land in Russia.

Between the prospect of a major expense that would cut seriously into my budget, and the idea of landing in Provideniya without anyone there to sail my boat back, I decided to go meet up with Martin and Ronnie at Teller, a village sixty-eight miles north of Nome. They would take a taxi to meet me there.

Just ten or so hours away from Provideniya, I was turning the boat about. That was when my battery decided to go dead so that I had no automatic pilot to allow me to take my eyes off the course for even a minute. I called Martin and asked him if he could find me a spare battery.

Clamped on to the tiller twenty-four hours a day, soaked through and frozen solid, I was surfing over stiff waves, each coming so soon after the other that when the triple hull of my trimaran often plowed into the next wave, I was oh so close to tumbling forward, ass over elbow. With my rudder suspended helplessly in midair, I lost control of the sailboat twice, and I was just seconds away from capsizing. With my sails winched up, I zipped along at sixteen to eighteen knots. I bent every nerve in my body to master my speed in such a way that I would climb up the face of the waves instead of plunging into them. Land wasn't far off, but if I was swept overboard, there was no way I could swim to it. In these icy waters, I would be dead of hypothermia in minutes.

I was beginning to regret having acquired a twenty-four-foot sailboat; it was much too small for the Bering Sea, which was definitely living up to its reputation. This error in judgment might wind up costing me dearly.


Three days after setting course for Teller, I entered its natural harbor, where the water was finally calm. Martin and Ronnie were waiting for me on the beach. A guy named Joe Garney took us in and fed us a spectacular pancake breakfast complete with salmon that he had caught and smoked himself. Joe remains one of the outstanding faces of true generosity that I met in the Far North.

The next day the weather reports were favorable, so Martin, Ronnie, and I set our course for Russia. For the first five or six hours, we sailed along in fine weather, making ten or twelve knots. When night fell—or the shadowy dusk that passes for night at that time of year—the wind died down, and so did our speed.

When morning came, everything changed in a few minutes.

A cyclone and an anticyclone were converging in the Bering Sea at the very moment we were sailing across it, and we were battling sixty-knot winds. With all sails reefed except for a storm jib, we were zipping along at fifteen knots. Clamped onto the tiller, I suddenly saw the vertical wall of a breaking wave off to one side.

There was a good chance we were about to capsize. And Martin and Ronnie were belowdecks, poring over their charts. I steered sharply to head the boat straight into the wave, which broke right over me! Only my instinctive reflex of grabbing onto one of the boom sheets kept me from being swept overboard.

Once I regained control of the boat—and of myself—I discovered that I had lost all my bearings. At that very moment Martin burst out of the hatch and pointed.

"Over there!" he said. I obeyed without thinking, and as a result we narrowly escaped being hit by another breaking wave. The waves were rushing in all directions, completely unpredictable, and the squalls were driving the rain horizontally and tearing off white cascades from the crests of the breakers. Visibility was practically zero. Ronnie and I were taking turns struggling to maintain control of the boat.

The coast blocked the wind. The water began to grow calmer as we approached it, and I played out some sail. But at the mouth of the Provideniya Bay, we were brutally battered by a sixty- or sixty-five-knot wind, which turned the boat over on its side! It skidded along on just one float, like a car on two wheels. Ronnie was at the helm, Martin was in the cockpit, and I was on deck. I lunged at the mainmast to free the halyard and then went forward to pull in the sail to keep us from capsizing completely. I had the sail half rolled up when the boat landed on its "feet" with a resounding "sla-a-a-ap!" and reverberations that we could feel in our shoulders. The wind on the bare mast alone pushed us along at six to eight knots.

Tired but content, we sailed into Provideniya Bay. Once we entered the shelter of the harbor, the wind died away as if by magic and the sea became calm. Ronnie unfurled a bit of sail, Martin pored over the charts, and I sat holding the tiller.

Soon the town came into view, and then the massive outlines of its blocky buildings. It had been thirty-six hours since we left Teller, but time seemed to have run backward. As I looked at Provideniya, I felt as if I had fallen into a hole in the space-time continuum and traveled fifty years back in time.

( 6 )

# Welcome to Russia!

T HERE WERE PRACTICALLY NO LIGHTS VISIBLE in the windows of the rows of buildings. Only fishing nets containing a few meager provisions—in the absence of electricity they served as refrigerators—gave any sign of human life. Looming over the phantom construction yards, cranes that had been frozen in place for months stood like skeletons over heaps of smoking coal. Coal is the only fuel used for heating there. Military vehicles that had been abandoned for decades cluttered the wharfs. Rusted hulks of half-sunken ships obstructed the port.

The grim grayness and decay of the place was strongly reminiscent of the Soviet Union under Stalin. I suspected that the rest of town would be in keeping with what I had seen already.

It was close to 10:00 P.M. when we sailed past the harbor tugboat. The sailor aboard waved wildly at us, yelling to make it clear that we were forbidden to tie up at the wharf. We were expected to drop anchor in the harbor and wait there for the customs agents and the Coast Guard to come out and board our vessel. We knew all of this, but we were exhausted. The ocean had wiped us out, and we wanted only one thing: to feel dry land under our feet.

The man on the tugboat pulled out a bullhorn with which to bark orders at us.

I came about sharply and yelled, "Do you speak English?"

Apparently he didn't. I sailed straight for the dock amidst a shower of "*Nyet! Nyet!*" which I pretended not to understand. Martin and Ronnie leaped to the dock to tie up. The sailor on the tugboat shined his spotlights on us and kept on yelling the whole time.

Hiding out in the cockpit, we sipped our beers and waited for the repercussions of our disobedience.

Martin and Ronnie each had a three-month visa, but it was a Russian visa without the special invitation required to travel to Chukotka, which meant that they were here illegally. They had not planned to stay in Provideniya, but setting back out to sea in such bad weather would be too dangerous. The plan was for them to charter a plane to take them back to Nome, and I would load my trimaran onto the next freighter, wherever it might be bound.

The Russian Coast Guard arrived on the scene in their intimidating uniforms and green-visored caps. They examined the boat with suspicious glances. We invited them to come on board to take care of the formalities under shelter from the icy rain that had begun to fall, but they refused. They demanded of us a declaration that we were not transporting any prohibited goods including ivory, drugs, or any illegal passengers; a detailed inventory of the contents of the boat; and a roster of the boat's crew. We spent a solid hour fulfilling those requests. Then the officers ushered us aboard their tugboat to fill out the rest of the paperwork.

Packed into the dimly lit wardroom, we sat there completing forms from another era. All the blank spaces for the year began with "19." The harder we tried to break the tension, the grimmer the expressions on the soldiers' faces became.

One of the two officers on board was named Dmitry (nicknamed "Dima"). He was the customs officer and spoke a few words of English since he had studied in Alaska. He pulled out of one of his pockets a zippered leather case containing a series of stamps; out of another pocket, a case containing an inkpad; out of a third pocket, an assortment of fountain pens. He puffed a few hot breaths onto the inkpad to moisten it and then pulled out a sheet of paper to test each of his stamps one after the other. He lined up our passports on the table in front of him and began stamping them, rhythmically, in a sort of absurd, interminable dance, performed by a cog in a well-oiled bureaucratic machine. It all unfolded just like a scene out of some bizarre movie.

Once he had completed his ritual, Dmitry said with a straight face, "Welcome to the future!"

I sat openmouthed, absorbing the irony of it all. Of course, what he meant was that we had crossed the international date line, and so it was now, in fact, a day later than in Alaska.

He asked me if I had any weapons. I told him that I carried a rifle.

"Prohibited! I will have to confiscate it." It did me no good to argue that in the wilderness that I was preparing to cross, I would need a rifle to defend myself; Dmitry would have none of it. Martin was sent to get the rifle, which was still in the boat. My GPS suffered the same fate— also prohibited. The argument that I needed it for safety purposes, in order to report my location to my wife, carried no more weight than the other.

Luckily, what we handed over were merely decoys! I had learned my lesson from my misadventure in Igloolik, and I had brought two rifles and two GPSs. The real ones were carefully stowed at the bottom of my luggage.

But I wouldn't have much of a chance of using them yet—at least according to the Coast Guard officers who informed me that I didn't have authorization to travel in Chukotka territory. I was aware this might be a problem. Because a nuclear power plant had been built in the area to provide electricity to eastern Siberia, the peninsula had become a high-security militarized zone, off limits to anyone without special authorization.

In order to help secure me a permit, one of my sponsors got in touch with the multibillionaire businessman Roman Abramovich, who was

also the governor of Chukotka. Abramovich, who was originally from
the capital of the Anadyr province, had reinvested part of his immense
fortune in the economic and industrial revival of the peninsula. He put
us in touch with Alexander Borden, the deputy governor, who was in
charge of foreign affairs. Borden had an entry visa issued; authorization
to cross the province was supposed to come later. Unfortunately, Borden left for Moscow and then went on vacation to Mongolia. My file,
which he must have taken with him, could not be found.

Although I was allowed to enter the country, I couldn't go one step
farther. After stamping a last few stamps onto our passports, the soldiers ordered us to stay on board our boat for the night and to show up
at the customs office the next morning at ten o'clock, when they would
inform us what they had decided about our case. Then they climbed
into their old Jeep, which one of them started up with a crank.

To think that in Alaska, just ninety miles away, I could come and go
without anyone even thinking of asking to see my documents. To think
that in any American or Canadian port, I would only need to go to the
police station, where entering the country was a simple formality.

Soaking wet and crammed together, the three of us shared two
sleeping bags, and we spent an icy cold night worrying. The next day
beautiful weather gave us a more complete view of Provideniya. Or
what was left of it.

During the 1970s, the Soviet regime decided to make this town the
chief point of entry for the Northeast Passage. It was a deep-water port
with about three hundred feet of clearance and could thus accommodate large ships. Moreover, it was sheltered by a glacier, and even at this
high latitude icebreakers wouldn't be needed to clear access to the harbor more than two months per year. The Soviet plan was to make Provideniya and Murmansk, an established Soviet port of supreme
importance, twin port cities of equal importance, each of them the ter-
minus of a major maritime line.

Provideniya grew at a breakneck pace until it had a population of
more than ten thousand, and then, for reasons as mysterious as all the
inner workings of the Soviet Union, all its great projects were cancelled.
All of a sudden the city no longer received supplies of food and other

primary necessities. The beer plant shut down, the industrial bakery that supplied bread for all of Chukotka padlocked its gates, and most of the inhabitants left the city.

The barracks on the opposite shore of the harbor were also abandoned. Their huge rundown walls housed only border guards, customs officers, and the employees of the airport. Martin and I found Dmitry there, who told me that the border guards intended to interrogate me thoroughly and that I would need an interpreter. When I assented, he called a certain Vladimir Bychkof.

Half an hour later, a forty-year-old man arrived. He was shorter than me, with a brilliant gaze. Vladimir, who had earned an MBA at the University of Anchorage and who spoke excellent English, was the interpreter aboard the *Quak,* a large Russian icebreaker that transported joint Russian and American teams of scientists. He also worked as a guide on occasion, and he owned his own company, YUR Trans Services, which managed logistics for American and Canadian mining and land companies operating in Russia. In short, if there was anyone that could help me solve my problems, it was him.

Vladimir was surprised that he had never heard of me. I explained that Alexander Borden, the deputy governor of Chukotka province, was supposed to be seeing to my file personally, but that I had not received any notification from him or anyone else. And, apparently, no one in Anadyr had thought to alert Provideniya of my expected arrival. What's more, no one had bothered to tell me what Vladimir now explained: that after one of the very few explorers who ventured into Chukotka—a Japanese explorer—had been killed there the year before, only a very few authorizations had been issued to travel there, and they all required the explorer to bring along a chaperone! So it seemed that unless I had a travel companion who was acceptable to the authorities, I would not be allowed to cross the territory.

If I had only known, I would have started looking for a companion six months ago.

Vladimir asked me to give him a couple of hours to make a few phone calls, and he parked us in a café—Provideniya had no hotels or restaurants—where they served cabbage-and-potato soup with a side of rye bread. When we got back to the boat, an enormous freighter was unloading construction materials on the same wharf. The captain, a friendly Ukrainian who spoke perfect English, told me that he was hoisting anchor the next day for Korea.

Could he take my trimaran with him?

"No problem, Mike. I'll be leaving practically empty. I've got plenty of room." I'd just have to check with his bosses, a Dutch shipping company. Then I could turn my attention to chartering the plane to take Martin and Ronnie to Nome.

But maybe there was another option. According to the latest weather reports—supplied by the Ukrainian captain—yesterday's storm had yielded to a forty-eight-hour window of good weather. That would be long enough for Martin and Ronnie to reach Nome by sea. They were ready to give it a try, but there was still a degree of risk and I left the choice up to them. We agreed that if the six o'clock forecast confirmed the earlier predictions of clear sailing, they would start off immediately. Through Vladimir, I notified the customs officers and the Coast Guard so that everything would go off without a hitch.

At 6:00 P.M., half a dozen soldiers stood at attention around the trimaran while I unloaded the equipment I would need for the rest of my expedition. The weather report didn't come through until 6:30. It was favorable. The soldiers put a few more stamps on Martin's and Ronnie's passports, asked them to fill out and sign the last few forms, and the soldiers handed over to them, with an honesty worth mentioning, the rifle and the GPS that they had confiscated from me.

My brother and his skipper weighed anchor, and I gave a wave goodbye from the dock.

Martin and Ronnie hadn't yet piloted the trimaran out of the confines of Provideniya Bay when the chief customs officer pointed to my gear piled up on the wharf and said something that Dmitry translated for me: "Now we are going to search all that."

"All that" meant my kayak and half-a-dozen bags containing my provisions, my tent, my sleeping bag, my fuel supplies, my camp stove, my clothing, and so on. Also in the pile were my .45 Magnum, the GPS, and the satellite phone—all illegal—which I had wrapped in a waterproof tarp and stuffed in the bottom of the next-to-last bag, under a pile of clothing.

If any of these items were discovered, I would be expelled from the country and forbidden ever to return. It would spell the end of the expedition.

I asked the chief customs officer if he wanted to dig through everything himself or if he preferred for me to empty the bags myself. Luckily, he let me do it. Starting with the first bag, I unpacked everything, each piece of equipment, explaining the whole time in great detail what it was used for and how it worked. Then I took a long time carefully repacking each object and placing it carefully back into its proper bag. I opened my fifty food rations one after the other. In short, I did everything I could to drag out the process as long as possible, but the chief customs officer wasn't fazed. And, in fact, my camp stove held his attention for many long minutes.

At around seven thirty I began to detect in him the first signs of impatience. My one-man show had been going on for more than an hour, and he had been due back at his quarters at seven. But he still wasn't giving up. We finally arrived at the bag of forbidden objects, which I opened as slowly as possible with my heart racing. In slow motion I took out a parka, some socks, a mitten, a second mitten. When there was nothing left but a thin layer of clothing on top of my gun and my GPS, I tried a poker bluff by shaking the open bag under the officer's nose.

"Look, there's only clothing." And finally he cracked!

"That'll do," he said, with a disgusted grimace. With an enormous—but discreet—sigh of relief, I hastily covered up the forbidden material, though I offered to allow him to inspect my repair kit and my waterproof neoprene slippers. He refused and walked away.

Dmitry looked at me and said, "I hope you aren't carrying a weapon." I replied by asking him if it was possible to buy one in Russia.

Maybe from an Inuit hunter," he said, "but that would be against the rules." We piled all my equipment into an old Russian truck, and Vladimir got in and drove. The few words we exchanged demonstrated for me that he was an okay guy and that I could trust him. His wife had stayed in Alaska, and he could have done the same thing after finishing his studies. However, he harbored a profound loyalty to his country, and he returned to live in his hometown of Provideniya.

He offered me, in a neighboring gray concrete apartment building, the apartment of a woman who had gone on vacation for two months. The price was twelve dollars a day. It would be like being at home, except that at home I wouldn't be under the equivalent of house arrest.

The next day Vladimir Bychkof called one of his friends in Anadyr—Nikolai, a sled-dog driver—who would accompany me to Pevek when the time came. I couldn't get over my delight. All the same, my joy over this important piece of good news was mixed with disappointment that I wouldn't be able to travel alone and that I would have to adapt my style to match the pace of another person. But Vladimir explained to me that Nikolai and I would be traveling independently, and we would rendezvous just before reaching each village and military outpost along the way. We would set off together, then split, and so on—the arrangement suited me perfectly.

Now I just had to resolve the problem with my authorization, but Alexander Borden still couldn't be reached.

The days passed.

Vladimir and I spent part of the time making phone calls, sending faxes all over the planet, exploring every contact or lead imaginable. Cathy was moving heaven and earth—all to no avail.

In the meantime, I stayed in shape by hiking in the nearby mountains and kayaking in the bay. In town, people stared at my red parka, which clashed with the gray surroundings. I would greet their stares with a wave and a hearty *"Privet!"*—meaning hello. The men and women all looked as if they had survived a nuclear war.

Even though I had been traveling solo for nearly a year, it was in Provideniya that I first began to feel genuinely lonely. But it all changed quickly as I made the acquaintance of one person, who introduced me to another, and so on. People took interest in my journey, were fascinated by stories of my adventures, and bombarded me with questions. They sympathized with my bureaucratic plight. Basically they adopted me as one of their own. Bottles of vodka, which were very cheap here, emerged from pockets. Even though everyone here lives beneath—in many cases, far beneath—what would be considered the poverty line in Europe, no one would let me pay for anything, and people lavished their generosity on me. Paying no attention to the fact that I was technically under restrictions by the authorities, families invited me to come stay with them.

None of the buildings had elevators, the staircases were steep and crooked, and tiles were falling off the walls. In the few apartments that were occupied, the poverty was heartbreaking. Between the cracked walls, a table, a kettle, and bare cupboards were often the only furnishings. However many of these apartments I saw, I had a tough time believing that people still lived like this in the twenty-first century.

Under a bare lightbulb—often the only lightbulb in the apartment—I would be offered vodka, sausage, orange slices, and black bread. They would sing Russian songs for me and tell me about life in Provideniya—where hot water was available only occasionally, where electricity worked twice a day on fixed schedules. When the electricity was about to be turned on, women would get ready to do their cooking, and children prepared to do their homework. There was a feverish buzz of activity in that short span of time, and then it was back to night . . . and a melancholy calm.

Dmitry showed a depth of heart and intelligence that soon made us fast friends. He was less of a stickler for the regulations than his fellow guardsmen, and sometimes that got him into trouble. He did his best to broaden the views of those around him—a challenging job, no doubt, but Dmitry was an idealist.

He took me to a Russian *banya* (sauna), where fifty people showed up to see the madman who wanted to walk across Siberia. People smacked one another with *venik*, bundles of leafy birch branches. Questions flew as if it were a press conference, and Dmitry interpreted for me. I even saw a few Russian journalists who asked for interviews.

No one had told me that any foreigner who arrives in Provideniya has three days to go and report his presence to the police. One week after I got there, the police—who had seen the article and the photographs that a journalist had published in Chukotka's main daily newspaper—summoned me to the police station.

While he was accompanying me to the police station, Vladimir Bychkof happened to glance at my passport and stopped short. The passport contained an official invitation from the provincial government, along with a visa for one month! Alexander Borden had given me an entry visa for thirty days even though I had expressly requested a visa for three months, which I expected to renew once I was in the country. Furthermore, the one-month visa was effective not from the date of my entry into Russia but from the day it was issued—which was one month ago on the dot!

And so I was already technically in violation of my visa, and I was put in a guarded residence. How Western of me not to have double-checked the dates! This sort of carelessness can be very costly when you are dealing with a powerful bureaucracy like they have in Russia.

Just for starters, Vladimir and I were both given fines—eight hundred rubles for me and, for having found me a place to stay, five hundred rubles for him. Then the police turned the case of my expired visa over to the FSB, the former KGB.

That same day a major and a lieutenant from the intelligence agency questioned me in Vladimir's office. How had I arrived here? Who invited me? Who exactly was I working for? Why didn't I have the required papers? I mentioned the name of the deputy governor, and I told them that a second visa was supposed to be on its way; but, of course, I couldn't prove anything. The interrogation dragged on until three in the morning. I was exhausted, but I kept insisting that my file was in the hands of Alexander Borden. The FSB agents finally decided to try to call him and—miraculously!—managed to reach him. Borden vouched for me. He knew who I was and was astonished to hear that I had only been issued a one-month visa.

The FSB wound up admitting that I was acting in good faith. Nonetheless, it was a matter of standard procedure at this point. I was going to be put onto the next plane for Moscow, and after that, back home. In short, I was being expelled from the country.

It was nothing short of catastrophic. Once deported, I would be forbidden to return to the country for a year!

The next day Dmitry and I called Alexander Borden. The deputy governor fully appreciated the close call I had had with the authorities and committed to do what he could. In the meantime, Cathy contacted Ian Banner, one of our friends with the Richemont Group and the Laureus World Sports Awards, who reached out to Bernie Ecclestone, president of the International Federation of Formula One racing. Ecclestone in turn spoke with Viacheslav Fetisov, the Russian minister of sport. Fetisov called me to get an explanation of my situation and promised that he would intercede on my behalf. I had some key political connections, but it seemed that even they couldn't keep me from being deported.

Bychkof, Fetisov, Borden. Each of them tried separately to persuade the FSB not to make my expulsion grounds for a year's prohibition of my return. At least let me wait in Alaska for authorization to return to Russia, they argued. Unfortunately, my American visa was in my second passport, which had by now made its way back to Switzerland. And so the FSB couldn't even send me back to the United States. Willing to try anything at this point, I offered to have my brother bring me

my second passport with the American visa that would allow me to return to Nome.

They agreed to this plan, and I called Martin right up. He hopped
on the next flight to start his journey out to the Russian Far East.

Before I knew it, I found myself before the tribunal that would determine my fate. The decorum was intimidating: a podium draped with
red velvet, a Russian flag, neon ceiling lights. A line of judges, an official
interpreter, and two magistrates made up the tribunal that would review my case and decide my punishment. Numerous border guards
were called to testify. Vladimir served as my lawyer. I was seated in the
second row, right behind him. The Coast Guard officers testified one
after another.

Since the proceedings took place in Russian, Vladimir translated for
me in English that I wasn't going to be fined. That was actually a bad
sign because I then expected to be told not to return to Russia for a
long time. But instead I got surprisingly good news. I wasn't barred
from returning to the country. The court recognized that I had been
acting in good faith. As a result, I was authorized to leave Russian territory and to return whenever I liked—this time with the proper documents, of course.

During the course of the ensuing, interminable formalities, the various parties filled out pounds of forms, in keeping with the cumbersome
local tradition that I was starting to get used to.

So I had been sentenced to go back to Nome to wait for authorization to resume my expedition across Chukotka. I had been hoping
that I would be allowed to wait in Provideniya, but no Russian official could overlook the expiration of my visa. After all, a visa couldn't
be renewed on Russian territory except in cases where it was physically impossible to leave within the stipulated time—because of accident, bad weather, or the like—and, even then, only for the duration
of the problem. That is what I explained to the residents of Provideniya who were sad to see me go, which touched me deeply. But the
main emotion I felt was relief that my expedition wasn't going to end
here in this bleak outpost. I would continue. It was just a matter of
time.

◆ ◆ ◆

It was Thursday. I theoretically had until Friday to leave Russian territory aboard a Bering Air plane I would have to charter to take me to Nome. However, the airline officials told Cathy, when she called to charter the plane, that they would need three days to obtain permission to land at Provideniya. And since they didn't fly on the weekend, I was stuck there until Monday. Problems began to develop once again.

Amazingly, Cathy managed to accelerate the process. She pulled strings to schedule the plane for Friday, and since Martin was supposed to land Friday morning in Nome with my passport and American visa, he could just board my plane to bring them to me.

The timing was perfect. Too perfect, as it turned out.

The flight from Seattle to Anchorage was delayed, preventing my brother from getting to Nome on time, and preventing me from returning to the United States. Fortunately, Vladimir was able to persuade the authorities to extend my visa until Monday. That was something.


On Sunday my wife received an e-mail from the U.S. Bureau of Customs and Immigration, informing her that I was forbidden to set foot on United States territory, and that was the final word. They extended this order to my brother Martin, too, who was on his way to Alaska at that very moment!

No one wanted me anymore in either Russia or the United States. It was as if I could no longer move in any direction, like a king who finds himself in checkmate.

It turned out that the reason for turning me away was that I had entered American territory without reporting my presence. Of course their information was wrong! At the first American town I had reached, Kaktovik on Barter Island, I had reported to the authorities, who had informed the Bureau of Immigration. At first, Immigration had wanted to send agents to screen me but then decided against it, requiring only that I report my departure from American territory— which I had done just before leaving Point Hope.

As for Martin, I knew that he had all the papers, all the stamps, and all the visas required.

Cathy contacted the American authorities who had jurisdiction, and they quickly agreed that it was a mistake. The e-mail had been sent by an ill-informed and overzealous official. Crisis averted.

On Monday morning the Provideniya airport officials called me to say that the weather had cleared up. The plane was expected soon, and so was I. One hour later Martin stepped out of the plane with my passport. I showed my American visa to the border guards so that they could authorize me to board.

Then the officer noticed that my Russian visa had expired three days before. I explained that it had been extended until today. Unfortunately, no one had thought to inscribe that extension on my passport. I no longer had the right to leave Russia!

When I was informed that I had to start over from scratch, going through all the formalities of requesting an extension of my visa, I exploded. "Well, I'd like to know what you guys want! First you say I can't stay here, you expel me from the country, and now you refuse to let me leave! Look at that plane! I chartered it just for this trip because you ordered me to! It cost me a fortune! And now what am I supposed to do with it? Send it back?"

This outburst compelled the officer to call his supervisor, who just happened to have with him the official stamp to extend my visa. He stamped my passport, and charged me one thousand rubles.

To avoid the risk of being searched again the next time I entered Russia, I left all of my equipment—carefully packed—with Vladimir. A backpack was all the baggage I carried. Without bothering to open it, my friend Dmitry asked me solemnly whether I was carrying any forbidden goods or if I had anything to declare. I answered no, and this time it was the truth.

After completing that last formality, I marched straight to my plane, passing between two lines of border guards whom I saluted as I passed.

The soldiers surrounded the plane until it began to taxi. I heard the pilot's voice as he identified himself and asked the control tower in Russian for permission to take off. The plane halted momentarily at the end of the runway and then began gathering speed for takeoff.

We briefly flew over Provideniya before tipping the wing in a turn, heading due east on a course for Nome, Alaska, USA—a city where I had never expected to set foot again.

Time passed slowly—between Jeff's cabin, Gerry's trailer, and the Breakers Bar.

Martin had first made the acquaintance of Jeff Darling, buying a new battery for my boat in Jeff's auto supplies store. Jeff then invited him to a barbecue at his house where he had met Gerry Allan. And that's how I happened to have two friends from the minute I arrived in Nome. I made lots more friends in no time, including Sandy, the woman who owned the Polaris Bar, and Olga, her mother, who was a big-hearted baseball fan.

Like those I'd encountered everywhere else in Alaska, the people of Nome were remarkably generous to me, helpful in every way possible. Like so many inhabitants of the Arctic, they were sincere, straightforward, and considerate of others, in part because they live in such harsh conditions. To be here is to be a member of the family. There is no other way to survive.

At the end of September 2003, I still languished in Nome, where I had returned on September 10. Cathy, my sponsors, and most of my relatives doggedly pursued their inquiries with the Russians to try to move my case forward. My friend Dmitry in Provideniya also did his best with the meager tools available to him. Nothing seemed to be working.

On a lark, Cathy also requested a one-year visa for me over the Internet to see what would happen.

◆  ◆  ◆

From what you've read thus far, you might think that nothing works in Russia. The truth is that things just work differently. Russian time is different from time elsewhere, and you have to learn how to make Russian time work for you. You need to learn to be patient until just the right moment—which is impossible to predict—when someone, somewhere in the bureaucratic maze, decides that it is time to sign or stamp the form that you need.

This game of patience is also a game of nerves. It's a cloaked weapon that the Russian administration uses to discourage "undesirables" like me. Only one thing was certain about my bureaucratic struggles: trying to force the issue would be as pointless as Don Quixote's fight against the windmills.

On October 1, I was informed that Cathy's online request was granted and my authorization should arrive in two weeks. But in two weeks, it would have started snowing in Chukotka, and I didn't want to be caught crossing the mountains through huge drifts of snow in white-out conditions. I wanted to get across them before winter arrived.

Later the same day, the problems were piling up faster than snow in a blizzard. Vladimir Bychkof, who had never stopped assuring me that things were moving in the right direction, suddenly told me that he was no longer in charge of my case. The FSB had told him in brusque terms where he stood when I was still in Provideniya: "No visitors, no problems. That guy's not going anywhere." But he kept working on my behalf only to tell me now that he was powerless? He was trying to get me to give up, too. There was no other way to interpret it.

Could Vladimir be an FSB agent himself? Since they were clearly looking for any excuse to keep me out of the country, maybe someone had discovered that I had fought against the Russian-supported troops in Angola? But that was eighteen years ago! I was definitely starting to become paranoid. I couldn't help thinking that behind this torturous process, there had to be something more than the basic Kafkaesque nature of Russian bureaucracy.

Then came good news for a change. Nikolai, the tour guide and sled-dog driver based in Anadyr, whom Vladimir had contacted on my behalf, would continue to work with me. Apparently my Web site had boosted his excitement about the project. Not only was he still willing to work as my chaperone—because I had to have one—but he was even willing to vouch for me officially.

That was not an insignificant commitment. If anything happened to me—and especially, I suspected, if I broke a law or violated a regulation—he could forfeit everything he owned, as well as his civil rights. In short, the FSB could then destroy him.

Admittedly, he was asking for one thousand dollars a month for his services, which is ten times the average Russian salary. But, after all, it did seem fair that there be compensation commensurate with the risk he was assuming. It seemed like a reasonable price to pay for my freedom.

Not long thereafter, Nikolai called to tell me that the FSB had sternly warned him not to sign the document vouching for me as my guarantor. When he asked why, they told him that they were not at liberty to explain. He asked that this recommendation be provided to him in writing. They refused. And so Nikolai signed the document and officially stated that he was vouching for me. I admired his courage and I thanked him with heartfelt gratitude.

It was October 23, and the two-week wait that had been predicted on October 1 had long since passed. I still hadn't received my authorization. I was beginning to think that the wait might really go on forever.

If the stonewalling continued, I knew what I would do: I would go back to Provideniya under the guise of picking up my gear and provisions, and, instead of returning home, I would secretly set out to cross Chukotka. Once I was in the mountains, it wasn't likely that they would call the army out to go after me. After all, I wasn't really a problem for the Russian authorities except when I was right under their noses, forcing them to decide what to do with me.

I would run a serious risk of being caught, which would almost certainly end my expedition, but giving up amounted to the same thing.

At long last, on October 23, I received a response from the Russian authorities that I was authorized to continue my journey across Chukotka starting on November 20. That was a long time to wait, but still, I was beside myself with happiness.

I called Cathy to ask her to send me my winter equipment—at the end of November the ocean and rivers would all be frozen, and I would no longer need my kayak. And if she brought our daughters, we could spend a little family time together.

Nikolai was required to accompany me along the route established by the Russian authorities, all the way to Ambarchik, on the border between Chukotka and Yakutia. We agreed that he would not travel or camp with me; we would meet up at planned points a number of days apart. If everything went the way I hoped, we would almost never see one another. That way, I could continue to travel alone and still comply with the orders of the Russian authorities.

The famous mountains of Chukotka continued to haunt my dreams, and I could already feel myself setting foot in this territory, one of the most remote and pristine places remaining on the planet. I knew that it would be terribly tough to cross this territory in winter, but months of inaction had built up such fury inside me that I felt as if I could move mountains—or at least climb over them in just about any weather imaginable.

The interlude was over. I was once again equipped for winter travel. I had a few more things to check and I would be ready to leave. I returned to Provideniya to resume my journey.

❖ ❖ ❖

Nikolai was supposed to fly in to meet me. But in the Anadyr area, around the Gulf of Anadyr, the weather conditions were so bad that sometimes planes couldn't take off for months at a time. And so I was left to wait again.

Vladimir Bychkof invited me to his wedding, and our differences were swept away. I had the pleasure of enjoying a real Russian wedding, which lived up to its reputation. We ate, drank, danced, and at dawn we were still at it.

Nikolai finally arrived on December 12, and I had a chance to meet him at last. He was a "Chukchi," meaning he was from Chukotka. He had participated in the Iditarod, the famous March sled-dog race that followed a thousand-mile course between Anchorage and Nome, and he spoke perfect English. Moreover, he had an American visa, which was unusual for someone from Chukotka. Apparently he had left his sled and his dogs in Alaska. At first he was planning to take them with him on our trip, but after thinking it over, he decided that traveling by snowmobile was the wiser choice.

I had always assumed that, even though I had no other choice, at least I would be in good hands with this man, who was a native of the Chukotka Peninsula, a sled-dog driver, and a hunter. But when he got out of the plane with no gear other than his animal hides, I began to wonder. And when I discovered that, for his own security, he had recruited a second Chukchi named Ivan—the escort of the escort, as it were—I wondered some more.

"I am responsible for my own survival, and you are responsible for yours," I warned him. "I won't give you shelter and I won't feed you. You are entirely on your own."

"That's fine with me," he said.

Five days of preparations were still needed. I supplied Nikolai with a complete set of gear, which I had to teach him how to use, including a lesson on pitching the tent. I also had two snowmobiles for him and Ivan shipped in from Nome. Then we had to get the vehicles ready, assemble our sled, and draw up an inventory of provisions.

The big departure took place on December 17, 2003—a long four months after I first set foot in Russia. I left Provideniya all alone; Ivan and Nikolai were scheduled to meet up with me later. It was twenty-two degrees below zero, and the white city and its frozen fjord made a much different impression than the one I had when I landed there for the first time in August.

Here, and in Nome, I had watched three seasons and four months go by—time that I could have used to reach at least the Lena River, which flows into the Laptev Sea, and to cross its immense delta before the spring thaw. But this was no time for regrets. I would be able to make some progress now, and that was what counted!

The whole town came out to watch me leave. In the crowd, I recognized "Dima," the customs officer; Igor, the phys-ed teacher; Sergei, the dentist; and all the other friends I had made during my stay. Each of them had tried to persuade me to wait for spring before venturing out into the wilderness. I thought back to Arctic Bay and how my friends there urged me to take the same precautions.

I set off onto the harbor around which the city was constructed—it was my triumphal boulevard. The residents were clustered along the shoreline, and they cheered and waved encouragingly. They had all known that I would leave one day, but they had stopped believing it would actually happen. For that matter, they still refused to believe that I could cross the entire country on foot, since it was likely a journey that they would never undertake.

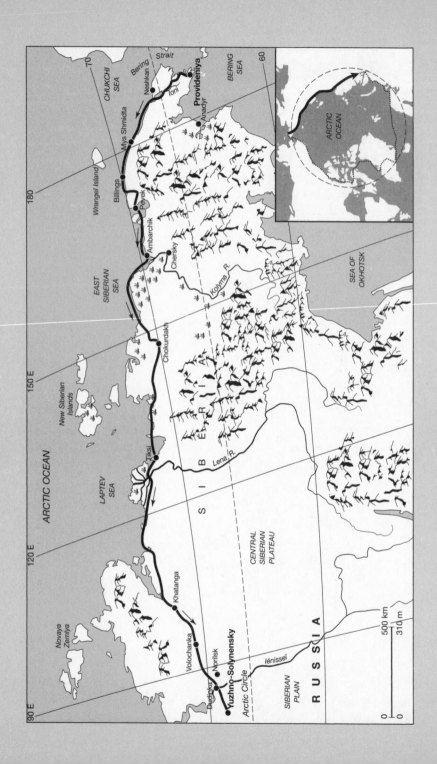

# 7

# To Die Just a Little

Because the rivers were all frozen over, I had been forced to abandon my first plan, which was to kayak out of Provideniya. It was now also out of the question to follow the coastline on foot because the violent currents kept ice from forming in the Bering Sea.

The end result was that I would head toward the nearby mountains now, skirt them along their eastern flank, follow the coastline north for the few miles where it was frozen, and finally cut directly across the mountain range to hook up with the river that flowed straight to Lake Ioni.

My goal was to complete my tour of the Arctic Circle by the following Christmas. I was still sticking to my rule of never descending below the Arctic Circle, unless I was forced to by an impassable obstacle or bureaucratic problems.

At last I was entering the mountains of Chukotka. It was permanently dark this time of year. A strong snowstorm was blowing snowflakes from one mountain valley to another, and as I approached each pass I could feel a blast of polar air chilling my face. The rocky outcrops that stuck up through the blowing snowdrifts suggested this landscape's harsh brutality, while the frozen lakes lay dormant in thickening blankets of white. The countless valleys were punctuated by rocky massifs, sketching out an intricate snow-sunken labyrinth, which was constantly challenging to navigate.

Once again I felt as if I had traveled backward in time, and not fifty years, as at Provideniya, but at least a century this time. The landscape itself had a more primitive character than all the places I had already traveled.

At the end of the first day, I met up with my two companions nineteen miles north-northeast of Provideniya, in the little village of Novyi Chaplino, our first planned rendezvous point.

However, on the second day, on the pretext of going to get fuel at the village of Yandrakinnot, Ivan disappeared with his snowmobile. Something told me that we wouldn't be seeing him again.

On the fifth day Nikolai headed down the wrong valley and got lost in the mountains, so I had to go looking for him. My "guide" was apparently so unfamiliar with the terrain that he was endangering his life and my own. He had been born 180 miles north of Provideniya in a little coastal village named Nachken, but the Chukchis, like the Inuit, never traveled in the winter darkness and knew very little about how to read maps.

After twelve hours of searching and an entire day wasted on his account, I finally found Nikolai, trying in vain to climb a slope that was too steep for his snowmobile with the added weight of pulling his sled. Once he unhooked the sled, the snowmobile climbed the slope quickly and easily, and the sled plummeted down the slope. However, the snowmobile became lodged more deeply in the snow and still did not manage to reach the top of the ridge.

I spent four hours—at a temperature of twenty degrees below zero and in total darkness—climbing the hill myself, in a state of rage fueled by the certain knowledge every step was wasted effort. I seriously considered then and there abandoning my so-called guide and continuing alone.

When I finally got up to his elevation, Nikolai was sitting in the snow next to his vehicle, lost, white-faced, and clearly upset. He was a man in distress. My lips were frozen, but my anger had dissolved. Although minutes before I had wanted to kill him, I helped him get his snowmobile free and back on the road.

Not only did Nikolai not know how to read a map, but he had no idea of how to use a GPS. When I offered him one of mine, he thanked me warmly, trying desperately to conceal the fact that he didn't know how to use it. I spent two days filling this gap in his knowledge, simplifying it through a method that consisted of programming his GPS for a specific point on the map and then entering "go to" so that the device would lead him to the selected location where I would then catch up with him.

Nikolai was hauling substantial reserves of fuel on his sled, and in order to top them off he had to make detours to the various supply points along the way. These resupply missions became twice as frequent after Ivan disappeared and therefore caused him to burn twice as much fuel in the process. Each time he left, I would mark his route on the map and set his GPS so that he only needed to drive the course marked out for him until the GPS displayed: "You've reached your destination."

His next refueling was twenty miles away, and on the return he needed only to follow his own tracks back to the point of departure where he had left three empty gas cans to mark the spot.

I reached the appointed location before him, so I pitched my tent and waited. A few hours later, a terrible blizzard darkened the night with a wall of driving snow. Nikolai should have arrived a long time ago, and I began to worry about him.

I finally decided I would go look for him, but just as I emerged from the tent, I saw the headlights of his snowmobile. He rushed into my tent the way a drowning man swims toward a life raft.

He had just started back, he told me, when the blizzard started to blow. Since he could no longer see his tracks, which were buried by the snow, he had gotten lost. Since he didn't really trust the GPS, he had decided to find his way in "the Chukchi way." But in the pitch black of night with a blizzard whipping all around him, finding three gas cans sitting out in the middle of nowhere was a futile exercise. He realized that he was likely to die without gear for spending the night in the elements, so he finally decided to turn on his GPS. He started off slowly, following the device's directions. Just ten yards from my tent, which he hadn't even seen, the GPS told him that he had arrived. The GPS device had just won a new convert.

From that point on, Nikolai stopped arguing with me about the routes I proposed.

One morning, after spending a night in a hut so old that it was nearly falling apart but still sheltering me against the wind, I turned into a valley where I noticed fresh dog tracks despite a rough snowstorm blowing around me. Their owners couldn't be too far away. After traveling another one-and-a-quarter miles, I distinguished a hulking dark-brown shape that appeared and disappeared in the snowy fog. As I drew closer, I marveled at the sight before me—it was a *yaranga*, the traditional dwelling of the Chukchi Inuit.

These enormous reindeer-hide tents, which vaguely resemble the teepees of Native American Indians, contain a smaller squarish tent inside, which is also made of reindeer hide. This structure is based on the age-old principle of layers of insulation. If it is forty below zero outside, then it will be five degrees below zero inside the first tent, where they do their cooking, and much warmer inside the second tent, where three seal-oil lamps provide both heat and light.

I had come suddenly into contact with a way of life that hadn't changed in the past century. Whether it was the dwellings or the clothing, everything here seemed to be unchanged. The Chukchi Inuit still dress in sealskins and caribou hides, they still make their sleds by hand, and they eat frozen reindeer and seal meat. Dogs are still their only means of transportation, and their only means of sustenance continues to be reindeer herding.

These are the original Chukchi people who have their roots in Mongolia. While the Inuit live on the coast and draw their living from the sea, the Chukchis make their living inland.

For the moment, however, I couldn't see anyone. There were no dogs outside, only a few wooden sleds. I climbed inside the tent on all fours. I still saw no one. I took off my skis without drawing any attention. True, the howling blizzard must have drowned out all sounds. Finally, I announced my presence with a yell. A moment later, a piece of the wall of the interior tent flew up—there was no door, to preserve the heat inside—and a head poked out, flush with the ground, as if poking out from under a sheet. I stood upright, and the perspective must have made me look like a giant. Two almond-shaped eyes fixed in the tanned and tousled face stared at me in a blend of amazement and panic, and the head disappeared. I waited. A few seconds later, the wall of the tent was lifted again, more cautiously this time, and this time two heads poked out.

The two Chukchis spoke to me in Russian, the official language of the former Soviet Union, established by law throughout all of its territory and for all its peoples on threat of imprisonment. Unfortunately, I still couldn't understand a word of Russian.

Suddenly embarrassed at the idea that I might have disturbed or frightened these people, I turned and fled. In this blizzard I wouldn't travel more than a mile or so before having to stop and set up camp. I had barely left the *yaranga*, though, when its occupants—who had quickly thrown on warm clothing—caught up with me and, pulling me by the sleeve, led me back inside. In the antechamber, they helped me to take off my parka and my snow-covered trousers and invited me, dressed in my polar undergarments, into the square tent that is the heart of their household.

I sat down with two men and a woman, the wife of one of them, on a small reindeer-hide carpet where the seal-oil lamps stood burning. The three Chukchis continued their conversation while gobbling down a meal of walrus meat—rotten walrus meat.

According to a traditional recipe, they bury the walrus meat during the three months of summer, and the heat of the sun begins the process of decomposition. The smell carries for miles. Then they dig it up and leave it outdoors when the weather turns colder and allow it to freeze. They slice it up and eat it on the dark winter days. It is an especially prized Chukchi delicacy.

Since I was a guest, they offered me the best part. I brought the chunk of flesh to my mouth, doing my best not to smell it and repressing my impulse to vomit. I chewed on it, trying hard not to taste it. Since I made signs that it was yummy, my hosts pushed the board on which the entire slice of meat lay on display toward me. I took another bite, and I realized that this rotten meat tasted of cheese. "Stinky cheese," admittedly, but still, cheese. Not so bad, after all. Hunger had its way, and I did justice to the food that my hosts were offering, to their intense joy.

Nikolai, who had followed my tracks, caught up with me in the *yaranga* and served as my interpreter. Astonished to learn where I had come from, and even more amazed to hear where I was going, the Chukchis offered to let me use their sleds as a means of transportation. When I explained why I couldn't accept their offer, they had a hard time understanding.

They were delighted to meet their first Westerner. I was even more delighted than they, after my lengthy battle with the Russian bureaucracy, to be in contact with such kind and genuine human beings. My trek across Russia was starting out nicely.

That night, on a reindeer-hide floor that was too small for me to stretch out my legs, Nikolai and I shared the bed of an old Chukchi man, his wife, and another member of his family. Everyone pulled on the single blanket—made of reindeer skin—to try to cover themselves.

For the road, my hosts offered me a large chunk of rotten walrus meat, an enormous portion of whale meat, and some Eskimo fritters made with flour and seal oil. I wanted to offer them some of my rations in return, but they refused to accept them, insisting that I would need them for such a long journey.

However, in this territory where polar bears were constantly passing through on their way to the fish-rich waters of the Bering Strait, carrying such aromatic foodstuffs might well be dangerous. I wrapped part of it in hermetically sealed plastic bags and gave the rest to Nikolai, so that he could offer it as a gift to the inhabitants of the next village.

My guide Nikolai told me he thought that our daily distances were too long. Even though he was on a snowmobile and well outfitted by me, he was still terrified at the idea of being forced to spend a night out in the open. It was true that he still had trouble pitching his tent and that his heating stove didn't work. I began to get the impression that he saw our expedition as a sort of excursion into the countryside.

He became increasingly dependent on me. On three occasions he spent the night in my tent, which was designed to hold only one person, obliging me to feed him and warm him using up my own reserves of energy and benzene. On this treacherous and almost unexplored terrain, in the nearly permanent darkness and extreme cold of the Arctic night, I found myself supporting the extra burden of a "guide" whom I had to look after and take care of.

A Chukchi like Nikolai should have been able to survive the conditions here better than me, theoretically, since this was his own stomping ground. But we had traveled relatively far from his hometown, and the Chukchis aren't accustomed to moving around much, especially in winter. He had a hard time believing that I could march twenty-five miles a day under these conditions.

We agreed that he would stay in one village until I reached the next one on our route. He would then join me on his snowmobile, and the next day he would drive ahead of me to the village after that one. In this manner he wouldn't have to camp or cook for himself. If after three days I didn't see him arrive, I would know that something had happened to him and I would go looking for him. If he ran into trouble when he was ahead of me, I would almost certainly find him along the way.

We had already crossed over the first range of mountains when Nikolai informed me that he had barely enough fuel to make it to Yandrakinnot, the next village, and that he was unwilling to run the risk of traveling there alone. He used my satellite phone to call members of his family who lived in the village in question and asked them to bring him some fuel.

We waited for them together, but no one showed up. It is true that this was the season of end-of-year feasts and celebrations, and so the inhabitants of the region rarely sobered up this time of year. The mission must have been forgotten amid the empty bottles of alcohol. Nikolai then called on one of his friends, a Chukchi hunter like him, but this fellow demanded one hundred dollars a day to transport the fuel. Finally, as a last resort, he called some cousins of his from another village, Lorena, who promised to bring him some fuel. I had the feeling that we would be there for a while.

We waited in a hut in the middle of the tundra on the shores of Lake Ioni. I began to boil over with impatience. It had been twelve days since we left Provideniya; we had covered 250 miles on foot but only 125 miles as the crow flies!

I suggested to my guide that if he liked, he was free to forget about me and just go back to his comfortable home, but he wouldn't hear of it.

The days passed. We finished off the provisions given us by the Chukchis of the *yaranga*—whale *maktak*, reindeer, rotten walrus—which allowed me to economize on my travel rations. I did a little repair and maintenance work on my equipment, and I helped Nikolai improve his map-reading and his solar-navigational skills, even though the sun wouldn't be of much use this time of year.

Nikolai spent hours playing with his GPS, which is the best way to learn how to use it. Since his people lived in reindeer-skin tents, he knew nothing about the art of building igloos, and it was I—now a master igloo-builder!—who taught him.

He deepened my knowledge as well. I discovered, for instance, that it is common practice for a Chukchi, feeling that his end is drawing near, or simply tiring of life, to ask a younger Chukchi to help him to die. He will choose a place that is dear to his heart—the mountain pass where he killed his first bear or the valley where he went on his happiest hunting party—and have his son or grandson take him there. The young Chukchi is then obligated to kill his father or grandfather. The older Chukchi returns to the wilderness, which has fed him and kept him alive for so many years. That is why, in Chukotka, you will frequently find graves in the most out-of-the-way and unexpected places.

It was in this little hut in the middle of nowhere that we spent a New Year's Eve enlivened by the bottle of vodka that Nikolai had the inspiration to bring. At midnight we made our wishes. I wished that I would return home before the end of the year that was just beginning.

I still harbored some resentment against my guide for all the days he had made me waste, but I avoided letting him know to keep the atmosphere from becoming tense. He needed me and I couldn't abandon him. I could see that if this turned into a regular thing, I would have to continue on my way and allow him to catch up with me when he could. I couldn't endanger the expedition just for him.

When his cousins from Lorena finally brought him his fuel, Nikolai and I had been sitting there waiting for seven days! We set out again the next day, me on foot, and Nikolai at the head of a squadron of snowmobiles, since the two fuel couriers were following the same route. They were going to help him transport his fuel reserves to Nutepelmen, where he would wait for me. I would arrive in five days.

Nutepelmen was the first place where I was required to report my presence to the authorities. In this case, the authorities meant the mayor of the town, who would radio the exact date I came through his town to the FSB.

Day after day the winds shifted, and the temperatures changed radically, rising from forty degrees below zero when the Siberian anticyclone froze the tundra to five degrees Fahrenheit. The snow, which clung to the sled like sandpaper, turned to slush when the thermometer rose. The Canadian winter had not offered such sudden rises in temperature. But there my average distance was never more than nine miles a day or so, while here it was twenty-two miles a day. This was because I had made the best of the experience of my first Arctic winter, and the hostile terrain had by now become familiar. I was operating like a well-oiled machine.

In the almost complete darkness, I skied along hunched over to push against the squall. The wind blew so fiercely that it regularly tore my hood off my head. It was hard to put it back on because my gloves were so thick. I had to take them off to put my hood back on and then slip them back on as quickly as possible, and then warm up my hands. Each yard was a victory.

When I got about ten miles from Nutepelmen, I was literally pinned down by the power of the wind, which was driving the temperature down as well. My face turned into a mask of ice, which my blood could no longer warm. My facial muscles became temporarily paralyzed. I could no longer open my mouth. My nose was frostbitten again, as were my left cheek and my eyelids. My hands were still working so that I was able to pitch my tent quickly and get out of the wind, but the cold was so extreme that even inside the tent I couldn't manage to warm up.

The next day the violence of the storm kept me trapped in my tent. It was impossible to move. I was now one day late for my rendezvous with Nikolai, and he was going to start worrying about me. Twenty-four hours later, I decided to try to make some forward progress, but the instant I put my nose outside of the tent, I realized that I wouldn't be able to cover two miles.

A few more hours went by, and the wind died down a bit. I set out again, and that same evening around six o'clock I arrived in Nutepelmen, an old village of 150 inhabitants, half Chukchi and half Inuit. The darkness was pierced by a few dim lights barely visible through the filthy windowpanes. The dogs barked all around the dilapidated old huts that were heated by the coal furnaces and lacked running water.

It seemed that all the doors opened at once. Nikolai had warned the entire village that I would be coming, and the dogs had just announced my arrival.

When I told Nikolai that the wind had been blowing so violently that it made it impossible for me leave my tent, he answered that it must be because I had marched over a grave. The spirit of the dead man was furious, and this was how he showed his displeasure. Or, of course, it could be the new moon, which always washed its face with a strong wind before reappearing.

Mys Shmidta, 125 miles away, was the next checkpoint where I had to report my presence to the authorities. Throughout the Cold War, Mys Shmidta (*mys* means "cape") was a military base with a garrison in a state of almost permanent alert with missiles, radar, and fighter jets ready to take off at any moment. I could expect to see some ghosts from that bygone era.

A few miles from Nutepelmen lay the burned-out wreckage of a helicopter that crashed there a year earlier. Seven people had died in the accident. The villagers insisted that I should avoid the place, even if I had to detour around it. The Chukchis, despite being capable of murdering their old people when asked, were also fearful and superstitious where death was concerned. When I refused to change my route, someone confided in me the secret of warding off the attendant bad luck: I would need to carry a small bottle of vodka and empty it at the crash site.

The weather had cleared up when I got near the orange-and-blue wreckage of the plane, which had been chartered by a scientific team to film bears. The helicopter had been following a bear a little too closely, at too low an altitude, when it turned sharply and the blades brushed the ground. In order to make my friends from Nutepelmen happy, I performed the ritual libation.

The reason that the scientists had come here to meet their fate a year before was that this coast is a Mecca for bears. I didn't see any bears at the moment—if those specks on the horizon weren't a mother and her cubs—but their tracks were everywhere. I made camp well inland and away from the shore where the breaks in the ice attract bears.

The cold and the wind were so harsh that my pulmonary alveoli began to freeze in my lungs again, triggering that same horrible sensation of being strangled. According to schedule, I was supposed to pass through here four months ago. This was definitely turning into a bad habit with me: being at the wrong place at the wrong time.

Nikolai had gone on ahead and would wait for me in Mys Shmidta. Finally I could make progress unhindered, without having to worry about him.

Our thorny relationship had gradually developed into a genuine friendship. I had come to understand that he was a humble and sincere man. He told me that he had learned more in the course of a month traveling with me than he had in the rest of his life. This touched me deeply. And when he needed my help, I didn't forget that I was indebted to him for even being there at all. He was the only one who had the courage to vouch for me, with all the risks that that involved.

I wondered what it was that the FSB wanted to keep me from seeing by requiring Nikolai to keep me on a specific itinerary. A rocket-launching pad? An atomic power plant? As far as I could tell, there was nothing anywhere in the region—nothing but mountains and tundra.

In any case, there was little danger of me seeing even the outlines of the landscape, since my horizon was restricted to the beam of light from my headlamp. And that was just as well. These identical valleys and mountains never seemed to stop rising, one after the other, and it was enough to sap your courage and turn you into a defeatist. At least the darkness offered the spice of the unknown. I would find out that there was an uphill climb only when it became necessary to start climbing, and therefore I wouldn't have to dread the impending uphill struggle. Moreover, as is the case with blind people, my other senses became more acute. I had become so accustomed to anticipating danger that I could sense it on the other side of a hill or a pile of ice. I knew the significance of each and every noise. I could hear a seal rubbing itself on the ice, or a bear or wolf heading in my direction.

When I got to Mys Shmidta, the wind was blowing at speeds of over forty miles an hour, and I couldn't see any farther than two yards straight ahead of me.

The town's gray and broken-down buildings stretched along the coast. With their shattered windows, its barracks were as much relics of a bygone age as its abandoned control towers. In the distance I could make out the lights of a gold mine that was still operating. These relics stretched for twenty-two miles.

The first people I met were the border guards. I was looking for a place to camp, and I happened upon their station. Once again I found myself face-to-face with human brick walls who were assigned to enforce pointless regulations. They began with the suspicion—of course—that I must be a spy. And who would be paying me? To spy on what? These questions never passed through their minds. Nikolai, who was waiting for me, returned to help me with this situation.

For me, urban, military, or commercial centers in the Arctic generally contained two sorts of people: those who had the power to complicate my life and those who wanted to take my money. The two categories often overlapped. That was why I did everything possible to avoid them.

The former military base, which was now a huge fuel dump, was a sort of capital for the practically nonexistent population. The governor was also the chief of the fire brigade, as well as a physician. In this icy hamlet, depressing and windswept, no one said hello, no one spoke to me, and no one answered my questions. In the darkness, hoods pulled over their faces, people would run to buy the black bread or the canned food that they needed, before returning to hole up in their houses again. I would see them crossing the streets, dark and fearful silhouettes that always seemed to be running away from something. I had no desire to stay here a second longer than was strictly necessary, but the storm pinned me down there for twenty-four hours.

As soon as possible I got back on the road—on the ice, actually—along the coastline. After 155 miles of marching on the Chukchi Sea, I reached Billings, my next checkpoint. My sled was growing lighter, and my average daily distance was about twenty-five miles despite the darkness and the still very harsh cold.

At Billings I stayed in the home of a hunter named Alexander

Machkov, whose wife, Elena, made me reindeer-skin socks and gloves. He wanted to give me a bear skin that was eleven and a half feet long, the largest one I had ever seen. Unfortunately, I had to refuse the gift because I had no room on my sled.

Alexander taught me some interesting things about local customs. He explained that the chief of police, who pushed the art of corruption to the verge of caricature, had reportedly gone into the house of a trapper who had taken more than his quota of foxes and had impounded his pelts without a word. The trapper, who was on the wrong side of the law, was in no position to object, so the police chief nonchalantly sold the furs for his own personal profit.

I noticed that the merchants selling snowmobile fuel were hard at work. But Alexander said that the fuel that these street-corner swindlers were pawning off on certain unsuspecting visitors was diluted with water, as much as fifty percent! If used, the water would freeze in the carburetor and the engine would explode. Having been duly warned, Nikolai bought his fuel at a polar weather station that wasn't far off.

I left after two days. At a rate of twelve hours of marching each day, I worked my way along the length of the Chukotka Peninsula, gradually progressing toward Long Strait.

No other human beings lived in this part of the world. At least that's what I believed, until I happened on an out-of-the-way hut, no bigger than a table. I pushed the door open. Between the bed and the heating stove, a man, his *chapka* (warm Russian hat) pulled down over his eyes, was snoring, collapsed against the wall, obviously drunk, on the verge of slipping into an alcoholic coma. He woke with a start, startled by the light of my headlamp, and yelled, "My God! Oh my God! Take whatever you want, but don't hurt me!"

I left him to sleep it off, and I moved into the cabin—even smaller than his—next door. The next day he discovered that I wasn't just a bad dream, and—after some laborious attempts at explanation on my part—he welcomed me warmly.

His name was Alexei. He was a prisoner of the vast wilderness that surrounded him, like some prehistoric beast trapped on an island by the continental drift. How had he wound up here? The few words that we managed to exchange despite the language barrier allowed me to guess that the Komsomolsky mine, not far from Pevek but farther inland, bought his fishing catch to feed the miners during the summer. In the winter he lived on his savings and hibernated. I got some idea of how intoxicated he had been the night before when he told me that he made his own homebrew, called *samogon,* and that he drank the one hundred and ninety-proof alcohol that the mine supplied him to burn in his heating stove and his lamp!

To him I was not a spy but a long-lost brother. We immediately hit it off. Alexei admitted that he missed civilization but that the simplicity of his life was sufficient to keep him happy. I could see what he meant, looking at the permanent grin on his face and the twinkle in his eye. He was happy with what little he had, and he didn't want to accept any help or supplies from me. I learned a great deal from Alexei and his own ways. I hadn't appreciated anyone's company so much since I had entered Russia.

I spent two days with him. He wanted me to stay longer because he said that the sixty-degree below zero temperatures would never allow me to make it to Pevek alive—but I needed to keep on moving toward my goal.

The little town of Pevek was located on the Chaunskaya Bay. The shortest way there was to hug the coast, staying on the ice. But Alexei had warned me that the area around Cape Shelagski, just outside the mouth of the bay, was nothing but a dumping ground for huge blocks of ice that were impossible to traverse on foot. The only way through, according to him, was to cut across inland by climbing over the mountains. There was a valley that led to a frozen river, which formed an ice route that would take me straight to Pevek. But the important thing was to find the pass leading to this all-important valley. And in the permanent night, I would be very lucky to find it.

I walked through valleys and climbed over mountain passes. My face was completely frozen. I had the sensation that someone was stabbing my face over and over. A number of wolves followed me from a distance from the moment I left Alexei's hut. I felt that I would never find the pass that he had described to me.

In the meantime, I needed to rendezvous with Nikolai. He was coming directly from Billings, and I had entered the position of our rendezvous point into his GPS. I wasn't far from the rendezvous point when a furious windstorm blew up.

As I approached the pass on the other side of which we were supposed to meet, the windstorm threw up a veritable wall of air and snow, blocking my way. I struggled mightily to get through. Each time I got close, I would hit a breaking point where, fuming with rage and helplessness, I would feel my skis begin to slide inexorably backward. When I would turn to regain my traction and my balance, my sled would be hit sideways by the howling squall, which, like a crashing breaker, would sweep it off the ground and hurl it down the slope, dragging me with it as it went.

I had to get through somehow. Nikolai was waiting for me on the other side, and he had no camp stove and no provisions. That is the only thing that gave me strength to keep on pushing and, finally, to make it through, despite the frostbite to my face and the indescribable cold. Otherwise, I would just have camped at the base of the mountain until conditions improved a little.

This battle that I came so close to losing left me with some scars. I began to wonder for the first time in so long: Why am I doing this? Why should I keep on suffering the way I am? No one lives or travels like this, in the dark, in the worst weather conditions on the face of the earth. Why should I? But I shook myself out of it. In my situation this defeatist state of mind could be the most dangerous toxin of them all. I was disturbed to see that I had let it creep up on me, caused by my anger at having to travel this region during the worst season of the year, when I had planned everything carefully to avoid this very thing. It was caused by the suffering and the humiliation, after having hauled a sled weighing 330 pounds up the side of a mountain, to be hurled back down the other side, ass over elbows and tangled in my harness.

Once I made it over the pass I was sheltered from the wind. I skied downhill to the tent where Nikolai was waiting for me to spend our last night together. From Pevek he would take a plane back home to Anadyr. His contract required him to accompany me to Ambarchik, on the border with Yakutia, but he was exhausted, frostbitten, and terribly homesick. His three-year-old daughter was waiting for him at home, and he was in a hurry to get back.

When he asked me if I would mind if he left me a little earlier than planned, I accepted eagerly, despite the friendship that had grown between us. The faster he went back home, the sooner I would have freedom of operation.

If everything went according to plan, his plane would leave Pevek even before I got there, just two days from now. So we settled our accounts. We had agreed on a fee of one thousand dollars per month; we had left about sixty days before (mid-December to mid-February), so the total worked out to two thousand dollars. That was two years' salary for the average Russian and a good deal for him. Of course, though, he had also been an invaluable help to me. Nikolai had been crucial to me in administrative terms. He had cost me time, money, and effort, but he had taken an enormous risk in vouching for me, a risk that had allowed me to push on.

I figured that we were all square.

To get over the pass and join Nikolai, I had had to travel for eighteen hours instead of ten in order to make my twenty-two miles. That was an average I was determined to maintain, whatever the cost. I would do anything to avoid suffering through a third Arctic winter, which I felt more and more certain every day would be my breaking point.

I was pushing the envelope every day now. I was driving myself a little too hard without a doubt. I wouldn't stop until I could no longer feel my hands, my feet, my face—just before the frostbite really took hold. I wouldn't start off again until feeling returned in my limbs, or else I could easily lose my fingers or toes. But each evening, as I warmed up my GPS in my sleeping bag, I would have the satisfaction of reading my progress.

Two days after Nikolai left, by following the valley and river that Alexei had told me about, on what amounted to a straight line, I beat my own Russian record with thirty miles covered in eleven hours of effort.

The next day, February 7, at a temperature of forty-seven degrees below zero, I had the sensation that frostbite had penetrated down to my bones. But I had finally reached Pevek. I spotted this "urban" waste-land from a distance, because the coal and oil heat that got residents through the winter blighted the sky with its sooty fumes and pollutants and sent runoff into the sea.

An old woman who looked out her window as I arrived through the grayish snow, like a statue carved out of hoarfrost, ran downstairs and embraced me. She insisted that I come into her house to warm up. I thanked her but declined the offer in the few words of Russian that I had picked up, and asked her to point me toward the weather station. She refused to listen and insisted on giving me a cup of hot tea.

Just then a police car sped by. The instant the driver saw me he jammed on his brakes, and the vehicle swerved to a stop in the middle of the street. Four men in uniform piled out and lined up in front of me, Kalashnikovs at the ready, to block my way.

"*Dokument!*" barked the chief. I was frozen to the bone, I had been marching for days, and I had marched even longer than usual to reach Pevek in a single day. I was well beyond fatigue, and the words that I wanted to hear from my fellow human beings did not include "*doku-ment.*"

I lowered my head and kept on walking, ignoring the uniformed men completely. One of them walked toward me, and for his trouble got the metal tip of one of my skis full on his tibia. He howled and shouted again, "*Dokument! Dokument!*"

I kept on going. The four men jumped into their Jeep and went ahead to set up a roadblock a half-mile down the road, in front of the police station. Once I got there they forced me to make a sharp right turn to enter the police station and continued to ask for my papers.

I answered that I urgently needed to go to the bathroom. No response. I was exasperated by this point, my nerves were on edge, and I finally cracked. There, in the middle of the police chief's office, I dropped my trousers and squatted to take a crap. After a horrified moment of silence, the shouting broke out twice as loud, and they literally carried me to the toilet.

I showed them my papers and explained that I had a guide. Luckily, Nikolai's plane had not yet taken off. They found my former guide at the polar weather station, brought him to the police station, and he confirmed everything that I had told them. When the policemen continued their nitpicking, he rose to the occasion: "You wouldn't be capable of going where this man has been!" And when they asked him for his authorization to cross Chukotka, he answered, "I don't need one. I am in my own country here! You are the ones who should have to show me your authorization!"

In fact, the border guards had been informed that I would be coming. But they wanted to show their power, using me as a demonstration of their authority. And, admittedly, when we first met, I hadn't been very cooperative.

After Nikolai's lecture, the border guards' attitude improved. They offered me tea and even showed a certain degree of respect. Their colleagues in Provideniya had never believed that I would get to Pevek, which could be reached only by sea or by air. But I had arrived there, and moreover I had done so during the coldest months of the year.

They questioned me at considerable length concerning the exact route that I had followed to get there and everything that I might have seen along the way. I answered the first part of the question with my GPS, which recorded all my successive positions. As for the second part, if there had been anything "sensitive" for me to see, they needn't have worried. I had been traveling in the total darkness for two straight months, and I had barely seen the ski tips mark out my path in front of me.

I spent another night in Nikolai's company at the polar weather station on the outskirts of Pevek. I waited for him to leave while treating my frostbite.

I had told the border guards that I would be leaving Pevek on Friday the thirteenth. They had written that date down and explained that I absolutely had to leave Pevek on that day. But Nikolai's flight was delayed by bad weather, and so was I.

The atmosphere grew tense. In the tiny, cockroach-infested room we were sharing, the soldiers—usually drunk—would burst through the door at any time of the day or night, demanding to see my passport, inventing all sorts of excuses to extort money from me. I would invariably reply, "Ya ne ponimayu," which means "I don't understand." Nikolai was uncomfortable. The Russians hate the Chukchis and tend to treat them like dogs. Fortunately, he was one of the representatives of his community to the government in Anadyr, which made him something of a VIP.

Finally, his airplane arrived. This time we said good-bye for good.

On February 15, I still couldn't leave because of the bad weather. That day, a policeman came to see me and told me that, since I had not left on the thirteenth and was also without my guide, I was once again in violation of the law. I explained that none of that was under my control. I suggested that I could leave immediately. He refused to allow that. It was too late now. He was going to arrest me and send me back to Switzerland.

With that, he left and went to find his fellow policemen. It was now or never. Seizing this unexpected opportunity, I packed my gear and got ready to leave.

"Stop!" a friend of Nikolai's shouted, someone whom I had got to know there. "Before you leave, everybody has to take turns sitting on your sled.

I sputtered, "What?"

"It's Russian tradition. Before a traveler starts off, he and everyone who is present need to sit one by one on his baggage. Then you can be sure that the traveler will have a good trip."

It did me no good to explain to him that if I waited another minute before leaving, there would be no journey at all. He insisted. I relented, if only to save my breath. One after the other, we all sat on my sled together, and then they wished me bon voyage.

By the time the soldiers got back, I was gone.

I set off straight across the ice, over Chaunskaya Bay. Once I had crossed the peninsula at the far end of the bay, I would hug the coast again. The soldiers wouldn't chase me over the ice. They weren't equipped to go out in extreme cold. They would be risking their lives, and they knew it. And just like that, once again, it was just me.

Behind me, Pevek was vanishing into the distance. Ahead of me—215 miles away, but ahead of me all the same—Ambarchik and the Yakutia border, along the Kolyma River. No more FSB, no more guide. I was finally free!

There was only one problem: the last time I had been resupplied was two months ago. The authorities had refused to allow my team to come to Pevek, and I was beginning to run short on fuel and food. The food that I had been able to obtain along the way was both too heavy and too low in calories, but I had nonetheless purchased some provisions in Pevek. I used them to make my regular rations last longer, but they weren't enough. In such frigid conditions I needed to ingest ten thousand calories a day. I burned two thousand calories just while sleeping.

I absolutely had to get provisions in Ambarchik.

I had only one goal in mind, to cross into the territory of Yakutia. This region is one of the most deserted places on the planet. There is not a single inhabitant in the entire Kolyma Plain, all the way to the village of Chokurdakh on the Indigirka River. There would be no one to cause me any trouble.

Of course, I would need a permit to travel through Yakutia, and I still hadn't received it, even though I had requested it at the same time I asked for the permit for Chukotka—four months ago! The border "town" of Ambarchik, which had once been one of Stalin's most terrible gulags, was now nothing but a weather station manned by three people. There were no police, no border guards. I should get through without difficulties.

Cathy suddenly dampened my optimism by telling me that the authorities were refusing to issue permits to my team to travel in Yakutia. They would only authorize them to spend one hour with me in Ambarchik. One hour!

Jean-Philippe and the others would have to charter a helicopter in Chersky, ninety miles to the south, on the Kolyma River to travel to Ambarchik—and then leave again after one hour! That wouldn't be worth the cost, and we had too many things to do.

So it was decided that we'd try to rendezvous again farther along. But farther along meant Chokurdakh on the Indigirka River, roughly the same distance away as the distance that I had already come from Provideniya. Since there was no alternative, my team set about getting the necessary documents to travel to Chokurdakh, and they were successful.

As for me, I would simply have to adapt my route to these new plans. I had originally planned to stay on the ice of the East Siberian Sea as far as Tiksi, just before the mouth of the Lena River. But Chokurdakh was well before that, and far inland. I would therefore have to cross the entire Indigirka plain overland to reach Tiksi.

I skied along on the ice, and the beginning of the day promised nice weather. I was only a few days away from Ambarchik, but since I no longer had any reason to stop, I decided to cut across the bay so that I could pass between nearby Cape Bear and Bear Island.

The north wind began to blow. Soon it was blowing harder than I had experienced during the entire expedition, roughly seventy-five or eighty miles per hour. The wind swept away the layer of snow, and the bare ice became a skating rink where my skis no longer had any traction. I was constantly being knocked to the ground where I would continue to slide on my belly like a curling stone.

As soon as I recovered a semblance of stability, I turned southward so that I would have the wind at my back. When the wind was blowing from the side, it tended to lift my sled up in the air and take me with it.

I was literally being pushed toward Ambarchik, along the cliffs that kept me from seeking shelter on dry land in the shelter of their lee.

Since it was impossible to pitch my tent in these conditions, I had no alternative but to keep on moving.

I marched on without stopping for forty-eight hours, lashed by blowing snow that reduced visibility to zero. The wind pressure on my harness was such that it crushed the layers of air and clothing that normally protected me from the cold, and frostbite started to afflict my sides. I had set up a system that allowed me to transfer the pressure from my sides to my shoulders, but then my arms began to lose circulation and my elbows froze.

In the midst of this windstorm, which was blinding me and preventing me from using my GPS, I managed to set my course by moving forward at a consistent angle to the wind, and I ran straight into the polar station of Ambarchik.

At that moment I was thanking heaven for my first Arctic winter, the one that I spent getting from Arctic Bay to Committee Bay. The experience that I had gathered during that winter had certainly just saved my life. I could have easily died. And there was no reason to think that I might not die yet.

Despite everything, I have less appreciation for the nice weather in the Arctic than for those moments when nature is on a rampage. Its demonstrations of power trigger in me a mixture of fear and respectful enthusiasm. I had needed to come this far in order to witness the true power of the elements, a power in comparison with which it is really understatement to say that we are insignificant creatures.

◆ ◆ ◆

I moved into the Ambarchik weather station to wait for the provisions and the fuel that Nikolai had appointed someone else to bring me, via Chersky. Thus I would have enough supplies to reach Chokurdakh, where I would have my next real resupply.

My courier was, in fact, the man to whom I had sold Nikolai's snowmobile in Pevek with the condition—these vehicles are in short supply up here—that he would use it to help me out, in case of need. I waited eight days, and then two natives of the Sakha, as they call Yakutia here, arrived. They brought me three gallons of fuel instead of the five gallons that I had been promised, and a very incomplete array of rations. What was missing had been stolen or lost. Their muddled explanations kept me from understanding.

Two gallons less fuel meant twenty-four days without fuel. Even more serious was that the diesel fuel had soaked into much of the food, making it inedible. I separated out what could be salvaged, and I supplemented it with provisions that the occupants of the polar station generously gave me out of their own reserves.

The Kolyma Plain, which began beyond Ambarchik, is an expanse of thousands of square miles of wet tundra with countless small lakes and deep rivers whose waters melt the permafrost, stretching out in immense, slow curves and twists. This is the most frigid part of the Arctic. During the coldest part of the winter, a record temperature was set here of 101 degrees below zero!

During the winter it is covered with a thick layer of ice that smoothes the surface and makes it relatively easy to cross. All the same, I chose to reach Chokurdakh from the sea, which represented a detour of 125 miles. And that's not counting the obstacles presented by pack ice, stretches of open water, and bears. However, I knew from experience that it would be seven or eight degrees warmer on the ice of the East Siberian Sea than on the permafrost of the tundra. What's more, this was the beginning of March and the sun was beginning to appear again, which meant that I could hope for a very slight rise in temperature. That rise in temperature—since the sun would be reflected off the ice—would be more noticeable on the sea ice than on dry land.

I skied across the frozen sea in a permanent blizzard, without a compass or a GPS, once again orienting myself by the angle of my course against the direction of the wind. In this absolute whiteness, it was impossible to see the shoreline between the ocean bristling with ice and the tundra absolutely without relief, just a few feet above sea level and just as white as everything else.

Two days after I left Ambarchik, one of my tent poles broke in two, smashed by the power of the raging storm, something that had never happened to me before. As it broke, the aluminum shaft tore the fabric, creating an L-shaped gap through which wind and snow entered the tent. The cold made it impossible for me to take off my gloves to fix the tear with needle and thread, so I warmed up a roll of silver duct tape, and I used it to close the hole. When I folded up my tent, I would just need to take care that this bandage stayed flat; otherwise, the duct tape would freeze and shatter like glass.

But twenty-four hours later, my do-it-yourself repair was beginning to show signs of fragility. I was forced to stitch it back together from the outside. I had to work bare-handed because it wasn't a job that could be done with mittens on. It was forty degrees below zero outside, and every thirty seconds I had to go back into my tent to warm my hands over my stove.

For five days running I had managed to follow a straight trajectory that took me close to land, between the Kolyma Plain and Bear Island. But my average daily distance dropped steadily because of the difficult surface of the pack ice and because of my growing weakness, which resulted from my inadequate diet. Each night I had to stop a little earlier. It would take me a full hour to brush off the snow that covered my clothes, filled my boots, and blew into my tent. By economizing on food, I had affected changes in my metabolism that, for the first time, made me gradually, almost undetectably, lose control of my own organism. To make up for the shortfall in calories, I drank more water. Any extra effort would then make me sweat excessively. A layer of ice would form on my skin under my clothes and chill me to the bone.

Days and days passed without the tiniest sign of human or animal life. This frozen desert is desolate in ways that make it even emptier than any of the actual deserts that I have crossed. There was not a footprint or paw print anywhere in this part of the world, not even the bear tracks that I had come to expect. It was as remote and surreal as if it were on an alien planet. I suffered almost physically from the sense of abnormality I experienced there. I walked along as if I was in one of those dreams in which you wonder when it is going to topple over the brink into the realm of nightmare.

When Cathy told me over the satellite phone that Annika and Jessica had won their ski competitions, I felt a sense of pleasure and pride that made me briefly forget about what I was enduring. I wanted to share my fatherly pride with someone. When, as I got closer to land, life finally manifested itself in the form of a fox, I climbed up onto a small butte to yell after the fox, with all my strength, "Annika and Jessica won the slalom and the downhill competitions!"

To conserve on the fuel I still had, I began to melt less snow and drink less water. As a result, my exhaustion became so extreme that my body finally refused to obey my mind's commands. My legs worked in slow motion. When my sled hit a bump, I stopped short. It took an incredible effort to haul it over the tiniest obstacle.

I was covering just five and a half miles per day. I was practically standing still, and I didn't even realize it. Cathy made me aware of it by asking me over the satellite phone what was going on. I would never make it to North Cape at this rate.

Just as I was reaching my breaking point, a will greater than my own took charge and forced me to stop, spend a day or two in my tent, eat until I had my fill, and drink until my thirst was quenched. The provisions and fuel that remained might not get me as far as Chokurdakh, but one thing was certain—I would never get there at all if I kept on moving like this.

✦ ✦ ✦

This complete halt restored my strength and my speed, and now my daily distance was hitting twenty-eight miles on the good days. I was back to eating ten thousand calories a day, which also helped to lighten the sled and increase my speed. But Chokurdakh was still far away, and even at a quickened pace my provisions would be gone long before I got there. I considered the possibility of hunting. But hunting what? And how? There wasn't the slightest sign of life in the surrounding area.

The four months of that terrible winter had worn me down. I was making mistakes that I didn't used to make. One day when I was hauling my sled along, I suddenly felt an abnormal cold around my crotch. I lifted my parka and realized that I had left my fly open. It was impossible to grab the zipper with my mittens. I had to stop, pitch my tent, light my heating stove, warm my hands, and unfreeze my zipper before I could close my fly—an hour and a half to do something that would have taken two seconds if I hadn't been so careless in the morning.

The mouth of the Indigirka River, which would take me to Chokurdakh, was about sixty miles away when a bank of dark clouds appeared on the horizon. The day had been dead calm with hardly a breath of wind. But there was a sort of palpable menace in the air, something electric and indefinable. And suddenly the dark line advanced from the horizon straight at me. In the space of a few seconds, it swept over me like a tidal wave, and everything went white.

I told myself that it was a passing weather front and kept trudging along, assuming that it wouldn't last.

It lasted two days.

Once again I found myself turning my back to the wind to keep my sled from flying away, obliged to keep on moving because the raging storm kept me from pitching my tent. The wind kept me from even opening the sled. Without food or drink, I was growing weaker. The stronger gusts would regularly throw me to the ground, push me along the ice, and pile swirling snow up on me. And each time, I got back to my feet. Until I had been battered one time too many, and I stayed down on the ground.

I had been moving forward through the storm for twenty-four hours. I could almost immediately feel the snow covering me up. But I didn't feel cold because my exhaustion had dulled my senses.

With my body and my face glued to the ice, all feeling lost in my hands and feet, I was letting myself slide gently under. I had demanded too much of my strength. Nature was stronger than me; I accepted my defeat. I was so tired that I preferred to die, and, for that matter, it didn't hurt a bit. Cutting your veins in a warm bathtub must produce the same pleasant sensation of distance. With my eyes closed, I was letting myself flow into an absolute state of rest. No more pain, no more cold, no more leaden sled to haul . . .

Moments before I dropped off forever, a voice that could have been mine suddenly started to question me: If I found myself in such a predicament, it was only because I had believed in myself, right? Hadn't I believed in myself in the face of all the reasons not to, in spite of everyone who said I didn't have a chance? And all the people who had believed in me, who had helped me, who had supported me—was I going to let them down? What about my wife and my daughters?

As if through a mist, I suddenly saw Annika and Jessica the day I left North Cape. My boat was slowly moving away from the wharf, and my girls were calling out to me, "Papa, we know you can make it. You're going to make it, and you'll come back home to us." I could hear their voices coming from far away.

All at once it became clear. I couldn't die that way. I had no right. It would have been too easy. A mysterious force seemed to come and lift me up, tear me off the ground, stand me up, and my feet began to count out the paces again, one after the other. I continued without stopping until the next day.

Once the storm became a little less intense, I decided to try to pitch my tent. Exhausted by forty-eight hours of continuous effort, I desperately needed to sleep. It was fifty-three degrees below zero, and the wind was still blowing at thirty-seven miles per hour. I drove a first stake into the ice, as usual, while holding the fabric flat so that the wind wouldn't get a grip on it. The tent opened up like an umbrella, and at that same moment, the squall ripped out the stake and the tent flew up into the air. I hung onto the tent poles, but the tent picked me up and threw me over my sled. I held on with all the strength I had left in me. If I lost my tent, I was a dead man.

I finally managed to pin the tent to the ground by lying on top of it, and I then fastened it to my sled. After that, I succeeded in pitching it. Minutes later I was inside the tent with the stove burning, and the feeling that I was safe at last. By tossing snow into the red-hot pan atop the stove, I managed to create a sort of Turkish bath in the tent, which allowed me to heat my lungs as well as the rest of me. That did nothing to dull the intolerable pain of my frozen face, which felt as if it were being stabbed with daggers.

For a moment I had thrown in the towel. I had been beaten, and I had teetered over the abyss. I panicked at remembering how easy it had been and how tempting. The first time I nearly succumbed to the elements, near Committee Bay, I had demanded too much of myself due to a lack of experience. This time, however, there was no excuse for having pushed myself to that point of risk. On the other hand, I had seen once again that the determination to survive is stronger in human beings than any other force.

When I woke up, I gobbled down a double ration in an attempt to throw a little more coal into the boiler, and I recovered my strength. That storm, by forcing me to move forward without stopping, had made me cover forty-five miles all at once! I wasn't far from the mouth of the Indigirka. And another carrot dangled in front of me: on the satellite phone Cathy confirmed that fresh supplies were awaiting me in Chokurdakh.

On the tundra of the Indigirka River delta, the wind blew constantly at over thirty-five miles per hour. One evening the guy line of my tent broke; once again I came close to losing the tent. The squalls dramatically reduced visibility and—even though it was late March—kept the temperature under forty degrees below zero. Each step forward was a Herculean effort to pull my sled through the thick snow. Once again my average distance dropped sharply, even though I was out hauling my sled for the same number of hours every day. When I had the wind at my back and snow underfoot, I tried the kite. But the snow was too soft, and I bogged down in it. I started to snowplow and wound up facedown in the snow, being dragged by a crazed kite that spun madly in all directions. I held on desperately to keep from losing it.

Once I had regained control of the situation, I folded up my kite until things were a little calmer. I didn't want to run the risk of a broken leg at this point.

I did my best to follow the path of the Indigirka River, but its curves and meanderings were only lengthening the distance I had to cover. And its icy surface, covered with windblown snow, wasn't much better to travel over than the tundra.

Sixty miles from Chokurdakh, I spotted a tiny cabin on the vast plain. Smoke was pluming upward. As I got closer, the inevitable dog began barking, but no one appeared. Since night had already fallen, I pitched my tent outside the front door. I had just finished when headlights pierced the darkness, accompanied by the distinctive "beep-beep-beep" of a snowmobile.

The master of the house was back. He got off his vehicle and shook his head. He wasn't going to let me sleep outdoors.

It must have been at least eighty-five degrees in the cabin, where a peat fire was burning. Even in my undergarments, I was sweating as if I were in a sauna. There were two real beds and a table with a loaf of fresh bread on it, baked by my host. Pavel was a Yakut, which is to say that he was a native of the region. He was the master of this hundred-square-foot palace built in the middle of hundreds of thousands of square miles of absolutely nothing. Amazingly enough, this evening he had a guest.

In contrast with Alexei, the alcoholic fisherman I had met before reaching Pevek, Pavel had not made his cabin into his principal residence. This was his fishing hut. He lived in Chokurdakh and was planning to go back the next day. Because I was going there too, he informed me that I was to stay in his home there as well.

After a comfortable, warm night, weighed down with provisions that Pavel had given me, I set out again across the tundra toward Chokurdakh. We would meet again in about three days.

Chokurdakh was a small town with a population of eight hundred, where a statue of Lenin that had been spared from demolition constituted just about the only curiosity. But for me it represented a significant milestone—I had completed one-third of my Russian journey!

I moved in with Pavel and his wife, Tanya, who were happy to welcome the first foreign visitor to their town that anyone could remember.

After this monthlong stage starting in Ambarchik, I was left without any remaining rations or a single drop of fuel, and I was at the end of my rope. The two days' lead that I had on my team gave me a chance to recover my strength. Pavel and Tanya fed me generously on caviar, a staple food supply here that seemed to be as inexpensive as rice in China.

When Jean-Philippe, Sebastian, and Raphaël arrived, we didn't waste a minute. I not only needed to restock my provisions and my fuel; I also needed to replace certain pieces of worn-out gear that were no longer reliable. Normally this was equipment that you might use once a year. But I lived and worked with my gear twenty-four hours a day for months on end, and I was subjecting it to ordeals that went far beyond your ordinary winter excursion.

We set off immediately after my resupply, and it was a beautiful day. Pavel and Tanya bid me farewell with lots of tears and vodka.

Now there was nearly permanent daylight, and the thermometer had climbed back up to thirty-five degrees below zero. My team followed me to get a new set of pictures. Pavel and one of his friends escorted them in their snowmobiles.

I started out by traveling twelve and a half miles in the wrong direction, along the Indigirka River, because I thought I could make quicker and easier progress that way. This detour led me to a cabin where I rejoined the others for the night. The next day I headed due west toward Tiksi and found myself on the open tundra. A change of scenery!

After three days Jean-Philippe and the others left me to my fate. There was no one but me, looking out alone over the immense Indigirka Plain, which extended all the way to Tiksi. As if she had sensed my sudden case of the blues, Cathy chose this perfect time to call me on my satellite phone and tell me that she and the girls were going to be able to come visit me in Tiksi. (It wouldn't be too cold, so this was the perfect season for it. The idea that I would soon be able to hold them in my arms again—I hadn't seen them since Nome, seven months before—already made me feel as if I could fly.

Meandering between white hills and white plains, I carved my path through the snow, focused on the rendezvous with Cathy on April 22. There are few flights to Tiksi and they all require a complicated series of connections. I absolutely had to make my arrival there coincide with the arrival of my family, who would also be accompanied by some of my friends and sponsors.

As always, my mind wandered during these long days of marching along. The tendency was accentuated during the Russian portion of my expedition because, with my mind less occupied with technical questions, it was freer to think about other things. I would randomly pick out from the shelves of the library of my memory, books that I hadn't thought of in twenty years. Images would resurface. A classmate whose mother had bought him a pair of odd shoes for Christmas. Those boys on motorcycles who tried to steal our satchels and our lunchboxes one day when we were all bicycling to school together. My father taking me to see Vasco da Gama's cross during a vacation.

The sedimentary layers of new information that are laid on top of the old information every day of our lives and bury it forever were suddenly gone, and paths were opened to parts of my mind to which I previously had no access. Without becoming a nostalgic advocate of the good old days, I will say that I believe that every minute lived is a treasure that helps to make us better people. It helps to polish up those memories and lessons from time to time.

The wind began to work in my favor by hardening the snow, which helped me to go faster. The piles of snow it sculpted were minor obstacles now, and their angles served as compasses once again. My daily average climbed to more than twenty miles, and I was halfway to Tiksi. Despite the resolutions I made before reaching Chokurdakh, I couldn't resist the temptation to get out my kite. That day I beat my Russian record: fifty-two miles in one go!

When the wind died down and I was skiing across a flat and immaculate vastness, I crossed the implausibly huge tracks of a wolf. They might have been tracks of the animal that had been scouting me out at a distance for the past day or so. I remembered Simon's lessons and tried to see whether its fur was short on the side, which would mean it belonged to a pack and was therefore a potential danger, but the tracks weren't quite fresh enough.

Part of my brain was permanently on guard. But when the huge white pheasants of the Arctic sailed over my route, I forgot all my concerns and stood blissfully watching them go by.

The snowy surface had become less stable and more irregular. I would frequently happen upon stretches of "cardboard," crusts where the ski would slip under and remain wedged there. Luckily this never happened while I was using the kite.

In order to get to Tiksi by April 22, I would have to cover between twenty-eight and thirty-one miles daily. I was not far from that average, but the weather was deteriorating. Snow was falling heavily, visibility was dropping to zero, and I was getting bogged down in the snow.

I could see nothing but white. My sense of equilibrium lost its points of reference, and I wobbled and pitched, seized by nausea. To see a little more clearly, I removed my sunglasses, which were misted over and covered with frost. The refracted sunlight burned my eyes, and I was soon afflicted with snow blindness. I had that horrible sensation that I had first experienced in Greenland that made my retinas feel as if they were being sandpapered. No matter what, I had to keep moving.

Three weeks after leaving Chokurdakh, I was on the frozen water of the Laptev Sea. But the fracturing of the pack ice made my progress as slow as the cardboard crusts and the hollows of the tundra. And despite the permanent daylight, the snow was falling harder and kept applying the brakes to my sled.

My eyes were slowly getting better, but I desperately yearned to see something—anything—that wasn't white. A little color, for the love of God!

I projected out my progress, and I would be sixty miles from Tiksi, on the ice of the Buor-Khaia Gulf, when Cathy and the girls arrived there on April 22. If only all of that snow hadn't bogged me down.

I buckled down, though, and made double-time. A few days later, I was in the homestretch. That last day I covered twenty-eight miles over fifteen hours in spite of blinding snow conditions. I had really pushed myself to and past my limits, but it wasn't fatigue that caused me to stop a half-mile short of town.

There were three places on my map called Tiksi! The first Tiksi was the airport and the former military base. The second Tiksi was the outpost of the border guards. The third Tiksi was the town proper.

I had gone well beyond my strength to get here, and I felt incapable of setting out in search of my family. Perhaps they were nearby, perhaps far away. At two in the morning, no one could tell me anything, and I was running the risk of freezing to death.

I decided to camp on the ice near the shore, hoping that my family would find me, but I learned later that when, an hour or two later, Cathy and my daughters came down to look along the shoreline, they didn't see me. I was hidden by the large structures of the port.

In the morning I walked through the town of Tiksi, and I was overwhelmed by the crowd—or what seemed like a crowd to me after all the time I had spent without seeing another human being. The whole village had been waiting for me. They cheered me as if I were a homecoming hero, and they pulled me toward the little hotel, the Mariak (the Sailor), where my family was still sleeping.

I knocked on their door. Cathy was still groggy, and she screamed with surprise when she saw me at the door. My daughters jumped out of bed. It was pure happiness.


The Siberian port town of Tiksi had once been a major industrial center. The machines were no longer running here either, and the population had shrunk from ten thousand to two thousand. The wharves were still haunted by the gaunt silhouettes of the rolling gantry cranes. Yesterday, more than six miles away from town, I had seen them looming over the horizon like a strange banner marking my finish line.

A group of Groupama representatives had accompanied Cathy and my daughters. We were all invited by the mayor to a series of impromptu celebrations being held in our honor. A woman who spoke English—the only one in town—acted as our interpreter and accompanied us everywhere. The clan is a central element of the culture of the residents there, who were mostly of Mongolian origin, and they were especially touched by the fact that I had met up with my family.

I spent as much time as I could with my daughters. I asked them about school and sports. I was interested in hearing all of their stories, no matter how trivial. I tried to make up for lost time as much as I could. Above all, I reminded them that, even when I was gone, I was still with them, that I still loved them just as much, that they were more than ever the most important thing in my life. All these things might have been more obvious if I came home every evening at the same time, so I thought it would be useful to put them into words. And in fact, what we shared during those few short days was a concentrated session of familial love and togetherness.


I was also proud that I had achieved a considerable triumph by crossing the Indigirka Plain and reaching Tiksi just four months after leaving Provideniya! If I kept up this pace, I would cross all of Russia in less than eleven months according to my predictions. I would disprove all those who had told me that it was impossible to do in less than two years.

I happened to run into a Dutch sailor, Henk de Velde, who had left Provideniya the previous August to make a run through the Northeast Passage. Not far from here, though, at Cape Chuluchkan, his sailboat, the *Campina*, had been caught in the ice and was still blocked in the port of Tiksi. The irony was that even though I left Provideniya on foot four months after he left by boat, I had caught up with him. And he wasn't going anywhere anytime soon.

I couldn't get any sleep in the hotel room. The heat, the bed, the curtains—I wasn't used to any of it. In any case, I had lots to do. Using what Cathy had brought, I adapted my equipment to the change of seasons that was underway. It was the beginning of May. I would continue to march over snow, and it would remain about ten degrees below zero in the coming weeks, but I was done with temperatures of twenty degrees below zero and lower. From now on I wouldn't be wearing as many layers of thermal clothing. I would need to wear thinner socks to reduce the perspiration, and I would wear a lighter Gore-Tex parka.

When, five days after I arrived in Tiksi, my wife and daughters boarded their plane and flew home, I missed them much worse than the last time we had been separated. Luckily I was slowly getting closer to returning home.

I spent the night on the iced-in sailboat of my new friend and fellow adventurer, Henk. The next day I could leave the boat and set off immediately.

But when morning arrived, I just couldn't go. I just couldn't get motivated. I had devoted all my energy to leaving the family I loved. I needed to put a little space between the warmth of my family and the icy solitude I was about to plunge into. I needed a breathing space to recover my strength and prepare myself mentally for the challenge ahead. I spent another day aboard the *Campina*, inventorying my equipment.

Now I was ready.

✦ ✦ ✦

On the ice of Buor-Khaia Gulf, I set out for the delta of the Lena River. I figured that I was in time to get across before it could thaw. But just twenty miles out of Tiksi, the storm pinned me down for forty-eight hours, a prisoner in my own tent. I feared that the fury of the squall would break up the ice in the delta.

The following day I wolfed down breakfast in my haste to leave. The northeast wind came to my rescue, and I unfurled my kite. I was traveling lighter than when I arrived in Tiksi, and I made an incredible distance of more than forty-five miles.

When I reached the river mouth, it was covered with a thick, unbroken layer of ice, amounting to a solid, masonry-like bridge linking the two banks. Unfortunately, the sandy sediment that the Lena River carried down in its waters had been churned into the ice, giving the surface a rough consistency that snagged my skis and my sled. At every snag I would take a tumble. All the same, switching off between ski power and being pulled by my kite, I managed to cover seventy-five miles that day! That was three times my average distance traveled before arriving at Tiksi.

At this rate I could even reach the town of Khatanga, on the Khatanga River, before the thaw. And I might make it all the way to Dudinka, on the Yenisei River, with my present supplies. So I decided to push my scheduled resupply back from Khatanga to Dudinka. I also planned to hold a press conference in conjunction with that resupply point to mark the symbolic moment when I switched back to my kayak for the last part of my journey.

The winds held up; in fact, they got stronger and stronger until I was forced to reduce the size of my kite to the area of a large handkerchief.

After setting a new distance record—eighty-seven miles in one day!—I returned to the snowy tundra, and a thorny underbrush began to poke up through the snow. There was twenty-four-hour daylight now, and the relatively mild temperatures around five degrees meant that frostbite wouldn't be a problem anymore unless I fell in the water. All around me, the Arctic wildlife was performing its spectacular springtime show, which reminded me that mother bears and their cubs ought to be emerging from hibernation just about now as well.

With the help of my kite, I was making terrific distance, but the danger of falling or hitting an obstacle meant that I couldn't let my concentration slip for a second. Likewise, I couldn't let up the constant strain of bracing knees and arms to hold the kite. I got tired faster than I did when skiing normally, and at the end of each day there was no feeling left in my legs. They were exposed to the racing wind, and my legs wound up going numb and stiff as two wooden sticks.

The horizon clouded over once again, visibility dropped as well, but the wind kept blowing. Pulled by my kite, I covered more than seventy-five miles one day, and I ached all over; it was just about time to stop for the night. All of a sudden, out of the corner of my eye, I caught a glimpse of a sort of rim, and on the far side of it was . . . nothing. I wasn't completely positive that I had really even seen it. All the same, an alarm bell went off in my brain: I was very close to the Popigay River, and streams of water tend to dig out deep grooves into the tundra soil, creating steep drops along either bank. The ledges alongside these steep river valleys rise as much as thirty to fifty feet straight up, and they easily crumble beneath the weight of the unwary passerby, carrying him down and burying him beneath tons of snow.

When a huge gap suddenly opened up in front of me, I swerved on my skis and stopped short. But my sled, carried forward by the momentum of its 330 pounds, went sailing past me and tipped over into the void. An instant later it was dangling over the void, and I was struggling fiercely to keep from being dragged down after it. At last I managed to get a bit of slack into the harness straps, just enough to release the carabiner and unhook myself. The sled dropped like a boulder and hit the ground about fifteen yards below, hitting a deep layer of snow that broke its fall.

Everything had been going so well—and then suddenly *this*. This accident—which could have ended so much worse—was a warning.

In any case, I could afford to slow down a little bit at this point. I had covered five hundred miles in seven days and, unless I had another accident, I would cover on a single set of supplies the 1,250 miles between Tiksi and Dudinka! That's longer than the distance from Canada to Russia via the North Pole. If everything went well, in less than five months I would be catching sight of the cliffs of North Cape.


But I came very close to never seeing anything again. The next day I hit another ledge at full speed in a thick white fog, and this time went sailing over it without even a chance to slow down, like a ski jumper lofting into the air. My flight was snapped short by the weight of my sled, and I dropped like a brick; the fall, fortunately, was relatively short. But my sled, which came plunging down after me, landed on the side of my thigh. A classic blooper, yes, but an especially painful and dangerous one.

Lying in the snow next to my sled, I felt certain that my leg had been broken. And the physical pain was nothing compared to my horror at the idea that this marked the end of my expedition. Gradually, however, the pain subsided and I regained the use of my leg. Apparently it was nothing serious. When the sled hit me, the depth of the snow had absorbed the impact.

That was my second—and perhaps final—warning to slow down.


I arrived in Khatanga sixteen days after leaving Tiksi. Without counting the three days I was confined to my tent by the storm, that made 750 miles in thirteen days, or slightly over fifty-five miles a day, which was not too shabby!

The little town of Khatanga, set in the middle of the northern Siberian Plain, is closed to visitors except those who have a special permit. At this point in the spring, it was transformed into a sea of mud because of home-heating and car exhaust. I found the relative heat that reigned here very unpleasant. Luckily, shortly after I moved into a sort of family bed-and-breakfast where I was the lone guest, a heavy snowfall freshened up the atmosphere a bit.

Because I had canceled the resupply in Khatanga, I was deprived of the Russian Army maps that I needed to make my way to Norilsk and Dudinka. Cathy faxed me copies and I managed to piece them together into an overall area map.

I prepared to set out along the frozen surface of the Khatanga River. My destination was Volochanka, midway to Dudinka. But locals warned me that the microclimate that prevails on the Putorana Plateau would push warmer waters into the icy waters of the Khatanga and begin to thaw its surface. In other words, I wouldn't be able to reach Dudinka, on the Yenisei River, unless I changed course.

Should I head straight west across the plain? That would be impossible because of the vast and dense pine forests that cover the taiga, the dense woodlands that abut the tundra. There was only one solution: to follow the Kheta River south by southwest until I reached the village of Volochanka, which risked that the whole region might be flooded by the spring thaw before I could reach it.

I left Khatanga after just forty-eight hours there. My race against the spring thaw resumed.


The bed of the Kheta River cut a furrow across a landscape that was entirely new to me: the taiga, which was just like the tundra but with trees. The trees—armies of short, scrubby pine trees stretching out to the horizon—were the first ones I had seen since setting out on my expedition.

I dragged my sled along the frozen river, trudging through a mixture of mud, sand, dog excrement, and garbage of all sorts.

The next day I tried using my kite, but my skis got caught on an invisible sandy surface concealed beneath a thin layer of snow, and I went sprawling onto the ice. My nose was bloodier than a crushed tomato, but I covered seventy-one miles that day in spite of it.

The following day however I couldn't make more than twenty-six miles. I was caught in a heavy snowstorm, and the strong westerly wind kept me from using my kite.

The thermometer was climbing, and the snow grew soft, clumping up beneath my skis in heavy packets. Between the oatmeal underfoot and a solid white fog through which I was traveling blind, I was making only minimal progress. To top off my problems, I discovered that there was pack ice on rivers as well. Luckily the fractured pack ice that the currents and eddies of the Kheta River created only forced me to make a few minor detours. To compensate for the delay that the pack ice caused me, I decided to indulge in a twenty-four-hour makeup day.

The wolves, which had remained out of the picture until now, began to follow me again. From time to time I would glimpse one or several. They followed the same tactics as their Canadian cousins, who had stalked me from a cautious distance on Saputing Lake: trap their victim on a frozen lake or river where there was no escape.

Clearly they were hesitant about attacking me—I looked so different from their usual prey—but I knew they never lost sight of me. I could sense their presence, even when I couldn't see them.

There was also a dog that had been following me for a number of days, and from a much closer distance. It was a Siberian husky that must have lost its mother, and it was probably hoping that I would feed it. Unfortunately, I had no food to spare for the dog. But when I thought it over, I couldn't stand the idea of letting it die of hunger. After all, at the speed I was traveling, I would likely have plenty of provisions to make it as far as Dudinka. The backup supply of stale bread that I had packed away somewhere would make a very respectable bag of crunchy treats.

The dog kept on following me and slept outside of my tent every night. I decided to call him Arktos. He became my best friend.

Day after day I kept in a corner of my mind the image of that cliff at North Cape, which constituted both my starting line and my finish line. I had etched it into my memory so that I could visualize it whenever I needed and tell myself, "That's where I'm going."

+ + +

With just a few dilapidated huts and a handful of isolated but friendly inhabitants—once they got over their surprised fright at the sight of their first foreigner, who was, no doubt, a spy—Volochanka was a ghost town. In four or five years it would probably no longer exist.

The first person I met there was the real owner of Arktos. He was delighted to get his dog back and thanked me effusively for having brought him back. I was going to miss his company, but it was certainly better for everyone this way.

From here I was planning to follow the Kheta River until it joined the Piasina River, which I would then follow to the Yenisei River. But the locals told me that 125 miles from here the Kheta had already thawed. I would only be able to walk on the ice for about four more days.

After careful consideration, I decided not to head north to reach the Piassina River. Instead, I would walk along the Putorana Plateau and cross Lake Piasino, on a line with Norilsk, which would then take me on to Dudinka.

In the taiga, the snow was melting in patches. Wild geese, ducks, swans, hares, and foxes reappeared in a world that could finally feed them again. Huge herds of caribou crossed the plain. My old buddies the bears were there, too, but only to be glimpsed at a distance. They were brown bears, though—not very aggressive and rather shy compared to their polar bear cousins.

This plain in northern Siberia is a veritable nature preserve where an incredibly rich fauna frolicked as it had thousands of years ago, no doubt because there were no human beings to disturb them.

The rushing torrents of meltwater that poured off the Putorana Plateau made the streams and rivers overflow their banks, sweeping along with them muddy ice floes and the occasional full-fledged iceberg.

I crossed a succession of rivers, doing my best to keep my balance as I made my way across drifting slabs of ice.

Some rivers were covered with a crust of snow as fragile as paper. The instant my attention wavered, I would drop through into the icy water, and clambering would only assure that I would freeze all the sooner. At five to fifteen degrees, it was still plenty cold for that.

On other rivers the layer of ice was covered with water, which undermined its structural strength. One of these water-covered mirrors collapsed beneath me, and I found myself standing thigh-deep in water. All around me, the ice was shifting and cracking. I held my breath and did my best to spread my weight, to stress the ice as little as possible.

I was permanently soaked now, as was my gear.

What with the treacherous snow, the melting ice, and the overflowing rivers, springtime in the Arctic is no easier a season on the traveler than winter. In fact, it's worse in many ways. In the winter you are prepared for the rigors of extreme cold. In springtime, because the weather is not as harsh, you tend to be less cautious, to lower your guard, which only makes it more dangerous.


A sudden cold snap firmed up the snow and made it thicker, which allowed me to launch my kite for a few hours. But when the tundra began to turn into marshland, I was forced to ski along the bed of the Avam River, which was flooding its banks. I was walking knee-deep in water. I was beginning to understand why, in Khatanga, people had told me that I would never make it to Dudinka.

I needed to get there, though, and fast! Otherwise, I would be forced to swim.

I decided to begin marching at night—night being the dimmer part of the daylight—just as I had in Canada and Alaska because the few-degree drop in temperature made the ice more solid and firmed up the snow. I decided to venture for the first time off the icy surface of the river Avam to cut across its oxbow curves. As a result, I was forced to fight my way through a pine forest. My skis, my sled, and the straps of my harness continually snagged the resinous branches as I progressed.

The snow was so deep that I regularly sank chest-deep into it; the horizon was so restricted that I had no landmarks to refer to. It felt as if I was walking in place.

When I made it back to the Avam, after ten hours of exhausting struggle, I realized that my shortcut had taken two hours longer than if I had stayed on the river. I continued to move forward, and finally I left the watershed of the Putorana Plateau. Soon thereafter, I arrived on the shores of Lake Piasino.

I expected that it would be impassable, but it turned out that it was still frozen solid. The ice was no doubt not very thick, but I was ready to take a chance rather than being forced to detour around it, which would have taken me closer to Norilsk. It had become a habit of mine to avoid towns and human settlements of all kinds, especially bigger ones like Norilsk. The smoke and clouds of pollution, visible from dozens of miles away, depressed and disheartened me.

Lake Piasino was so big that once I moved out onto its surface I couldn't see the far shore—it was forty miles long. At the lake's southern end a river flowed in, making the ice especially fragile. That was why I was crossing the northern half where the river water had not yet warmed the top layer of ice. Even so, the unsettling cracking sounds that followed me as I walked gave a clear idea of how thin the ice was. I was skiing over glass, which gave me a cold sweat, but I made it.

My last resupply was in Tiksi, 1,250 miles ago, and I was beginning to run short on food supplies. Cathy and my team took advantage of the press conference they were arranging, which would be held ten miles outside of Dudinka, to bring me new provisions. My sponsors would fly the journalists in by helicopter and land them in the heart of the tundra. They would stay in two large tents pitched very close to my tent. That way, the journalists would feel as if they were really a part of the expedition.

When I reached the rendezvous point, I had to wait for my team. I learned that they had arrived safely in Moscow, but apparently the representative of our travel agency had taken them all out to enjoy a pleasant lunch while waiting to catch the flight to Norilsk, and he had forgotten the departure time! Incredible, but true!

I chose to wait where I was until they could catch the next flight.

I waited for six days in the middle of nowhere. If I waited much longer, I would be unable to cross the Yenisei on foot. Already the water was rising around me, and I was forced to move my tent.

At last they arrived from Norilsk. Helicopters carried the journalists to Dudinka, where I joined them on skis. Then I returned with them to Norilsk, even though I had sworn that I would avoid the town, for a few photo sessions and concluding interviews. Once they were back on their plane, I set off for Dudinka.

The Yenisei River, now in full thaw, carried only fragments of ice, bobbing along on its rushing torrents, which were fully four-and-a-half miles across! I hardly need to point out that it was useless to think of crossing in anything other than a kayak or another type of boat.

Unfortunately, my kayak, which was supposed to be delivered with my supplies, was still stuck in customs in Moscow. So, I improvised. I fitted a sort of inflatable dinghy around my sled, which made it look more or less like a motorless Zodiac, and I paddled across the river perched atop this odd contraption.

However, once I was on the far bank, I realized that it would be impossible to make any further progress, due to the lack of snow. I had planned to go on skis to the Tazovsky Gulf, but this waterlogged tundra was wholly impassable by skis. I couldn't even drag my equipment across it. That six-day wait for my team had proved to be very costly.

I returned to Dudinka to drop off my sled. Sergei, who was providing crack support work for my expedition from Moscow, would have it shipped back to Norilsk with my winter equipment. I set off carrying a seventy-pound backpack for the relatively short trek over the tundra toward the Messoyakhta River. My team would send my kayak there for me by helicopter, and then I would paddle along the river to the open waters of the Tazovsky Gulf.

I was carrying fifteen days' worth of provisions, an ultralight tent and sleeping bag, clothing that was waterproof and windproof, a smaller version of my camp stove, and a minimum supply of fuel. Where I was going, the rivers carried sufficient driftwood to make a fire whenever I needed to.

It wasn't long before I chanced upon the gas pipeline that Gazprom, the Russian company exploiting the vast natural gas reserves of the region, used to transport natural gas to Norilsk. The town required huge quantities of fuel to operate its nickel mines, which were among the biggest nickel-producing facilities on earth. The mines were the reason for the town's existence, and they were also the cause of the monstrous pollution that has ravaged the surrounding countryside.

The gas pipeline is about thirty years old, and it was built by the last prisoners of the neighboring Siberian gulag. These were the descendants, as it were, of the prisoners who built the Trans-Siberian Railroad on Stalin's orders. Around here there are still people who talk about those unfortunate souls who died of cold, sometimes frozen to the rails they were working on.

The enormous rusty pipeline—five feet in diameter and raised above the ground—runs for hundreds of miles all the way to the Messoyakhta gas field.

That was the direction I was headed, so I climbed on top of it and played at being a tightrope walker. It wasn't always easy to keep my balance. My backpack acted like a sail in the wind, which would shake me and make the pipeline sway at the same time. To make things harder, the pipeline was covered with a greasy rust-proofing that was horribly slippery. I would walk slowly and diagonally with my arches curving to the arc of the pipeline, but I still fell off and hit the ground a number of times.

On some long sections—especially rivers—the pipeline was suspended as high as fifty feet over the brown water in which I could see my shadow. I sometimes broke into a cold sweat as I carefully focused on staying upright and not tumbling into the river below.

Because the pipeline expands and contracts with changes in temperature, it is built in a zigzag formation between joints, where a little play was built into the structure. This gives it an accordion effect that allows the pipeline to become longer or shorter by a whopping two hundred yards over its total length of three hundred miles! The zigzagging shape was the cause of some minor added distance, but the countless rivers and lakes in the region were also the cause of more significant detours—when they were too broad, the pipeline didn't cross them, it went around them.

At the banks of the Malaya Kheta River, the "little Kheta," the pipeline vanished underwater. So I no longer had the option of walking on it. Wearing my waterproof suit—large chunks of ice were still bobbing in the water—I swam across, pushing my backpack ahead of me in an old can that had been sawed in half.

Another river, the Bolshaya Kheta, or "big Kheta," forced me to repeat this exercise (without a can this time because I couldn't find one). The river was a good half-mile across, and when I finally reached the opposite shore after an hour of swimming, its rushing currents had swept me two and a half miles downstream. It took me four hours, bogged down in a marsh where I felt as if I were running an assault course, to get back on course.

Between crossing the two rivers, the marsh, and the time that I spent getting back on my route, I had made just over a mile of actual progress in an entire day! And the two icy rivers, despite my waterproof suit, left me in a state of partial hypothermia that caused numbness and slowed down all my actions.

The weather had improved drastically, but it changes incredibly quickly in the Arctic. On a regular basis, short but furious rain showers soaked the tundra, giving it the rough consistency of a sponge. I had a pair of very high waders, like the ones fly fishermen wear, and they kept me from getting absolutely soaked when the winds grew so strong that I was forced to get down from the pipeline. I would alternate them with a pair of light, quick-drying sport sandals from Salomon that water gets into—and out of—easily. These shoes gave me an ideal degree of agility on the tundra, even if my feet did get a little chilly.

At night I wasn't exactly warm in my single-walled summer tent. The air no longer circulated between the double walls, and the tent would mist up quickly with the regular downpours and my own moisture and body heat.

During my hours of walking, I would hear no sound other than the uninterrupted whistling of the wind, broken now and again by the harsh cry of an Arctic bird, including a species of owl that communicates with other members of its species by gazing into the other's eyes—over distances as great as a half-mile! My feet would sink into the muddy soil with a regular hissing sound at a pace that has been stamped into my subconscious; the slightest slowing in the rhythm of that endless sloshing would alert me that I was getting tired, even before I began to feel the fatigue in my body.

In the permanent night of the Arctic winter, my sense of hearing had become as acute as a blind person's, and on the thawed tundra I felt as if I could now hear the seasons changing. My other senses developed equally. I could savor the smell of the sea for a long time before actually coming within sight of it. I could also smell the presence of any Arctic animal you care to name. I had become an animal myself—at least in part. That was the only way to survive.


After crossing the Bolshaya Kheta, I climbed back onto the gas pipeline. A few miles later I happened upon a cabin where a man lived who was responsible for monitoring the pressure in the pipeline. That was all he did, twenty-four hours a day, in shifts of fifteen days, just like all the other Gazprom employees in the region. Every four hours he would send in a pressure report to the main station, using a code name.

The gas-pressure measurer was named Tola, and I invited myself into his house to warm up and recover my strength after my two river crossings. He was delighted to have a visitor, and he pampered me. He gave me a haircut and treated me to a *banya*—a Russian sauna.

When Cathy told me that the customs people in Moscow were still holding onto my kayak and that I would have to wait another day or two for it, I told myself that I was as happy here, in "Chez Tola," as I would be on the banks of the Messoyakhta River.

When I set out again after two days, there was still ice on the lakes, but after forty-eight hours of relatively mild temperatures, there wasn't a speck of snow on the tundra itself. I saw this as a hopeful sign. This time, winter was really over. The Arctic had officially entered the season of mild weather.

In the land of ice, there are only two seasons: winter and the season that was about to begin. It lasts just two weeks. The brevity of the season means that when the snows melt, it is like watching a film being run fast-forward. The tundra shifts from brown to green in twenty-four hours. In the light that never dims, all you need to do is sit motionless and fix your attention on a given point and you can see the grass grow and the plants bloom—literally, not just as a manner of speech! From one day to the next, the tundra is suddenly dotted with nests. Life bursts out all over. Little ones must be raised to the age of molting so that their feathers will allow them to fly south before the brutal cold returns. Their apprenticeship in survival is a crash course—the foxes are out stalking them almost from the start. The tundra mice are out, sniffing and lifting their snouts into the air; ducks and swans rummage along the riverbanks; wild geese wheel through the sky.

The vegetation was in full bloom. I could sit down wherever I liked and stock up on mushrooms, stuff myself with blackberries by just reaching out my hand.

Unfortunately, the birds were stuffing themselves with blackberries, too, and there was now an abundance of bird shit on the pipeline, making it even slipperier than before.

And as soon as the lakes were done thawing, it was time for the mosquitoes to make their appearance. Swarms, hordes, clouds of mosquitoes were ready to devour on the hoof or the foot whatever animal they chanced upon, including humans. They only relented when the tundra winds swept them away. The rest of the time you just had to deal with them because they were an indispensable link in the chain of life there—they, in turn, would be eaten by fish and other insects.

My experience crossing the Amazon jungle four years earlier had given me a Zen-like attitude toward mosquitoes. Moreover, Tola gave me a very loose-knit sweater, over which you put on a sort of mosquito-net shirt. The little monsters couldn't get to me through the netting because of the thickness of the woolen yarn in the sweater beneath. As for the sweater itself, it was reminiscent of a fishnet, and it didn't keep me too warm, thankfully. On certain days during this short Siberian summer, the thermometer would rise to over eighty-five degrees!

If I compare this temperature with the coldest temperatures that I experienced during the course of this expedition—around seventy-five degrees below zero—then I can say I experienced total temperature swings of 160 degrees!

Just like the landscape, I changed in appearance at a startling rate myself. My frostbite blisters formed scars, and the skin on my face that had been scorched by the cold healed. I even had a suntan that any vacationer would envy.

My daily habits and routines changed just as quickly. For instance, when in conditions of extreme cold I needed to make a bowel movement, I wouldn't give in to the urge until the "third call," and I would be in such a hurry to get dressed again that I often lacked the time to relieve myself completely. During the summer, I would answer nature's call promptly, but I continued to get dressed again very hastily as soon as I was done relieving myself. This time it wasn't because of the hostile cold, but the millions of mosquitoes that would swarm like a tornado onto my excrement, my buttocks, and my private parts just as soon as I dropped my drawers.

The pipeline took me toward the little village of Yuzhno-Solynensky ("south bank") on the banks of the Messoyakhta River. It was the site of the last gas-drilling stations on the line, as well as the compression station that sends the natural gas three-hundred–plus miles to Norilsk, with a stopover at Tola's cabin.

Yuzhno-Solynensky was where I was supposed to pick up my kayak. It was going to be delivered to me in conjunction with the bimonthly staff rotation between here and Norilsk, via Gazprom helicopters. At least this time I could be certain that everything would run on time.

However, when I was twenty-five miles away from the rendezvous point, Cathy called to report that my kayak was lost! The shipping office confirmed that the kayak had been sent to Norilsk, and that's where it had vanished.

I thought my situation over. In the worst case, I could always hike as far as the Tazovsky Gulf, or even to the Gulf of Ob. But I would be stuck there, unable to cross twenty-eight miles of open water. And going around the gulf would force me to drop below the Arctic Circle, which I had stipulated I would not do if at all possible. In short, I absolutely needed the damned kayak.

A new logistical nightmare was beginning, in which I expected to go on a devious Russian bureaucratic scavenger hunt with the following goal in mind: to find the person holding my property and persuade him to hand it over with a smile in exchange for a sufficiently thick bundle of dollars. If the person failed to turn up, that would be part of the game as well. The longer it took me to find the kayak, the more urgently I would need it and the more I would be willing to pay for it.

The next day, a new and surprising development played out. My kayak had been found . . . in Moscow! It had never left the city, despite what the Gazprom office had claimed. There was another agreeable surprise: no one was asking for cash. Sergei, my contact in Moscow, promised me that my boat would be in Yuzhno-Solynensky in four days. We would see about that.

Since I was forced to wait again, I decided to wait on the banks of the Messoyakhta River at the home of another Sergei, the chief engineer of a fifteen-man machine maintenance shop. After two days I reckoned that it was time to start traveling again, and I was treated to the customary ceremony. First, you have to throw back a glassful of *samogon*, a homemade blackberry vodka. Then, in accordance with the tradition that I had experienced once before in Pevek when the FSB was after me, each of the men took a turn sitting on my backpack to bring me luck. Only after that ceremony was I allowed to resume my journey. Or, perhaps I should say, my pipeline.


At the end of the summer on the tundra, mosquitoes are replaced by an even more challenging breed: the *moskos*, known in English as noseeums, from "no-see-them." The tiny creatures don't suck your blood, they tear off patches of flesh. The resulting itch is even worse than what you get from a mosquito bite. The *moskos* got into my eyes, my nostrils, and even climbed up my sleeves as far as my wrists, causing an intolerable case of itching. Luckily, Sergei provided me with an effective remedy, a bottle of *samogon*. I only needed to rub it on the most sensitive spots to drive off the *moskos*. It worked like a charm!


This stroll of some 185 miles along the Siberian pipeline hadn't been easy, far from it. However, because of the extraordinary spectacle that it provided and the new experiences that it allowed me to enjoy, it had been a complete pleasure from one end to the other.

In Yuzhno-Solynensky, the Gazprom station chief, alerted to my arrival by Sergei, offered very generously to let me stay in his house while waiting for my kayak to arrive. Not once since Dudinka had I enjoyed anything less than an open-armed welcome, warm and generous. In this entire region where most of the jobs are linked to the natural gas industry, each person I met informed someone else farther down the road of my arrival. Each time I was greeted like a long-lost brother. It was a good excuse for a celebration as well, since most of the people here told me themselves that they had never seen a foreigner come through.

Russian bureaucracy is one thing, but the Russians are quite another—wonderful people, indeed. I'll miss them.

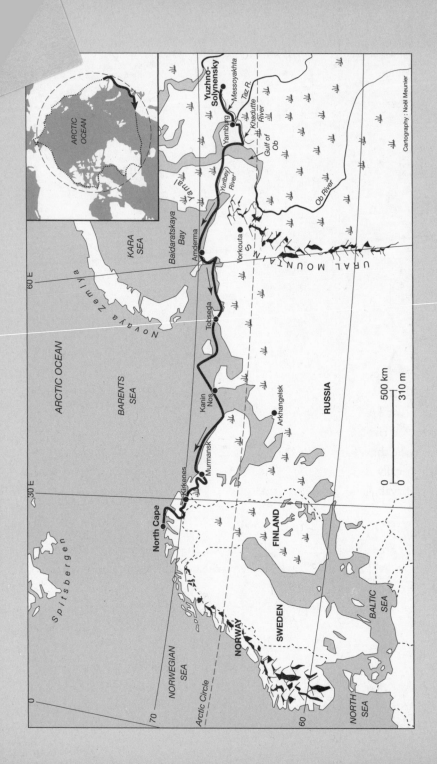

ARCTIC OCEAN

ARCTIC OCEAN

NORWEGIAN SEA

BARENTS SEA

KARA SEA

Spitsbergen

Novaya Zemlya

Yamal

North Cape

Kirkenes

Murmansk

Kanin Nos

Tobseda

Amderma

Baidaratskaya Bay

Vorkouta

URAL MOUNTAINS

Arkhangelsk

Yuribey River

Yamburg

Khadutte River

Gulf of Ob

Ob River

Taz R.

Messoyakha

Yuzhno-Solymensky

NORWAY

SWEDEN

FINLAND

RUSSIA

BALTIC SEA

NORTH SEA

Arctic Circle

70

60

0

30 E

60 E

0        500 km

0        310 m

Cartography : Noël Meunier

# 8

# The Last Man

At yuzhno-solynensky I carried out a number of scouting excursions along the banks of the Messoyakhta River to find the easily navigable stretches. Three rivers flow into the Messoyakhta so that I should be able to paddle as far as the Tazovsky Gulf. Although the rivers and streams swell and overflow when the snow melts, once the thaw is complete the water level drops until the riverbeds are practically dry. The period when most rivers are navigable, even aboard a kayak, is no longer than two weeks.

Three days after I arrived, the station chief woke me up in a rush.

"Mike! The helicopter bringing the new shift in will be here any second. It's bringing your kayak!"

I couldn't imagine how Sergei took care of the problem so quickly in Moscow. Certainly he had called on one of his many contacts and acquaintances, but in any case, he had done a great job.

I made an inventory of the damage the kayak had suffered: one broken paddle, various pieces of equipment missing. But the mast and the floats were still there, as well as the waterproof bags designed to keep my luggage dry. Part of the food rations that had been sent to me along with the kayak were missing, but I wouldn't need as many calories in the warm weather: four thousand calories a day would be enough. Thanks to the fishing net that Tola had given me, I would be able to fish. The Messoyakhta River was teeming with fish.

This river, like all the streams of the Arctic, would soon freeze over again. When I left again, the water was already so shallow that I had to slalom between the sandbars.

The river had plenty of curves that lengthened the distance I had to cover. After covering four and a half miles, I had gone no more than a half-mile westward. After covering thirty-seven miles of meandering, I had only covered nine miles in the right direction! One consolation was that it had started raining again, which lifted the water level a bit and accentuated the favorable current.

All around, the animals were full of vigor. The caribou waded into the river to escape the fury of the mosquitoes. Only their heads stuck out of the water, topped by their majestic antlers. Because they rarely heard me coming, they wouldn't notice me until the last instant, and then they'd start suddenly, their hulking bodies splashing me in the face with buckets of water as they hurried out of my way. The savage, magnificent spectacle continued. I didn't get tired of it and—after all the months I had spent in the icy, dead darkness—I would never tire of it.

To keep out of reach of the brown bears—less dangerous around here, but I was still not interested in running risks—I would camp in the middle of the river on the sandbars. I avoided pitching my tent on spits of land where they were likely to come to catch fish or play. After all, this is where they live. It was up to me to respect their territory.

While I slept, my fishnet, submerged in the water, prepared my meals for the next day. And the eggs, mushrooms, and blackberries with which the tundra abounded allowed me to vary my menus.

The days went by, and I hadn't seen another human being since Yuzhno-Solynensky.

The wind sprang up on me, blowing so furiously that it tore sand off the shoals and blasted it into my eyes, nostrils, and mouth. I had sand grinding constantly between my teeth. My paddle would catch the wind so that I would have to push it through the air on the up stroke before plunging it into the water. This effort, added to the work of pulling the 265 pounds of gear and food in addition to the weight of the kayak, made my upper body musculature undergo a sudden beef-up.

Since I hadn't paddled in quite a while, it took me five or six days to get back into the necessary shape.

My daily distances, fairly modest at first—nine, sixteen, seventeen miles—now began to reach twenty-five miles, just like when I was traveling on skis. The only difference was that the oxbow curves of the Messoyakhta River forced me to paddle more than sixty miles to travel the twenty-five miles of useful distance!

On July 16, I drank a toast to myself—of river water—and gave myself a birthday present of twenty-four hours of nonstop paddling, from midnight to midnight. The wind was soft, the weather was ideal, and I enjoyed a front-row view of the wilderness and magnificent fauna all around me, beneath the midnight sun. I felt like the most privileged man on earth.

As if it had been honoring a truce for my birthday, the wind began to blow hard the next day, making it virtually impossible to paddle. When the wind shifted, I took advantage of the opportunity to hoist the sail and put out the floats. The Americans who provided me with these accessories assured me that they were all-terrain and ultra-strong. I made the mistake of taking them at their word; at the first strong gust of wind, the whole assembly fell to pieces. This was all the more catastrophic because I was going to need that sail all along the course I planned to kayak from here to Tobseda, on the Barents Sea. I was going to need to cross that sea by sailboat before the storms produced by the series of autumn depressions made navigation impossible. I wasn't interested in waiting till next winter so that I could cross it on foot.

The failure of my mast support and float-arm structure would force me to paddle all the way to Tobseda. At my current rate of paddling, by the time I was on the Barents Sea, there wouldn't even be any windows between storms!

I was furious at the manufacturers. I felt as if they had stabbed me in the back! Their equipment might be guaranteed to "stand up to anything," as long as that was limited to summer sailing on Lake Geneva! To top it off, now the structure was deadweight. It would only slow me down to have to pull that much more weight with every paddle-stroke.

As I got closer to the mouth of the Messoyakhta River, with nary a human being nor a village anywhere in sight and nothing marked on my maps, I suddenly heard what resembled the distant roar of a tractor. The closer I got to the Tazovsky Gulf, the louder the sound grew. As if a small army of invisible steam shovels were working away somewhere nearby.

Suddenly, as I paddled out into the estuary, I saw an army of bull-dozers moving earth—ships, tugboats, machine-tools, and prefab houses being built. It seemed as if a city was being thrown up here out of nothing. If they were building a city out here, it ought to be possible to find someone to fix a mast support and a float-arm structure.

The first worker that I stopped and asked told me that the construction site was for the future natural gas field, which had just been discovered. It would be hooked up with a new pipeline that would run underwater for seven and a half miles under the bay. Workers were already welding together sections extending over many miles and then sinking them to be buried under the floor of the estuary. The future pipeline would deliver Russian natural gas to two of Gazprom's biggest customers: Germany and France.

I asked to be taken to the office of the chief engineer, a mobile home that could move with the project and that would soon be on the far side of the estuary. The engineer asked me where I had come from.

"Provideniya," I replied.

He paused for a beat.

"Buketa de Provideniya?" (Provideniya Bay?)

*"Da. In Chukotka."*

He jumped up and then plopped back down into his chair as if somebody had hit him on the head.

"What can I do for you?" he asked.

I explained briefly.

Instantly, the entire construction site—which must have cost hundreds of thousands of dollars a day to operate—came to a screeching halt. The entire staff gathered around my kayak and wracked its brains. There was no aluminum on the worksite, nothing but pieces of pipeline and welding materials. Each worker suggested solutions to my problem. Seeing how tired I was, the chief of the site suggested that I go get some sleep.

"When you wake up," he told me, "your boat will be fixed and ready to go."

Someone took me to the cafeteria, where I enjoyed a lavish meal and was given supplies of fruit and cookies. Then they showed me to a mobile home with two beds and a bathroom, where I had my first hot shower since Yuzhno-Solynensky.

Before letting me go to sleep, the chief engineer took me to his private den and pulled out a magnificent box lined with red velvet. It contained a bottle of Johnny Walker Blue Label Whiskey—a gift from a supplier whom he had helped to get a contract. He set two vodka glasses on the table and filled them until they were almost overflowing. We clicked our glasses and drank them down.

*"Davai, davai! Yesho raz!"* he cried. (Come on, come on! Let's have one more!) The Russians, I was beginning to understand, are never content with a single glass. My host threw back his precious scotch as if it were water. I drank more cautiously, since I hadn't had a drop in such a long time—except when, at each resupply, Jean-Philippe would bring one of the now-traditional bottles of Val de Travers absinthe from our friend the restaurateur, Pierre-Alain.

As soon as my head hit the pillow, I was asleep. When I opened one eye, seven hours later, my kayak was waiting for me on the doorstep. It was brand-new, ready to set sail. In that short period of time, the Russians had quite simply cut out of the alloy that made up the pipeline—and trimmed to the tenth of an inch!—an exact replica of my float arm and mast-support structure. And considering the metal they used, this one really might stand up to anything!

And in fact they told me, "Russian-made. Will never break!"

Because it is impossible to lay sections of the pipeline except when there is no wind at all and the sea is perfectly calm, the construction site has the most reliable weather forecasts. They warned me that bad weather was coming and that there would be a strong north wind. They expected the wind to whip up such heavy waves in the bay that it would be impossible for me to leave as I had planned. My only option, they told me, was to follow the Khadutte River. If I went up that river, paddling against the stream, following it in a south by southwesterly direction for about thirty miles, I would reach a bridge that does not appear on any maps. That bridge links up with a road that would lead me to the village of Yamburg on the Gulf of Ob.

I thanked everyone, but it seemed a feeble way of responding to the incredible generosity that I had been shown in that village that had no name. Soon the north wind was filling my sail, and I was zipping over the waters of the Tazovsky Gulf. Like the Bering Strait, it was shallow and therefore the waves were especially steep. As I went sliding over one of these towering waves, my extra double paddle fastened to the kayak acted as a wing flap that drove the bow of the kayak down and plunged it into the following wave. Suddenly I was almost vertical, my kayak nose down in the water, driven deeper by the wave that was coming up from behind me. I paddled furiously in the opposite direction to restore my equilibrium, but I could feel myself tipping over forward. If I capsized in the middle of the bay, three miles from shore, I would never survive!

At that very instant, flexing under the opposing pressures of the wind and the effort I was exerting on it, my extra paddle snapped like a dead branch, with a sharp crack. That's what saved me. Freed from the downward pressure, the kayak lifted its bow. I continued on with my "Indian-style" paddle. The two pieces of the other paddle remained fastened to the kayak, and I would find a way of fixing them sooner or later.

The waves carried me and the wind pushed me to the mouth of the Khadutte River. Just as I entered the river, the storm tossed me onto a sandbar. This final accident, after coming so close to going under entirely in the middle of the bay, confirmed my decision to take the southern route across the inlet. The people working on the pipeline were right—if I had gone across to the north with the wind against me, I would never have made it.

I would store their second piece of advice away for the near future: be sure that the weather is favorable before venturing out across the twenty-mile-wide Gulf of Ob, an inlet where storms are frequent and violent. Gazprom had lost barges there that were certainly much sturdier than my kayak.

I pitched my tent on the tundra alongside the Khadutte River. The next day I was delighted to still be alive when I set out to make my way through the countless meanderings and terrible currents of this river. I embarked after the wind had died down and allowed the seawater to flow out of the river. Unfortunately, once the wind died down, the mosquitoes also began attacking.

I was determined to avoid all unnecessary risks. I was still more than six hundred miles from Tobseda, so this wasn't the time to ruin everything. I could afford to be cautious, but not overly cautious.

The curves of the Khadutte River protected me from waves, but they slowed me down terribly. With the river flowing against me, the sixteen to eighteen hours that I spent paddling each day only yielded about twelve and a half miles of forward progress. On average I made about half-a-mile's progress for every two miles I traveled.

Maybe I should have turned north, now that the storm in the Tazovsky Gulf had died down. In any case, it was too late to head back. I focused on Tobseda, my goal.

I didn't stop even to pee during my long days. When I got out of my kayak, the blood had long since stopped circulating in my legs and I had a hard time standing up.

After three days on the Khadutte River, I finally discovered the bridge that they had told me about and a paved road that led to Yamburg on the Gulf of Ob.

I hauled my kayak out of the water, determined to stop the first truck that came by and ask the driver to take my kayak to Yamburg. I would go on foot.

Soon a big semitrailer came to a halt. The driver happily agreed to take my kayak and leave it at the police station in Yamburg, where I could show up later and claim it.

While my kayak was traveling ahead by truck, I walked along the road. It was an amazing sensation! I could hardly remember when I'd last walked on a paved road—in Provideniya, perhaps? The weather was nice. It all seemed too wonderful to be true.


And so it was. Thirty miles from the bridge, I found a roadblock in my way, sternly guarded by armed soldiers. On the ground outside their barracks, I saw my kayak. This spelled trouble.

"Where do you think you are going?" a soldier asked me.

"To Yamburg. Why?"

"Do you have a *proposk*? A permit?"

I pulled out my passport, I showed him my Russian visa, and I showed him all my various permits. However, at the Gazprom construction site, they had forgotten to tell me that Yamburg was a major private gas field, and access was strictly forbidden to all unauthorized individuals. The only way to get in was with a special permit.

The soldier told me without missing a beat that I needed to turn around and go back to Novyi Yurengoy, 250 miles to the south! That's where I would find the office that could issue permits for Yamburg. However, permits were issued only to people with a professional reason to gain access to the site. I was not going to travel five hundred miles on foot, round trip, just so someone could refuse to issue me a permit.

I insisted, explained, and argued for hours. But I might as well have been talking to the wall.

Even as I argued with the uniformed soldiers, I was wondering whether I should leave the road and go overland, across the tundra. The guards had warned me that if I tried that, they would have every right to shoot me! Another option was to return to the Khadutte River, paddle up it a few dozen miles and portage my kayak over to the Gulf of Ob. A third possibility was to double back to the Tazovsky Gulf, risking the choppy waters in my kayak. However, each of the two latter options would take an extra ten days, and I couldn't spare ten days. Moreover, the water level was dropping quickly in the Khadutte River, which would soon be impassable even by kayak. I had to make some forward progress by any means necessary.

I promised the soldiers that if they let me through, I wouldn't even go to Yamburg—I would go around the site and set out to sea immediately. The answer was still no, and they employed the eternal excuse: "We're just doing our job." How many times would I hear that phrase? They agreed to call their superior officer, and he insisted that I not be allowed to proceed.

Since I was required to wait at least twenty-four hours before leaving, they showed me to a sort of tiny lumber room next to the guard post, with a metal table for a bed. I called Sergei in Moscow.

"It's Friday night," he said. "I can't do a thing until Monday."

I had three days to wait, and after the three days Sergei made it clear to me that there was no certainty he would be able to get me through.

I had to make a choice: either I relied on Sergei and waited here, or else I decided not to run the risk and turned back, which would cost me fifteen days.

Maybe there were other options. I spent most of Saturday tinkering with my kayak, moving it, unpacking and repacking my equipment. Once the guards grew used to my presence and lost interest in me, I innocently moved the kayak to the other side of the barrier.

I still didn't know how I would make my escape, because once I was on the "right side" of the roadblock I wouldn't be in a much better position. The road stretched out, straight as an arrow and as flat as my hand for dozens of miles. There wouldn't be a thing in sight but me, and I would make an easy target, especially if I was dragging a kayak behind me.

But thirty yards past the gate there were two huts that served as warehouses for maintenance supplies. After three days of acrobatics, I managed to hide my boat behind them.

I had been stuck there for four days. To think that I had been congratulating myself for following the advice given me by the people back at the pipeline worksite. I might have done better if I had stayed with my original plan to follow the Tazovsky Gulf all the way to its mouth at the Gulf of Ob.

A plan began to take shape in my head. Trucks, after passing the roadblock, would sometimes stop by the maintenance service huts. If I could convince one of the drivers to load my kayak onto his truck and take it to Yamburg, then I might be onto something. I had walked from the roadblock to the maintenance warehouses a number of times without alarming the guards. Once my kayak was gone, I would only need to escape across the tundra, where they would never catch me.

I asked each of the drivers arriving from Yamburg if they could stop on the next trip just long enough to load my boat onto their truck. One finally agreed—the promise of twenty or thirty U.S. dollars helped him to make up his mind. He would pass through again on Tuesday and would load my boat on his way through.

The guards at the gate had seen me come and go, disappear and reappear, so many times that they hardly noticed me at all. I would head out farther and farther along the forbidden road, as far as sixteen miles, but I would always come back. Whenever anyone asked what I was doing, I would simply answer that I was exercising to keep in shape.

I hoped that I blended into the background so well by now that on Tuesday, at the changing of the guard—there is a change of shift every twelve hours—the soldiers would forget to tell the new shift to keep an eye on me. If that was the case, I would be able to make my escape easily.

On Monday Sergei told me that he didn't think he would able to resolve the situation through official channels.

On Tuesday there was no reaction from the guards after a whole day went by without their seeing me. That was a good sign. It seemed that my window was approaching. But my truck driver was late.

Just to see what was happening, I gave Sergei a call. He was ecstatic, "I did it, Mike! You can go! My friend from Murmansk, the general, spoke to the head of security for Yamburg. You have a green light. You can go when you want."

By the time I checked this out with the guards, the truck pulled up. Without wasting a minute, I loaded my kayak and got in. We set off for Yamburg.

The driver dropped us off—me and my kayak—at the harbor. I gave him a healthy tip.

The soldiers at the guard post had warned me that my permit was good for twelve hours, not a minute more. So there was no question of lingering here. I couldn't even get a night's sleep.

I went to see one of the security officers in Yamburg. His boss knew that my authorization had a twelve-hour limit, but he didn't. After a few minutes of friendly conversation, he agreed to keep an eye on my kayak while I took care of a minor formality, the sixty-mile round-trip that I needed to do on foot from Yamburg to the guard outpost and back in order to keep from breaking rule number one of my expedition.

In an alternating regime of walking and jogging, I spent most of the day covering that distance, taking advantage of a communications gap among the various offices. It was strictly forbidden to travel along that road except aboard a vehicle that had been properly authorized to do so. When I returned to Yamburg, the security officer was in a state of extreme agitation. He asked me where I had been. I gave him an evasive answer, saying only that I had been out for a stroll. He insisted that I leave immediately. Now he knew all about the twelve-hour limit. With my business accomplished, I was ready to leave anyway.

I paddled up the eastern shore of the Obskaya Guba—the Gulf of Ob. But after covering about sixty miles on foot, I lacked the strength to paddle much farther than six miles. I pitched my tent on a magnificent beach with the satisfaction of having solved a seemingly insurmountable problem and recaptured my freedom.

The next day I covered thirty-five miles, and I camped at Cape Parushnie, named for its tall, smooth cliffs. This is the narrowest stretch of the Gulf of Ob at twenty miles across. I had been warned that the crossing was dangerous because of sudden shifts in the weather. All the same, I set out at dawn on a calm, flat sea that, according to my barometer, should have stayed that way until I reached the far shore.

But when I was just three miles out from the eastern shore, a powerful north crosswind began to blow. The sea grew choppy and waves began to smash into my right side. If I turned so that I was facing into the rollers, then I would have a sixty-mile paddle ahead of me before I reached the next coast. Currents were forced together through the narrows, kicking up a chaotic series of waves that smashed together and down upon me from every direction at once. Twice, rollers swept right over me, coming very close to capsizing my kayak. I managed to keep upright and more or less on course. The Gulf of Ob had earned its reputation.

In front of me, high atop Cape Kamenny, I saw one of the radar surveillance stations that are the Russian equivalent of the American DEW Line. This station was doubtless designed to warn of any hostile forces approaching the nuclear submarine bases on the islands of Novaya Zemlya, between the Kara Sea and the Barents Sea. And after all, this spot was only 1,200 miles across the pole from Alaska.

After eight hours of nightmarish sea conditions, I was almost glad to be arrested once again by the Russian Coast Guard. From a distance they had noticed my sail heading for Cape Kamenny, a place—like so many others in this country—that was strictly off limits. My kayak was surrounded by men in uniform the instant it hit the rocky beach. Soaked, chilled to the bone, my legs numb, I couldn't think of anything but getting out of the kayak and relieving my intense need to urinate, a need that had had a veritable lockgrip on my bladder for hours. I came very close to peeing on a pair of freshly polished boots.

The boat stayed on the beach, guarded by two men armed with Kalashnikovs, while I was taken to the Coast Guard station. From there I called Sergei, who explained to me that because of the three-month period during which I had been stuck between Nome and Provideniya, most of my permits and authorizations—including the authorization to cross the Yamal Peninsula—had expired. There was no point in hoping that the soldiers would overlook that little detail. Fortunately, though, Sergei was as resourceful as ever.

"Give me a minute," he said, "and I'll make a phone call to my friend, the general, in Murmansk." Half an hour later, the officer in charge of the base hurried into the office and humbly begged my forgiveness for the inconvenience. It went without saying that I was free to continue on my way. And welcome to Yamal!

The bad weather and my exhaustion kept me from starting off immediately. I was given a place to stay in a building where the technicians who manned the neighboring air control tower stayed. Cape Kamenny was on the long-distance flight path between Europe and Japan, so planes needed to check in here on their way over.

One of the technicians brought me up-to-date on the weather conditions around Baidaratskaya Bay, which I would need to cross once I made it to the other side of the Yamal Peninsula. The bay should still be free of ice at least, which meant I could paddle across in my kayak. Still, it was at the very least forty-seven miles of open sea. If I sailed around it, it would take two or three days instead of one. It would become clear once I got there.

In the meantime, I planned to reach Baidaratskaya Bay by following the Yuribey River, which runs most of the way across the Yamal Peninsula. However, the Yuribey River was forty-five miles away. I could portage that distance, but I was in a hurry. Luckily for me, a helicopter pilot offered to shuttle my kayak there. All I had to do was to reach the headwaters on foot.

After two days of hiking, I lowered my kayak into crystal-clear waters. Unfortunately, however, the Yuribey River was worse than the Messoyakhta. Its oxbow curves and meandering course stubbornly refused to take me in the right direction. The river zigzagged like boot-laces, wending its way through hairpin curves, lurching northward, plunging southward, and even taking me toward the east at times! Moreover, the scrubby, overgrown terrain it ran through made portaging impossible.

My progress was pitiful. But I consoled myself with the thought that few human beings had seen the places that I was seeing.

On August 4, I celebrated the second anniversary of my departure. I had spent two full years in pursuit of this one goal, and yet it didn't feel as if I had been traveling that long. I paddled the whole day long, thinking about everything I had experienced in those two years. I ran back my mental home movies of Greenland, Canada, Alaska, and Siberia, fast-forwarding through them. Those twenty-four months seemed more like twenty-four hours.

I had announced that this journey would take me about two years, and I would have kept my word if it hadn't been for the red tape that blocked my way in Provideniya. If everything worked according to plan, I might not take too much longer than my stated goal.

On this same anniversary day, a white gleam on the riverbank caught my eye. I discovered a giant mammoth tusk jutting out of a heap of dirt and weighing at least 130 pounds. In my mind's eye, I could *see* them, those gentle, hairy pachyderms milling around me and munching sweetly on thorn bushes in a landscape that must not have changed all that much since prehistoric times. Then I thought about all the damage we have inflicted upon the planet. For how much longer will our children and grandchildren be able to make discoveries in places like this, the way I had just done.

A few days later I experienced a slightly less dramatic throwback. The Yamal Nenets live in tepees like the Indians of North America, but, like the Chukchis, they live by herding reindeer. They settle along rivers in order to fish. Each year they migrate great distances between the tundra to the north and the taiga to the south. They showed me their harnesses, the games they play, and they invited me to eat with them. I felt as if I established a bond with them dating back many centuries.

When I finally paddled out into Baidaratskaya Bay, the dilemma arose: coast around it or risk a straight crossing? Based on my experience in the Gulf of Ob, I had promised Cathy I wouldn't tempt the devil a second time. I was too close to the finish line to risk drowning now, but to waste two days, maybe even three, was difficult to swallow.

Hugging the coast would also mean making my way through the breakers every night in order to come in to camp on shore, and then heading back out through the surf the following morning. That is to say, I would be risking the loss of my kayak and my gear twice a day.

I therefore decided to try to paddle straight across.

The next day, after taking the precaution of drinking nothing from the time I woke up (I wouldn't have a chance to urinate during the entire crossing), I crammed as much gear and as many provisions as I could into the waterproof compartments of the kayak. I wrapped myself in a wind-breaker, gloves, and a waterproof hood and set out, ready for twelve hours of paddling.

The first few rollers caught me breathless and hurled me back up on the beach. But I managed to get through. Soon the shoreline was lost over the horizon behind me; the far shore was still too far away to see. Since I could use neither my compass nor my GPS, I set my course by the whitecaps on the waves and the direction of the wind. The sea was rushing to the northwest, and the waves ran perpendicular to that axis. The wind was blowing in the same direction. All I needed to do was to keep the wind at a forty-five degree angle to my face. If I followed the wrong course, I could very easily sail straight out into the Kara Sea and never reach land.

After five hours of paddling, I must have been—according to my dead reckoning—in the middle of the bay. The wind rose to a squall and blew straight into my face. The weather report had called for some strong weather, but the wind was getting stronger by the minute. I was soon drenched, and my kayak was weighed down by all the water that had sloshed in between me and my sprayskirt. It was getting darker and darker, and the waves were getting bigger and more threatening. The voice of reason was whispering to turn around and let the waves and wind push me back to shore. Otherwise I would be facing at least an eight-hour brawl that I wasn't sure I would win.

For the first time in quite a while, I considered the possibility of throwing in the towel. If I was going to have to hug the coast all the way around Baidaratskaya Bay, well then, that's what I would do.

But I wasn't quite ready to give up entirely yet. I held on and continued to battle against the wind and the waves with all my strength. Even though it was almost nighttime and I couldn't make out any land at all, I guessed that I was getting close to the west shore of Baidaratskaya Bay. The waves were growing taller and were making more noise when they broke, meaning that the bottom was getting shallower.

Three rollers in a row crashed into me, and I couldn't determine where they fit into the sequence of waves to get ready for the next one. The last big wave in the series caught me full on. I suddenly found myself in the grip of a wave that was driving me toward the shore, on and on. And then the water seemed to draw a big breath, and I was sucked back out to sea.

I couldn't see land, but it must have been about three miles away. I paddled furiously, making painfully slow progress toward the shore. Soon I repositioned myself along a line that allowed me to make use of the force of the waves.

I was finally tossed back up onto the shore, like a fish that the ocean no longer wants. My kayak was full of water, and my legs were so numb that I could no longer walk. I threw my paddle as far inland as I could and rolled the kayak over onto the shore so that I could drag myself out of it. Little by little, the blood began to circulate in my legs.

The crossing had taken eleven agonizing hours during which I was forced to urinate twice in my waterproof suit. I was happy that I had made it, but I swore an oath never to try to make such a challenging crossing in a kayak again.

I was too tired to go any farther, and I ended up pitching my tent so close to the waves that they soaked the base of my shelter.

Even after getting a night's sleep, I didn't have the strength to get out of my tent. I decided to stay in and sleep all day, in an attempt to recover. Unfortunately, I didn't have a drop of freshwater to drink, and since I hadn't drunk anything since setting out on the crossing, I was completely dehydrated. The lakes up on the tundra were blocked off by a butte of sand and permafrost that rose at least sixty feet into the air, with waves gnawing away at its base. But the Kara River poured into the sea a little farther along the coast. I would be able to fill up on freshwater there.


I started off again along the western shore of Baidaratskaya Bay. Despite the lack of freshwater, I had recovered sufficiently to paddle for sixteen hours in a row and cover fifty-four miles. All day long to my left, I could see the northernmost peaks of the Ural Mountains, crowned with permanent snow. On the other side of those peaks was Europe.

The temperature dropped like a rock to twenty-three degrees—it was still summer after all—but that was cold enough that the wind froze the water on my gloves, gluing them to the carbon handle of my paddle. This was yet another reminder that I had no time to waste if I wanted to avoid spending a third winter in the Arctic.

Fifty-two miles, fifty-one miles . . . After weeks of wending my way along lazy rivers, I had covered nearly 185 miles in three days, going against the current and into the wind.

On the evening of the third day, I was in a hurry to get to land to set up camp on the narrow shore, and at first I didn't notice the polar bear enjoying a bath in the grotto-pocked section of the cliffs. Just as my kayak ground into the beach, his head surged unexpectedly out of the water, and he stared at me with a pair of small eyes. I got back out to sea as quickly as I could (bears are quick swimmers). I wasn't too worried about the large number of bear prints that I was seeing on either shore of Baidaratskaya Bay, but I knew that in this period of the year when the bears were forced to leave the ice field, which was their main source of food, the bears were hungry and might well be dangerous. While keeping my distance, I filmed the bear as it came toward me, then retreated, reared up on its hind legs, clearly uncertain about exactly how to react to this strange yellow boat out of which half of a human was protruding.

As for me, I was going to pitch my tent farther along the coast—much farther along.

I ventured a little farther out to sea, just past the line of the breakers. I was right where Baidaratskaya Bay opened out into the Kara Sea. All of a sudden, a geyser jet of mist startled me. A magnificent white whale had just surfaced so close to my kayak that I could almost pet it! An instant later, it looked as if the sea were covered with choppy whitecaps, as if a wind had suddenly sprung up. But in fact these glittering flashes of white, stretching out as far as the eye could see, were dozens, even hundreds, of other whales, all frolicking in perfect formation as if a single whale had been multiplied geometrically with a cunning array of mirrors.

This was the second time that I had the privilege of witnessing such a magnificent and moving spectacle. It was a little more beautiful each time.


The next day big rollers forced me to move farther offshore in order to reach the port of Amderma with a tailwind. The temperature of the Kara Sea was between thirty-seven and thirty-nine degrees. I was permanently soaked, and the fierce winds practically froze me on the spot. Fortunately, after Amderma I would be moving into the Barents Sea where I would encounter the Gulf Stream again. The water temperature could climb by as much as four to six degrees, which would make a huge difference.

During the Cold War, Amderma had been a major military base with both naval and air installations. There is still a port, accessible only by air or sea, and it's sufficiently important to appear on all the regional maps. All the same, I felt as if I was entering a ghost town once again. The wharves were in a state of disarray, the port structures looked like rusted carcasses, and the wind was blowing piled garbage around in the streets. There was not a soul in sight.

I slipped between the two wharves of the port, where rusted ships seemed to have been tied up to keep them from simply sinking outright. The wind had dropped again, and the silence was distressing. I tied up my kayak and climbed up onto the piers.

There was still no one in sight against a backdrop of tall gray buildings that reminded me of Provideniya, high-rises of communal apartments with cramped space and boilers that would heat one apartment, which then heated the apartment above it, and so on.

I walked on, freezing in my neoprene slippers, wind-breaker, and water-soaked trousers.

At last I saw someone. A civilian. The man walked toward me and, wordlessly, examined me like the martian that I must have appeared to his eyes.

I asked if I was in Amderma.

"*Da, da*, Amderma," the man answered me.

"Is there a hotel here?"

The native stared at me, "No, why?"

"Where are the people?"

"All gone," he replied as if in response to a painfully naïve question.

When the military base had closed, the place had turned into a ghost town. In just a few weeks, the population had dropped from thirty thousand to four hundred. There had once been two flights a day into Amderma; that number had dropped to two per week, then two per month.

My new acquaintance invited me to follow him to his house. There he offered me a glass of vodka and cooked me a plate of eggs. After that he insisted on taking me to the *banya*. I had been urinating on myself so regularly in the kayak that I must have smelled just lovely. The man was in charge of the electric power plant (a diesel generator), where I enjoyed my Russian sauna. As filthy and exhausted as I was, it was a true joy.

When I told him that I planned to leave the next morning, he objected that with such bad weather, that would be impossible. It was cold, the rain was beating down relentlessly, there was thick fog everywhere, and huge waves were battering the coast. He had a point. I decided to wait for the weather to clear up.

He put my kayak into a garage crowded with trucks dating from World War II and gave me a place to stay at his house, along with his daughter, his son-in-law, and his grandchild.

I stopped by the border guards' station to report my brief presence and to receive official permission to stay in Amderma. At the nearby weather station, I asked for information about a possible window of good weather that might allow me to leave. They expected no breaks in the weather for at least the next three days. But the head of the office generously gave me some maps for the stretch of the trip to Tobseda. Since I had had no resupply since Norilsk-Dudinka, I was woefully short on maps. The maps he gave me—official military maps that were of no use to them since Amderma was no longer a military base—were wonderfully detailed and not available for purchase.

I had been at Amderma for two days, and the forecast was for at least three or four more days of bad weather. I couldn't afford to wait much longer. I would have to find some other solution.

I got an idea for an alternative route from an old bus driver. Every day this bus driver drove through town in his swaying, wobbling bus. He had to hand-crank the engine to get it started, and it had no doors or windows. The only form of amusement available to the townfolk was to pack into the bus and travel absolutely nowhere. In the rear of the bus, children would jump happily up and down on wooden benches that barely even suggested the form of proper bus seats.

The driver, during a conversation, suggested that I take a small road that, seven and a half miles from town, runs into Lake Totento, the town's reservoir. Running out of the southern end of the lake was a river that would take me to the sea and allow me to bypass the cape where the wind and waves were especially dangerous. According to him, it would take me three days.

The idea struck me as a good one, and I was so anxious to get moving that I didn't hesitate at all. I said my good-byes, once again.

But once I reached the lake, the cold, the snow, and a wind blowing nearly forty miles an hour kept me from going an inch farther. I resigned myself to the situation. The three men who worked at the pumping station offered me a place to stay, and I spent forty-eight hours fishing and contemplating nature.

Once the weather cleared up, I started paddling across Lake Totento, heading for shore. The landscape was all rocks and greenery, magnificent in the bright light. But a straying polar bear reminded me once again of the climate change that was blighting our planet. Global warming had cut this animal off from the ice field, its natural habitat, and had condemned it to try to eke out its survival in the midst of the tundra.

The river that drained the lake was dotted with rapids, and my sea kayak wasn't built to take river rapids. I was frequently forced to portage. Each time I was forced to do so, the process was hellish. I had to strap the kayak to my back with a system of straps and then haul it over the slippery, marshy tundra like a snail transporting its shell and making about the same speed: one mile an hour on average. It was enough to drive anybody insane. On this expedition portaging had only been a last choice, used only when I couldn't avoid it.

At least I no longer had to deal with ocean waves, and I never ran short on freshwater. And when I found myself at the bottom of a steep canyon, heading into churning whitewater, my trip began to take on the feel of a rafting trip on the Colorado River.

Despite the portaging, the three days that I took to reach the sea from Amderma had the feel of a holiday. I was crossing the imaginary line that separates Asia from Europe. As soon as I was in the Barents Sea, I could feel the added warmth of the Gulf Stream waters in my hands, just as I could sense a slightly warmer wind on my face.

At Cape Bolvanskiy Nos, or "White Nose," named after the color of the cliffs, freighters turn into the channel that runs between the mainland and Vaigach Island. I camped across from the strait and sat down to decide which way to turn next.

I also explored the nearby ruins of a former gulag. The tiny spyholes in the doors and the cells with grates in the ceiling spoke eloquently of the suffering that this place had witnessed and inflicted. It made me stop and think. My suffering meant so much less to me because I had been free to choose it.


Before me lay another choice of routes. This time I had to decide between paddling all the way around the enormous bay that opened out before me, or else attempting the longest crossing I had ever done by kayak. My experience in Baidaratskaya Bay had shaken me deeply and undermined my confidence, but it had also taught me a great deal, and it had made me stretch my limits. By now I felt as if I were capable of managing extreme situations in a kayak. The challenge was tempting. This was a chance to restore my confidence, and it might prove to be the last great challenge of this expedition.

At first, caution won out, and I hugged the coast for a while, which took me eastward, making the crossing even longer. Then, as if it was the most natural thing in the world, I changed course, turning ninety degrees to starboard and heading out into open water. All of a sudden, it seemed like the right thing to do.

The winds out of the west-northwest blew at thirty miles per hour; the currents were eddying around the little islands on the other side of the bay, making my job more complicated. My kayak filled with water. Despite everything, though, I was never overwhelmed by the situation and the crossing was actually less difficult than at Baidaratskaya Bay.

Sixteen hours after my change of course, I surfed to a clean landing on the far shore of the bay. I had won another bet and gained three days in the process.

When I tried to set out again toward Dolgy Island, daunting rollers made it impossible to get out to sea. I had to haul my kayak along the beach for seven and a half miles. The wind blew so hard that it covered the kayak in sand while I walked, and in the middle of the night I had to shift the location of my tent.

For two days running, the squall was so extreme that I couldn't even walk along the beach. Then conditions improved, and without wasting a second, I leaped into my kayak. Making distances of twenty-five to forty miles a day, I rushed toward Tobseda.

Farther along, the lashing winds and waves pinned me down for another two days. The temperature dropped back to fourteen degrees. The Gulf Stream had broken its promise.

Beyond an expanse of open sea protruded a cape, which stood between me and Chesskaya Bay, where Tobseda was located. I had a choice between making a direct crossing, doubling the cape and then heading down toward Tobseda or else hugging the coast, which would force me to portage again over the last few miles.

The twenty-four hours of good weather that the forecasts called for would be too short to attempt crossing the open seas. I would have to hug the coast, sail up the Pechora River, and portage about nineteen miles overland to Tobseda.

I reached the mouth of the Pechora River, where the huge industrial trawlers based at Murmansk and Naryan-Mar put out to sea. Naryan-Mar is a port located fifty miles upriver. Because dusk had fallen and I was paddling a waterway trafficked by enormous ships, I feared being crushed like a fly under an elephant's foot. I needed to find a place to stop for the night.

On the far bank of the Pechora River, I saw an isolated house. I headed for it, hoping that the inhabitants would take me in for the night. It turned out that the house was occupied by three forest rangers who worked on a nature reserve there. They welcomed me in and were able to instruct me how to navigate to Tobseda by following various waterways.

Their directions were correct, but the trek was tougher than I imagined. I spent the whole next day paddling from point to point, hauling my kayak over hills, swamps, and sandy tundra. It was a veritable decathlon and one of the worst days on land of the whole expedition. I made total progress of only five and a half miles in fifteen hours.

On my satellite phone I contacted Martin, who was on board my Corsair 28 trimaran. I had ordered a thirty-one-footer in the United States, but with delays in the container ships and various customs formalities, I decided to give up. I preferred to rely on the trimaran with which I had already gone around the world and crossed three oceans.

I asked Jean-Philippe and Martin to bring the boat to Kirkenes, Norway, on the Barents Sea near the Russian border. It would be an amusing little sail of 2,500 miles for them. Moreover, they would have to find an extra skipper who could pilot the boat from Kirkenes to Tobseda. When Cathy put out the call, Bernard Stamm was the only one to volunteer, maybe because sailing a twenty-eight-foot boat on the Barents Sea at this time of year wasn't really very tempting. Bernard, however, had successfully sailed around the world solo in a sixty-foot monohull, held the world record for crossing the Atlantic, and had taken part in the Vendée Globe round-the-world yacht race. He had plenty of experience and wasn't easily deterred. His response to Cathy's request was straightforward: he asked where he needed to be, and when.

"Tomorrow, in Kirkenes," Cathy replied.

"No problem," Bernard said.

Martin, Jean-Philippe, and Bernard were no more than a day's sail away from Tobseda. Raphaël Blanc and Sebastian Devenish would arrive simultaneously from the opposite direction by helicopter from Naryan-Mar.

The three sailors set out from Kirkenes and decided to dispense with the tiresome formalities of obtaining a Russian entry visa. It wouldn't be quite so simple for them to return; a helicopter would come to pick them up and take them to Naryan-Mar, where they would catch a plane for Moscow. But when the border guards realized that they had no legal entry visa, they were kindly expelled, and their tour was over as quickly as it started.

I was camped on the bay, five and a half miles outside of Tobseda, when my boat arrived, but unfavorable winds and sandbars kept us from hooking up. The next day I hauled my kayak over the tundra—once again—for four miles. Finally, I spotted from a high point the few abandoned houses of an old fishing village. This would be my last stop in Russia before embarking for the finish line. I completed this stage of my journey in my kayak, fighting my way through the waves to cross that last bay—to conquer that last challenge. For seven and a half miles I struggled against a wind that shoved me backward whenever I stopped paddling.

When I finally made it to the far shore, I still couldn't see my crew. I called Martin, and it turned out that he and others were many miles away on the same beach. I finally made out five tiny silhouettes slowly moving toward me.

Their presence meant that all the pieces of the puzzle were in place, that my boat was ready for me, that there was nothing that could stop me now. This time, the finish line was staring me right in the face.

It was a real delight to meet up with Jean-Philippe, Sebastian, and Raphaël, whom I hadn't seen since Norilsk; Martin, whom I had last seen a year and a half before; and Bernard, whom I hadn't seen for ten years. We fell into one another's arms, and we walked along the beach, unable to release our iron-tight grip on each other's shoulders. We talked, laughed, and poured forth our most gripping and hilarious stories. Martin hauled my kayak over the sand like a little boy pulling an inner tube. We reveled in the joy of being reunited.

That evening, in the abandoned weather station where they had set up camp, we enjoyed a small banquet of steaks, sausage, and fondue, carried all the way from Switzerland by Jean-Philippe, a gift from the restaurateur of the Six Communes. Not to mention various bottles of fine wine and a bottle of Val de Travers absinthe. There was plenty of food and drink to feast on for a number of days, which was just as well because my own food supplies were completely gone.

For forty-eight hours we worked to take as broad a range of photographs and video footage as possible for the book and movie about the expedition. I nursed my calf, which had been badly scalded a short distance outside of Amderma, when a fierce gust of wind had overturned a potful of boiling water onto it. (At least the cold had prevented any infection.)

The helicopter from Naryan-Mar, which we had chartered to bring Raphaël and Sebastian, came back to pick up the whole team. There were no sad good-byes. We would meet again soon.

When he got back home, Bernard Stamm stayed in touch with me and worked as a marine dispatcher to guide me toward the North Cape. Cathy, on her part, kept one eye on the weather and waited to inform me of the ideal window of opportunity. I couldn't expect a smooth ride, though. It was already September 18, and the low pressure systems spinning out of the North Atlantic would soon stir the Barents Sea and the White Sea up into a frenzy.

Jean-Philippe's departure was the most adventurous of the bunch. He took a domestic Russian flight from Naryan-Mar to Murmansk and intended to return again to Kirkenes to wait for me there. Unfortunately, when he landed, the police noticed that his papers were not in order, arrested him, and threw him into jail. When they questioned him, he admitted that he had arrived by boat, and that the boat was in Tobseda, where nobody could be reached to confirm the information.

Of course nobody could be reached . . . all that remained of Tobseda was a few old houses that the salty sea winds were progressively eroding. No one lived there anymore. There were no police, no border guards, no nothing. That was the very reason why I had chosen the place as a delivery point for my boat. Otherwise it would have been confiscated and declared contraband by the local authorities. At Tobseda, at least, no such danger.

This is the basic rule to follow with the Russian authorities: if you can keep them from knowing that you exist, they will sleep better and so will you. Otherwise you will just complicate their lives, and they will complicate yours a hundredfold.

It turned out that my assumptions about Tobseda were not exactly correct. There was no one left in town except for one person, Vasya.

He was an old man, exiled at the ends of the earth, penniless, without any resources or a goal in life. He merely awaited the end of his life like a sacrificial lamb of the former Soviet system. When the village had been evacuated after the fall of Communism or during perestroika—he couldn't really remember which—there hadn't been enough room for him in the last helicopter. So they left him behind.

He caught fish for sustenance, kept warm by burning driftwood that washed up on the beach, and treated his depression with vodka—although he drank less than he used to, he claimed. All this while waiting for his failing heart to stop beating once and for all.

His three dogs kept him company and chased away bears. From time to time, a haunch of reindeer meat, a gift from the Nenets, spiced up his diet.

Amazingly, he seemed content with his fate.

On board my boat, anchored in Chesskaya Bay, I was doing a little maintenance work when a storm blew up. Bernard had warned me that a nasty weather system was heading my way. Since I was in a relatively sheltered bay, I stayed calm and decided to ride out the storm where I was, waiting for the bad weather to pass. But it didn't pass quickly, and my anchor cable broke in the worsening seas. I dropped my backup an-chor, but it dragged along the seabed, pulled by my boat toward the shore by the powerful waves and then sucked back out to sea with the undertow that followed, only to be hurled back toward the coast by the next wave.

I had to get off the boat into the icy water to brace against my tri-maran. I literally used my body as a boatlift to keep the hull from tear-ing open against the logs and fallen branches that littered the sand of the beach.

I struggled with the boat off and on for two days. I was exhausted. In a moment of fatigue-induced distraction, I allowed an unexpected wave to throw my trimaran right at me, knocking me down; it wrenched and bruised my back. All the same, by getting under the boat, I got more leverage and was able to use the force of the next wave to haul it a little farther up the beach (it "only" weighed a ton and a half) and rest it on a log that poked out of the sand.

But the next wave lifted it still higher and then let it drop with a *Crra-a-a-cckk!*

That horrible sound was the fiberglass of the hull being shredded by the log! As far as I was concerned, it might as well have been the sound of my own bones breaking.

The noise stirred Vasya from the slumber in which his weak heart forced him to spend much of the day, and he rushed out of his house. He shouted to me to forget about the boat and save myself. I couldn't bring myself to abandon my boat, though. It was my ticket to North Cape and victory.

The waves grew so big and so rough that they washed up onto the tundra, well beyond the beach. I was going to need more force to pull the boat ashore. To that end I drove two sturdy tree trunks into the tundra and jury-rigged a winch with ropes and a pulley system that I found in the trimaran.

Vasya did his best to help me, despite his lack of strength . . . and then he collapsed. I threw his limp body on my injured back and carried him into his house. His heart was barely beating. I laid him on his bed and gave him the pills that he had said he needed in case of a heart attack.

When I had done everything I could for Vasya I went back outside and resumed winching my boat up the beach. It was a long distance to dry land, and the waves were rough. It was an endless, exhausting job. I was hauling the boat about two hundred feet an hour.

After the boat was secure, I went back to tend to Vasya. I spent the night next to the old man's bed, watching as he slowly recovered.

The next day I dug a trench beneath my trimaran, allowing me to put the boat in drydock without moving it. There was a gash sixteen inches long in the main hull. I then called Cathy and informed her that it would be impossible for me to make it to North Cape on September 28, as planned. She would have to cancel the small festival that she had organized for all the people who were planning to come up and welcome me back from my trip.

Yvan Ravussin prepared the resin and the hardener I would need to repair the hull, and attached instructions on how to use it. He sent someone to fly the package in to me, but customs officers in Moscow confiscated it en route.

Could I buy some where I was? Unfortunately not. Polyester resin is not available commercially anywhere in Russia. In spite of this, my miracle-worker friend Sergei managed to find some. Because it was illegal for the resin and hardener to be shipped by plane, they had to send it by truck, which would take an extra three days.

Sergei himself hopped on a flight for Naryan-Mar with the sandpaper, the little electric generator, the blowtorch, and everything else I would need for the operation.

As I waited for my repair supplies to arrive, it grew later and later in the season, and my chances of making it across the White Sea dwindled. What else could conspire to keep me from completing the final leg of my journey?

How about the Russian border guards?

When Sergei arrived in Naryan-Mar, they refused to allow him to board the helicopter to Topseda with my package. Then, when they learned from their colleagues in Murmansk that there was a questionable boat in Tobseda, they decided to board the helicopter with Sergei and see what was going on for themselves.

When they arrived, the officials questioned me interminably about the routes that Bernard, Martin, and Jean-Philippe had taken to get here. They wanted to see my logbook. I explained that I didn't have one because I had not come by boat. They did everything they could to make my life harder, as if it was just too damned easy! Their heavy boots left filthy marks all over my trimaran, which did nothing to improve my mood.

The tension mounted, and I finally lost it.

"Get off my boat!" I yelled. "Get the hell out of here! And find your way back to Naryan-Mar on your own! That's MY helicopter! I chartered it!"

Sergei tried to intercede and get me to calm down by discreetly reminding me that the border guards had the power to impound my boat if they felt like it. One of the officers even told me so in as many words.

And I roared back at him, "Just try it!"

Repairing my boat and leaving this place had become a religious mission for me. Anyone who stood in my way was going to be met with the ferocity of a cornered animal.

Eventually everyone calmed down. The border guards agreed to let me repair my boat and leave on the condition that I not stray any farther than twelve miles from the coast and that I stop off in Murmansk to report in to their main office. Their maritime patrols would help to ensure that I didn't "forget."


The helicopter took off again with Sergei and the guards, and I got to work. I heated the area around the crack because the resin wouldn't set at freezing temperatures (it was twenty-three degrees). After twenty-four hours of uninterrupted work, I had repaired the hull damage and my broken anchor cables. I was ready to go back to sea. Moreover,

Bernard reported that there was a three-day window of good weather, long enough for me to make it all the way to North Cape.

Now all I had to do was to use my improvised winch to move the trimaran in the opposite direction, back into the water. The sea level had receded as the storm subsided, and it took me almost two days to haul the ton and a half boat the five hundred yards back to the water. Vasya, who was feeling better, helped to the extent that his physical condition allowed. He was happy to have me there, and I felt the same way about him. In just a short time, a genuine friendship had developed between us.

To make the work easier, I moved the boat onto logs to roll it out to sea; my progress improved from two hundred to three hundred feet per hour. The sealed hole in the hull was holding, but each time it rolled over a log, the other side of the bow creaked in a way that I didn't like. Just a few yards from the water, the hull emitted an ear-splitting noise that said it all. I took a close look and saw that the crack that had opened was eight feet long!

I spent two more days winching my trimaran back up the beach to where it had been. I didn't have enough resin to fix such a large crack. And with the difficult crossing that lay before me, I couldn't afford to try a jury-rigged repair.

I could kiss Bernard's fair-weather window good-bye. And, frankly, I'd had enough. I wasn't sick of the expedition, but I *was* sick of things breaking, sick of fixing things, sick of equipment that wore out, sick of detours and the like, all just so that I could keep on going.

I called up Jean-Philippe, whom the authorities in Murmansk had finally released. He was waiting for me to arrive in Kirkenes. I asked him if he could come meet me and bring someone who could help fix the boat. My logistical supervisor found a Russian handyman in Kirkenes who demanded only one thousand dollars to do the work, everything included.

While I waited for the two of them to arrive, I dug a new "dry dock" under my boat, sanded and cleaned the crack, and cleaned out the hold of the trimaran in order to provide access to the break from the interior.

Once Jean-Philippe and the Russian arrived on the scene, we partitioned off the work area with tarps and set about repairing the boat, working from the exterior and the interior at the same time. By the generator-powered electric light, we worked all night long, blowtorch in hand, taking great care not to catch the resin on fire, and not to allow stray sparks to ignite the gases that the resin released in the enclosed space.

Without electricity and in the cold, the only way to dry the resin, unfortunately, was with a blowtorch. I crouched at the bottom of the hold with the blowtorch in hand, drying the resin, when . . . *Whooomfff!*

The interior of the boat suddenly burst into flames! I tried to peel away the layer of burning resin, but the heat had already melded it to the base layer. I beat at the fire with the palms of my hands, but that only fanned the blaze and spread the conflagration. I sprang out of the boat like a shot, shouting, "Fire, fire! Bring water, hurry! Water!"

The closest water source was the sea, and that was five hundred yards away! Jean-Philippe went galloping down to the shore with a bucket, beat every land speed record in both directions, lost half the water on the way back, and handed me a pail containing more sand than water. I emptied it over the flames, which sputtered, sizzled, and went out briefly, only to leap up again, burning more intensely than before! I grabbed a blanket and threw it over the fire, but the resin soaked into the cloth, and the blanket burst into flames! The Russian handyman threw on a little water that he had managed to gather, and the two pails full of water formed a pathetic little pond in the bottom of the hull. I scooped up water with my hands, sprinkled it over the fire, and finally managed to put it out. A black haze of thick, toxic smoke forced us all out of the cockpit.

The sight of this mess on a gloomy, gray day was so depressing that we decided to leave everything the way it was. We'd figure out what to do the next morning when we could think straight.

Meanwhile, I was already casting about for other means of travel to North Cape. My other boat was in Amsterdam, and it would take weeks to get it here. I knew someone in Kirkenes who had a sailboat, but if he came to pick me up, I would have to leave with him, and the last leg of my expedition would have to be run just like the rest of my journey—solo. There were no obvious answers, so I turned my attention back to the resources at hand.

Our faces were still soot-covered when we sat down to take an inventory of the damage. The interior was nothing much to look at, but the boat was fundamentally intact! The equipment that was being stored inside was okay as well. To top it all off, our repair work had been successful, which was a good thing, because there were no more materials to fix it with.

Jean-Philippe and our Russian friend helped me to drag the trimaran back down to the water. A few hours later the helicopter came to take them back to Kirkenes, via Arkhangelsk and Murmansk.

I reported in to Bernard Stamm and Cathy that, once again, I was ready to leave. Just then, a twenty-four-hour forecast of good weather presented itself. A narrow window, admittedly, but in that period of time, I should be able to get past Kolguyev Island and round the Kanin Peninsula.

My boat was in the water. After twenty days in Tobseda, where I had hoped only to pass through, the time had finally come to get back on the road.

All that remained was to say good-bye to Vasya. The old man walked toward me across the beach, and I embraced him heartily. He asked if I would stay, and I told him that it was impossible—I had a family and a home to get back to. Faced with the despair that I saw in his eyes, I offered to take him with me as far as Murmansk.

"No thanks," he answered. "What would I do in Murmansk but die? Here, at least, I might be able to live *my* life a little while longer."

I set off before sorrow could overwhelm me. In my insulated suit I swam to the boat, anchored just fifty yards off shore. I set sail and waved a last good-bye to Vasya, who stood motionless on the beach in his yellow oilskin.

As I was raising anchor, Vasya plunged into the water. Soon he was chest-deep in the waves. When I set my jibsail and my trimaran began to move, Vasya, now in the water up to his chin, held out his arms as if to keep the boat from leaving. His lips seemed to be whispering, "Don't leave me!"

My heart broke, but I knew that he was right. At this point in his life, he couldn't live anywhere else. To thank him for his help and because we had become close friends, I had given him all the Russian money I had left. It would be enough to charter a helicopter if he ever decided to leave.

As forecast, I enjoyed twelve hours of tailwinds and sailed westward, following a course between the mainland and Kolguyev Island. At nightfall the wind shifted, and Bernard, who was navigating for me via satellite phone, had me sail around the island toward the northwest.

The next day the weather was bright and clear. I shot like an arrow toward the point where I would shift course by ninety degrees, toward the Kanin Peninsula. When I reached the appointed spot, I made the turn with no problems. "You should sail at least four or five miles off the peninsula," Bernard warned. "The waves and currents are so violent there that there's a serious risk of being driven into the rocks." Duly noted.

Everything looked good from my perspective, but Cathy reported that a huge storm was lighting up the Doppler radar like a Christmas tree, and I was heading straight for it. Bernard confirmed the news, "There's a big storm dead ahead. Hold tight!"

I reefed my sails as much as possible, put away everything that could be stowed, and tied down everything above the deck. My main concern was that the storm might push me too close to Kanin Point, and then I would be at the mercy of the enormous waves breaking on the shoreline.

When the first huge breakers began to smash into the boat, water poured into the cockpit and short-circuited the electrical system. I had no more electronics, meaning no more automatic pilot. Clutching the helm, dressed in my waterproof suit, I fought against the storm as it made the boat dance like a cork in the midst of the huge, menacing white-capped waves. The squall grew in intensity; it was now bearing its full force down on me and would soon paralyze my boat unless I shifted the angle of my course by coming about into the wind. But I was too close to the peninsula to make the turn. I had no idea what to do next.

Eight hours after the beginning of the fierce storms, I called Bernard, who reported that the latest reports said the storm was expected to last eighteen hours, instead of the original twelve! On the other hand, the winds weren't expected to blow any harder than fifty knots. Since I clearly had no choice in the matter, I simply held on, ready to fight as long as necessary. My trimaran shot over the whitecaps and landed with a sharp thud in the black troughs between them. Between one lurch and the next, I spotted the rocky shores of the menacing cape of Kanin Peninsula. To escape its clutches, I took every opportunity to increase my angle from shore and put a little bit more sea between me and the cape. I met with little success in this regard.

The biggest waves I had ever seen in my life were breaking on the peninsula. If one of those behemoths caught the boat, it would be "sayonara" for me. I set a little more sail to scoot out to see a bit more, even though the wind was blowing so hard that it had ripped one of my decals off the sails. The decal was affixed at just one glue point, and it was flapping like a pennant in the gale-force winds.

I nearly scraped the Kanin Peninsula, but I made it through in one piece—just barely. After the weather calmed down just a bit, I was able to set some sail, take advantage of the wind, and set course in the right direction at full speed. I sailed straight across the White Sea to the Kola Peninsula, where I found a small bay relatively sheltered from still-rough weather conditions.

When the time came to take in my jib, I realized that the storm had warped the take-up reel. It was impossible to furl my sail and therefore—in theory, at least—to stop the boat. I "shocked" the sail by paying out the line entirely, so that it would go slack and I could haul it in by hand.

As I sailed into the bay, I noticed that another boat, much larger than mine, had already taken shelter there. I moored my trimaran next to its hull. It was occupied by a group of Russian biologists who were studying crabs on behalf of the fishing industry. They invited me to come aboard, have dinner, and spend the night. I fell asleep without much difficulty. I hadn't shut my eyes in sixty hours!

In the morning the biologists left. I sailed over toward a small abandoned observation post that was clearly a relic of the Cold War. I rummaged through it and found materials that I could use to repair my ship's furling system, which had broken under the strain of the gale.

At six the next morning I set sail again along the Kola Peninsula. Cathy and Bernard had promised bright, clear weather all the way to Murmansk. It was smooth sailing all the way, and at four the following morning, I steered into the mouth of the long inlet that leads to the harbor of Murmansk.

Murmansk serves a number of purposes as a Russian outpost. It is a military base for nuclear submarines, aircraft carriers, and icebreakers; an enormous shipyard and port for maritime commerce; and a veritable metropolis by Arctic standards with a population of four hundred thousand. Jean-Philippe reminded me over the satellite phone that it was not a place where I could casually sail in and tie a line to the first dock I saw. It was illegal to enter the harbor without a motor. Jean-Phillippe told me to announce my arrival over channel twelve on the radio and wait for a tugboat to guide me in.

I asked him to repeat that. We normally used channel sixteen for communications at sea. No, Jean-Philippe said, they had been very emphatic on the channel: frequency twelve.

But no matter how many times I called on that frequency (and I called more and more often the closer I got to Murmansk), I continued to get no answer. The closer I got, the narrower the channel became, and the shipping traffic grew more intense. As cruise ships and oil tankers began to appear, I sailed as close as possible to shore, turning on my automatic pilot when it worked while I called repeatedly: "Pilot boat Murmansk, this is sailboat *Arktos*. What is your location? Pilot boat Murmansk..." Still nothing. I was no more than twelve miles from Murmansk.

I tried again on channel sixteen.

Then suddenly a terrifying noise made me start. I was thrown forward as if the boat had just hit a wall. A jet of water sprang from the cabin floor.

My keelboard, which I had lowered to keep the wind from sweeping me sideways, had just ground into a reef! And at that very moment, the tugboat showed up.

"You shouldn't go through there," the captain of the tug informed me, "the draft is too shallow."

"Oh, thanks, I had noticed that! If someone had bothered to tell me a little earlier, that might have been useful!"

The pilot told me that I wasn't allowed entry to the port of Murmansk until my passport had been stamped by the border guards, and the border guard station was behind me. The tugboat hauled me back up the channel while I bailed by hand the water that collected in the boat up to the flotation line, in spite of my electric pump chugging away.

I eventually found myself tied up at a dock across from an official building, under the baleful glare of guards who were aiming their Kalashnikovs at me. On the satellite phone Jean-Philippe confirmed that I was not allowed to move until the Russian Coast Guard got there.

Unfortunately, they arrived sixteen hours later! For my part, that was sixteen hours of bailing out my boat without being able to set foot on the dock. All that, just so that the Coast Guard could confirm that Naryan-Mar had notified them of my arrival, stamp my passport, and announce that I was not authorized to dock in Murmansk. I waited another six hours for a tugboat to take me in to port, so I could repair my boat yet again.

Not far away, a boat was moored that I had seen somewhere before. It turned out to be Henk de Velde's—the explorer whom I had first met in Tiksi, where he was waiting for the ice to break up and free his boat. Apparently the ice wound up crushing his hull, and an icebreaker had conveyed him and his boat to Murmansk where he could have repairs done. He still planned to reach North Cape, but it looked like I would get there before he did. While we waited, he generously offered to put me up on his boat as long as I was in Murmansk.

◆   ◆   ◆

I had arrived at two in the morning, exhausted and soaked after three days without sleep, having spent most of that time bailing. I was stuck in my current predicament and could not leave unless assisted by a tugboat. The harbor cranes weren't operating this early, so I would have to keep on bailing until morning. Fatigue took its toll, and I didn't feel strong enough to go four days without sleeping.

A dock worker offered to install a pump in my boat that was usually used for fuel, assuring me that it would drain my trimaran in two minutes. And he would drain the boat whenever necessary so that I could get some sleep until the drydock cranes began to operate at nine in the morning. He offered his services for the moderate fee of one hundred Euros per hour. Here we go again . . .

I had no alternative. And after all, it wouldn't be for more than a few hours. However, later that day, at four in the afternoon, the gantry cranes still weren't working. The pump wound up costing me two thousand Euros. With the Euro equal to about one U.S. dollar, this was not pocket change.

The crane operator who finally showed up asked to see plans of my boat; he said that he needed to study the shape of the hull so that he could lift it and set it down without damaging it. I called Cathy and asked her to fax the plans.

First, the crane operator said, the boat would need to be hauled onto a floating crane—six hundred Euros an hour—which would take it to the hoist, which would in turn put it in the dry dock—for four hundred Euros more.

Of course, all of this work was connected. It was impossible to say yes to one piece and no to the others. The harbor mafia of Murmansk had me in its talons. It knew that I couldn't afford to lose the boat or the gear inside it.

To prevent my temper from causing an unpleasant incident, I decided to bow out of the negotiations entirely and to delegate matters to Jean-Philippe. After all, he was in charge of logistics for the expedition.

Jean-Philippe hired an interpreter who showed up and performed miracles of diplomacy.

All the while, I granted interview requests from journalists in town who had learned of my presence and my unusual expedition.

The interpreter was skillful in his negotiations, but we still wound up having to pay. But faced with the growing and endless demands of the Murmansk crowd, I decided to put off fully repairing the boat until I reached Kirkenes, Norway, which was about 185 miles from Murmansk and reachable by a paved highway. I needed only to pack the boat up on a boat trailer and catch up with it after two days of bicycling. Once the repairs to the trimaran were made in Kirkenes, all that would remain was a short sail to North Cape.

I had a boat trailer waiting for me in Kirkenes. However, a Norwegian freight company, Nord Cargo, wanted two thousand Euros to drive the trailer to Murmansk, put the trimaran aboard, and haul everything back to Kirkenes. I told them to take a hike and contacted a shipper in Murmansk, who took a look at the trimaran and said it would cost seven hundred Euros. Much better.

On my way out, I still had to deal with the exit formalities and harbor taxes. The officer in charge told me with a straight face that I owed three thousand Euros! I called Sergei in Moscow, and he told me that the normal fee would be two hundred Euros. I stopped the official, who had already begun to fill out the documents. I told him that there would be no need to check another box. Starting now, I would take care of everything—filling out forms, hiring transporters, and so forth.

But I had overlooked one vital detail: like everyone else here, the man had ties to the local mafia. Two hours later my transporter informed me that, for personal reasons, he had decided not to take my boat. It was clear that it was a courtesy even to tell me that. If he wanted to stay healthy, he needed to forget he had ever met me.

If that was how things stood, I announced that I would be doing my own repairs on the spot, and that I would then set sail under my own power. With the help of a local mechanic, I repaired the handle of my centerboard. Then I made preparations to weigh anchor.

Once they understood that I was about to slip through their fingers, the harbor union mafia began to relent. Once I was in a position of strength, I made them an offer. They would let me use my Russian shipper, and I would pay them two hundred Euros, in addition to what I had already paid for the pump and so forth. They were happy to make some money off me and accepted the deal.

What they didn't know—and I had just learned—was that there was at least four days of bad weather ahead, which would have kept me from going to sea anyway.

I left Murmansk on a Saturday on a bicycle I purchased in town. My high-end Trek mountain bike that had been specially designed for my needs was in Kirkenes, and according to Jean-Philippe, the bureaucratic obstacles to getting the bike across the Russian border were insurmountable.

The blacktop road to Norway ran down along a river, then crossed it and climbed back up on the opposite side. It climbed and dropped relentlessly, winding through a landscape of steep tundra, hills, and lakes. Unfortunately, the road was in terrible shape, pocked with potholes and covered with ice, not to mention the sleety mix of snow and rain that was falling from the sky. I took some spectacular spills as a result.

Winter had returned. My water bottle froze. To keep from meeting the same fate myself, I pedaled along without a break.

Midway between Murmansk and Kirkenes, I happened upon a checkpoint station where, once again, guards examined my papers and asked me the usual questions. My one-year Russian visa was still valid. I spent the night at a nearby sort of hostel that offered rooms for thirty rubles, about a dollar a night.

The next morning Jean-Philippe confirmed that my boat would arrive in Kirkenes the following day. I got back on my bike. A few hours later I arrived at the first Russian border post. Between it and the sec-

ond border post were twelve miles of road, accessible only to closed vehicles. However, Sergei smoothed out all obstacles in my way. Not only
did he obtain a special permit for me, but the guards welcomed me with
happy cries. This was a nice change from the usual routine. They even
waved me through with a smile.

I crossed the no-man's-land between the two Russian border posts.
When I reached the second one, the guards signaled to me to hurry up.
They resolved all the formalities in a hurry—a nice change, as well—
and ushered me ahead of the crowd of Russians who had climbed out
of their buses, suitcases in hand, and were preparing to spend endless
hours in line before they could enter Norway. In short, I got VIP
treatment.

The Russians must have been delighted finally to be rid of me. I
couldn't help thinking that if they had been this enthusiastic from the
beginning, they would have been rid of me a long, long time ago. Everyone's lives would have been much simpler.

A hundred yards farther on stood the Norwegian border guard station, which meant that I had done it. I had made it across Russia in approximately eleven months, just as I had predicted. Now there was
nothing that could keep me from succeeding. My trimaran would be in
Kirkenes any minute now. In the worst case scenario, I could still bicycle on to North Cape.

But I wanted to arrive the same way I had left: by boat. I wanted to
see the same cliffs I had been imagining for more than two years now.

To my great surprise, the Norwegian border guard was much less
friendly than his Russian colleagues. He looked at me with an air of
disgust, clearly seeing me as a hippie cyclist, bearded and filthy, who was
trying to get into his squeaky clean country. Luckily all my documents
were in order. He examined them carefully and asked me, "How long do
you plan to work in Norway?"

Once I got over my astonishment, I explained that I was coming to Norway only to complete my expedition. Afterward, I planned to go home. I swear!

He wasn't buying it. He was convinced I was a potential illegal guest worker. Therefore, he refused to let me in unless two reliable contacts in Norway would vouch for me. I gave him the name of Stig-Tore Johansen, who lives in Kirkenes and who had already helped us a great deal, and Børge Ousland in Oslo.

The guard changed expression, "You mean Børge Ousland . . . the famous Børge Ousland?" In Norway, Børge is a star, as well known as the king.

"The very same," I said. "He's one of my closest friends." From his sarcastic expression, I could see that he thought I was lying. I called Cathy to ask for Børge's phone number, which I didn't have with me. The guard began to treat me differently when he heard me mention Børge's name, but he completely changed his tune when he heard his voice on the other end of the line.

"There's a guy here named Mike Horn    " he started to say.

"Mike!" roared Børge. "Put him on!" The guard obeyed. Børge and I chatted for a solid fifteen minutes. When I hung up the phone, the man in uniform had changed his attitude considerably. Just to comply with requirements, he called Stig-Tore, who confirmed that I would be staying with him in Kirkenes.

I received the final stamp on my passport, and I peddled the last few miles into Kirkenes. Traveling along the icy road, I thought back on everything I had experienced and daydreamed about everything that awaited me. I began to prepare for the arrival, which I knew would empty me out once I realized that I no longer needed to set out again the next day.

A freighter traveling at full speed takes about six miles to come to a halt. How long would it take me? Since Murmansk, I had paid only the slightest attention to the rotten weather conditions that were brewing, which was a sign to me that I had begun to slow down from "expedition speed."

Stig-Tore and his family took me into their big beautiful home overlooking the fjord in Kirkenes. Showered, shaved, and rested, I began to look like a civilized human being again while I waited for my boat to arrive.

The boat was running a day late because of problems with the shipper. When it finally reached the Russian border, it was delayed due to new problems with red tape. Jean-Philippe, who was traveling with the boat, had to return to Switzerland urgently to deliver a lecture on his trip across Australia in a sand yacht, a trip he had squeezed in during some downtime on my own expedition. He had to hitchhike across the border to go catch his plane, leaving my sailboat at the customs station. Since I couldn't go back into Russia, I experienced hours of extreme anxiety, uncertain whether I would ever see my trimaran again.

But I managed to get my hands on it after eight hours of hard work through bureaucratic channels.

My boat was in Kirkenes. All that was left was to sail to North Cape. But that was barely a day's journey, and that would put me far ahead of schedule. The official date that Cathy and I had set for my arrival was October 21, 2004.

I decided to take advantage of this scheduling wrinkle to take a bicycle trip through the magnificent landscape of islands and fjords that stretched between where I was and my final destination. A 185-mile excursion, which I could complete in three or four days while enjoying the scenery, thinking, dreaming, and decompressing along the way. I would meet up with my boat at the end and cover the last few miles by sail. I would arrive—according to Cathy's predictions—wreathed in sunshine.

I biked along happily, all the way to a small fjord that just happened to be named Small Fjord, where Stig-Tore, two days later, met me on the road with my boat on its trailer. We spent a day putting it in the water and readying it to set sail. Piled on the trimaran were my bicycle, my kayak, and most of my gear—it was like a small-scale picture of my expedition. After my departure, Stig went back to his job as a professor and I set off on the last stage of my solo journey. The sail swelled gently in an ideal wind, and the boat began to glide out to sea. I moved along, a tiny figure beneath the immense cliffs of those majestic shorelines.

On October 20, I sailed into Skarwag, a small port town on the island of North Cape. Here I would be able to prepare calmly for the great moment of arrival, which was scheduled for the late morning of the following day.

I still had to prepare for that last step, and I still needed to be alone.

Cathy, my daughters, my mother, my team, and about a hundred good friends had arrived in Hönningsvag, the closest neighboring town. About twelve miles away from them, I spent my last night on my boat.

The next morning I hoisted my anchor for the last time. I set my course northward, so that I could turn about midcourse and sail straight toward the base of the huge promontory atop which stood the bronze globe that I had seen from below the day I left. At this panoramic vantage point tens of thousands of visitors each year look out over the Arctic Ocean, imagining the North Pole lying straight ahead of them over the horizon.

Up on that very perch everyone who was waiting for me that day looked out, imagining—not the North Pole—but the instant that a tiny twenty-eight-foot trimaran, barely visible in the vastness of the sea, would cross an imaginary line in the waves.

After I rounded a rocky spit, I could spot the cape dead ahead. There it was, the immense black cliff whose image I had carried in my heart for the past twenty-seven months. I could feel it spreading from the roots of my hair all the way down to the tips of my toes. I didn't dare close my eyes for fear it might vanish.

Fifteen minutes later I crossed the virtual finish line. In the distance, high above me, I could see a tiny, excited crowd, and in that crowd, I knew, were my wife and my daughters.

The emotion of victory was overwhelmed by the contentment of being back. The words that came to my lips were not, "I won" but rather "I'm home."

I reversed course and rounded the cape to drop anchor in a little inlet on the other side of the island. Jean-Philippe and Steve were waiting there to take possession of the boat, which they would sail back to Skarwag. I found this inlet before leaving twenty-seven months ago. From this inlet I had looked east and said to myself, "I'll be coming from that direction!" Now, in the same spot, I looked out in the same direction and thought, "That's where I came from!"

Striding with giant steps, I climbed up to the outcropping at the far end of which everyone was waiting for me. A helicopter flew overhead at regular intervals, each time carrying a new band of passengers, curious to watch from on high as I walked the last few feet. We waved at one another.

As I emerged onto the outcropping, I saw the white dome of the North Cape visitors' center and, in front of the building, a crowd. This time, their silhouettes were almost life-sized. The group moved toward me, and I moved toward them. There were cameras flashing.

The crowd slowed and halted to let three figures move forward. Cathy, Annika, and Jessica. My mother was right behind them. My wife and my daughters threw themselves into my arms. Cathy was crying and laughing at the same time. My daughters were tugging on my parka.

We walked along, all wrapped in a group hug. I could hear myself saying stunningly banal things like, "You all okay? Happy to see Daddy?"

I would find the words later—when I woke up from a long, deep, refreshing sleep.

# Epilogue

In the Arctic, when the sunlight shines through ice crystals, it creates a prism containing the entire palette of colors of this cold and magnificent world. Those twenty-seven months were a prism of life, a strong concentration of emotions and excitement. I experienced as much in that time as I had in my previous thirty-six years of life: fear, pain, joy, disappointment, euphoria, rage, hope, and despair, as well as happiness, in particular, with a special intensity. The expedition was an emotional roller-coaster.

I saw everything I had wanted to see, experienced everything that I had wanted to experience, and learned to handle disappointment and frustration as the inevitable elements of any journey, clarifying my own priorities at each step along the way. I learned something new every day of the trip.

When I came back, I was a different person—a better person, I'd like to think. I was a little humbler, a little wiser, a little happier to be alive, to live with myself and with those around me.

I know that everything that I lived and learned during those twenty-seven months would help me in all my future endeavors.

✦ ✦ ✦

My expeditions, although they remain physical challenges, increasingly resemble traditional rites of passage. I bring back such treasures of knowledge and understanding that the real reason I set out is to go and find more.

Now, when people ask me why I do what I do, I can truly reply, "Because the older I grow and the more experience I gather, the more questions I ask myself to which I have no answers. Because, in my view, pushing your own limits is the only way to know yourself and to grow as a human being."

The twelve thousand miles that I covered ultimately took me back to my starting point. I never really went anywhere; it was inside myself that I took a long, long walk.

My daily routines and way of life over the past twenty-seven months had become second nature to me. When I came back home, it took me a while to get used to the fact that I no longer had to pitch a tent every night or light my camp stove to make dinner. It took me some time to adjust to the fact that I didn't have to start off again every morning, to understand that I no longer had a geographic objective to attain, and that I had every right to stay still. It was time to accept life's complications rather than live as a man whose only goal is survival. It was time to stop thinking about myself and to start thinking about others.

I would need a period of time to reacclimate to the world I left more than two years earlier, a world that had changed quite a bit during my absence. (For instance, at the Geneva airport on my way back home, somebody stuck their cell phone in my face. I thought that they wanted me to speak to a friend, but they wanted to take my picture!)

After all these years of playing at survival the way that other men go to the office, I own nothing to show for it except for my own experience and the sum of the knowledge that I have accumulated. These are priceless treasures that no one can ever take away from me.

The long periods that I spent far away from the people I love, the sacrifice of basic comforts that most people enjoy, the physical and mental suffering, the frequent risk of death—these are just the less pleasant aspects of a profession that I chose for myself and that I generally practice with a smile on my face. I have a chance to live my dreams every day, and I wouldn't trade my life—or my dreams—for anything else on earth.

But I will soon be turning forty, and I can't keep practicing this "profession" indefinitely. Maybe I will devote the second half of my life to teaching values to troubled young people. I believe that I could teach them, in the context of difficult expeditions, a sense of determination and solidarity, and turn them into strong, respectable adults. Perhaps I will do just that . . . down the road.

But I'm not ready for retirement yet. The project I'm contemplating next will completely overshadow everything I have done to date and will combine all the most difficult aspects of each of my previous expeditions.

I would like to give Cathy a ring with a solitaire diamond. The ring would symbolize my trip around the Arctic Circle and the perfect path that I followed to be reunited once again with the ones that I love. The diamond would symbolize the sublime beauty of the worlds that I traversed, the hardness and glitter of the ice and its inestimable value, since it is itself the source of life. It also would signify the harshness of my journey, and the toughness that I had to develop in order to survive it.

After all this time, all this work, all these sagas, all the ordeals, and all the joys, I only want to say one thing, "I am happy to be alive." What did I leave behind me in the Arctic? A few footprints, quickly blown away. What did the Arctic give me? Experience and wisdom that I will take with me to my grave. It made a man out of me—a slightly better man, perhaps.

# Acknowledgments

To all those who helped and supported me before and during this expedition, I would like to express my gratitude and my friendship. None of this would have been possible without you.

**Main Sponsors**
Groupama Assistance; Mercedes-AMG; Mirabaud & Co. Private Bankers; Panerai Watches

**Partners**
Andaska; Eider/Gore-Tex; Town of Château d'Oex/Pays d'Enhaut; Julbo; Salomon

**Official Suppliers**
Corsair Marine; Ferrino; Prijon GmbH; Trek; Vade Retro

**Other Suppliers**
Ajungilak; Energizer; Global Satellite US; IBM Think Pad; Katadyn; Montana Sport Int.; Morand; Musto; Othovox; Toko

## Support Staff
Cathy Horn; Jean-Philippe Patthey; Martin Horn; Philippe Varrin

## Skippers—Boat Transport
Bernard Stamm; Pierre-Yves Martin; Ronan Le Goff

## Expedition Videographer
Raphaël Blanc

## Expedition Photographer
Sebastian Devenish

## Special thanks go to:
Børge Ousland; Support Group—Team Mike Horn; Johann Rupert and the committee of the Laureus Awards; Philippe Rochat; Steve and Yvan Ravussin; Thierry Legeret and Tiziana Camerini of TLRP